AUTHORS BY PROFESSION

VOLUME TWO

*This book is dedicated to
all my friends at
The Society of Authors
The Writers' Guild
and
The Royal Literary Fund*

AUTHORS
BY PROFESSION

Victor Bonham-Carter

*How authors, dramatists, and radio and screen writers
have practised their profession in their
respective media; their contracts and earnings;
their situation under the law
in respect of copyright, taxation, defamation,
obscene publications, etc.; their professional organisations;
their experience of literary patronage.*

VOLUME TWO

From the Copyright Act 1911
until the end of 1981

THE BODLEY HEAD
&
THE SOCIETY OF AUTHORS

British Library Cataloguing
in Publication Data
Bonham-Carter, Victor
Authors by profession.
Vol. 2: From the Copyright Act 1911 until the end of 1981
1. Authors, British
I. Title
808'.02'0941   PN155

ISBN 0-370-30600-7

Printed in Great Britain for
The Bodley Head Ltd
9 Bow Street, London WC2E 7AL
and
The Society of Authors,
84 Drayton Gardens, London SW10 9SB
by
Redwood Burn Ltd, Trowbridge

First published in Great Britain 1984

CONTENTS

Acknowledgements   11

Introduction   13

PART ONE: WRITING FOR PRINT

CHAPTER ONE   19
From the Copyright Act, 1911, to the 1920s
The Copyright Act, 1911. The book trade during the First
World War. Methuen prosecuted for publishing *The
Rainbow* by D. H. Lawrence. Rudyard Kipling and 'charity
books'. G. H. Thring, Secretary of the Society of Authors,
criticises publishing contracts. Stanley Unwin's defence in
The Truth about Publishing. The row between H. G. Wells,
H. P. Vowles and G. H. Thring. Thring's *The Marketing of
Literary Property*, with foreword by Bernard Shaw.
Florence Deeks versus H. G. Wells.

CHAPTER TWO   43
The 1930s and the Second World War
Thring succeeded in 1930 by Denys Kilham Roberts, who
transforms *The Author*. End of a literary era. Leonard and
Virginia Woolf's earnings as writers. Malcolm Elwin. John
Lehmann, Michael Roberts, and young writers of the Left
and Right. Cecil Day-Lewis proposes affiliation to the
Trades Union Congress. Lord Gorell at the Society. His
Libel Bill, 1929. Succeeded by Ian Hay Beith. Roberts's
initiatives. Recollections of the Society in the 1930s
by Elizabeth Barber. Relations with the Publishers
Association. Impact of the Second World War. Authors'
war committees and plans. J. B. Priestley. St. John Ervine.

Collapse of the Pinker agency. Margaret Storm Jameson's work for refugee writers at PEN.

CHAPTER THREE   66
Post-War Prospects
Composers form own Guild in 1944. Authors writing for
Government departments. Outlook in 1945. Shaw appoints
the Society to act as his agent. Agents discussed. Elizabeth
Barber succeeds D. K. Roberts as Secretary of the Society,
1963–71. Her successors, 1971–81. The Society's
Collection Bureau. Association of Authors' Agents, 1975.
Post-war taxation and authorship. Authors and social
security.

CHAPTER FOUR   86
Authors' earnings and Public Lending Right
Authors resist publishers' post-war attempts to reduce
royalty rates. Royalties on overseas sales. Full-time or
part-time writing. Walter Allen's *Critical Times for
Authors*, 1953. Surveys of authors' earnings and contracts,
1955–82. Comments by Richard Findlater. Public Lending
Right, 1951–82.

CHAPTER FIVE   110
Writing and the Law
A. P. Herbert. Obscene Publications Acts, 1959, 1964.
Professor Bernard Williams's Report, 1979. Censorship and
obscenity discussed. Defamation Act, 1952. PQ 17 case.
Faulks Report, 1975. Official secrets and access to
Government records. Closed shop legislation. Press charter
enquiry, 1976–7. The Society of Authors becomes a trade
union in 1978.

CHAPTER SIX   126
Copyright
The Writers' Guild and the Society of Authors. Breakaway
and rapprochement. Authors' Lending and Copyright
Society. Copyright Act, 1956. Copyright reform. British
Copyright Council. Whitford Report, 1977. Government
green paper, 1981. ALCS constitution. Piracy and
reprography. The new technology—video and microform.
Electronic publishing and authorship.

CHAPTER SEVEN   139
Freelancing
Incentives to write. Freelance journalism since 1900. Rise
and fall of periodicals. Decline of freelancing. Scales of
payment, 1952–67. Report by Jim Burns on 'little
magazines' for the Arts Council, 1971. Schools and tutors of
writing.

CHAPTER EIGHT   150
Patronage
Patronage of literature. Civil List pensions. 'Desert and
Distress'. The Royal Literary Fund. The state and the arts.
Honours. Literary Prizes. Support of literature by the Arts
Council. Writers' Grants 1964–81. The McGuigan Report.
Need for patronage if contemporary writing is to survive.

PART TWO: WRITING FOR PERFORMANCE

CHAPTER NINE   167
Theatre
Revival of drama in late 19th and early 20th centuries.
Introduction of box office royalty system. Dramatists
campaign for reform of censorship and a Managerial Treaty
with West End Managers. Rise in theatre costs during First
World War and afterwards. Attempt to form a 'Playwrights'
Union'. Role of the 'other' theatre. British Drama League
and amateur fees. New playwrights in the 1930s. American
Minimum Basic Agreement. League of Dramatists formed
in 1931. Impact of television in the 1950s. State patronage
of the theatre during Second World War. CEMA, Arts
Council of Great Britain, and H. M. Tennent's promotion of
new plays. The post-war subsidised theatre and grant-aid to
dramatists. Royal Court Theatre, John Osborne, and the
crop of new dramatists and plays. Alan Ayckbourn. Costs of
play production and returns in 1982. Proposals by the
Theatre Writers' Union.

CHAPTER TEN   205
Radio
Origins of the BBC. Broadcasting fees in 1923. Copyright
protection. A. A. Milne's criticisms in 1926. Collective

agreement for minimum terms. American radio fees in
1930. Playwriting for the BBC. Role of Performing Right
Society. Popular broadcasters in 1930s. Early television
transmissions. Growing dissatisfaction of authors writing
for radio during Second World War. Confrontation
between Society of Authors and BBC in 1947. Radiowriters'
Association founded in 1947. Some personal experiences of
radiowriting and broadcasting in the 1950s. Competition of
television. Pilkington Report, 1962. 'Broadcasting in the
Seventies'. Commercial radio and local radio. Annan
Report, 1977. Fees for radiowriting in 1980–1.

CHAPTER ELEVEN 240
Screen—Cinema
Early films and film makers. USA gains early lead.
Copyright protection. Cecil Raleigh's advice. Investigations
by sub-committee of Society of Authors in 1914. Rex Beach
on writing for films in USA in 1918. Film rights and film
deals in the 1920s. Scott Fitzgerald's experience as a
screenwriter. American dominance of British market in
1920s. Films Act, 1927. Rise of British 'verticals'. Impact of
the 'talkies' after 1927. Boom in British film industry in
1930s. Alexander Korda and others. Slump in 1938. Films
Act, 1938. Salaried screenwriters in Hollywood. US
writers' fight for recognition. Screenwriters' Association
founded under Society of Authors' auspices in 1937.
Screenwriting in 1939. Documentary films in Britain.
British film making in the Second World War. Rise of
Arthur Rank. Reports on the film industry. Currency
restrictions on film imports in 1947. Anglo-American
Agreement, 1948. Films Act, 1948. National Film Finance
Corporation. Reports on production, distribution and
exhibition. Some British films post-war. Ealing Studios.
Balcon, Danischewsky, Tibby Clarke. US anti-trust
legislation in 1948. Emergence of conglomerates. Drastic
fall in cinema attendances. New patterns of film making by
end of 1950s. 'New wave' of British films. Woodfall and
others. Film censorship. Williams Report, 1979. Further
Films Acts. Steep drop in British film production by 1981.
Film finance, film rights and remuneration of screenwriting
in early 1980s.

Screen—Television

Television in the 1930s. Re-started in 1946 after Second
World War. Advent of independent television in 1954–5.
Television flourishes late 1950s to early 1980s. Huge
demand for written material, especially original scripts.
Screenwriters' Association becomes independent of the
Society of Authors, and resists take-over by ACTT. It
registers as a trade union and adopts title of the Writers'
Guild of Great Britain. Fears of American invasion of British
television programmes. Terms available to scriptwriters in
1957. Collective agreements. Comparative rates for
teleplays in 1971 and 1982. Writing for educational
television. The precariousness of freelance TV
scriptwriting. Advent of videograms and cable television;
their impact and future possibilities. Direct
broadcasting by satellite. How to protect creators' rights?

Notes   297

Index   327

ACKNOWLEDGEMENTS

No one could write a book of this kind without a great deal of help. I have had just that from very many people. I wish therefore to acknowledge my debt to all who have supplied me with facts and figures and much other information, with authoritative advice and, not least, with encouragement to persevere. Some of my helpers do not wish to be mentioned by name; otherwise all authors, publishers and others whose works I have consulted for the purpose of reference and quotation are recorded in the narrative and the Notes. I am deeply grateful to them and, where relevant, to their agents or other representatives, who have given me the necessary permission. For this reason no separate Bibliography has proved necessary.

In addition I would like to express my thanks to all those who have patiently answered questions, who have read portions of the text, in some cases whole chapters, who have corrected the draft, and generally enlarged my understanding of the subject. In particular I am grateful to:

The Committee of Management of the Society of Authors for permission to use the archives, and all my colleagues on the staff of the Society.

Richard Findlater, editor of *The Author*.

Walter J. Jeffrey, General Secretary of the Writers' Guild of Great Britain, his predecessor Ian Rowland Hill, and their colleagues.

Martyn Goff, director of the National Book League.

Elizabeth Gotch, for fifteen years my assistant at the Royal Literary Fund.

The librarian of the British Theatre Association.

The librarian of the British Film Institute.

Dan H. Laurence, literary and dramatic advisor to the estate of Bernard Shaw.

Sue Harper, of the Department of Historical and Literary Studies, Portsmouth Polytechnic.

Also: Emmeline Baker, Evelyn Elwin, Mark Everett, Christopher Fry,

Richard Gregson, Lady Herbert, Antony Hippisley-Coxe, Michael Holroyd, Kenneth Hopkins, John V. Lemont, Roger Manvell, Molly Marriner, Barry Norman, Diana Raymond, Jessica Ritblat, Alan Ross, David Self, Bill Shine, Stanley Price, Malcolm Stewart, Heather Stoney, Claire Tomalin, and Harvey Unna.

Finally I owe a deep debt to my wife, Cynthia, for having endured frequent sessions of reading and consultation over the text at every stage from the beginning of the book.

Notwithstanding all this generous help, I must bear responsibility for any errors committed, and all personal opinions expressed.

V.B-C.

What do we as a nation care about books? . . . If a man spends lavishly on his library, you call him mad—a bibliomaniac. But you never call anyone a horse-maniac . . .

How long most people would look at the best book before they would give the price of a large turbot for it!

JOHN RUSKIN

Author—first published in May 1890—an invaluable repository for any researcher, since few events or questions of importance affecting authorship have escaped its columns.

Why, you may ask, did it take so long to write Volume One? The answer is simple. Barely had I got down to the job in the basement of No. 84 than I found myself gradually and inexorably drawn into the routine work of the office, which absorbed every minute of the three days a week I had agreed to put in for the Society. And when my task at Dartington was finally completed in 1966, the remaining two days were taken up by fresh employment as Secretary of the Royal Literary Fund, the authors' charity. So writing the history and organising the archives of the Society had to be squeezed into evenings, weekends and holidays. Even so it proved possible by 1969 to commission Sotheby's to negotiate the sale of the first large instalment of correspondence and documents (from 1884 to the mid-1930s, including most of the Bernard Shaw papers) to the British Museum (now the British Library), and then go on to complete the writing of Volume One nine years later.

Hard going as it was, Volume One had its relatively simple side, because 1911 could be said to mark the end of an era in which literary communication was restricted to print and the stage. Two media only. Since then several more have been added—films (the silent versions were already under way, but not significant for writers before 1911), radio, television, and more recently audio and video recording, reprography, and all the new technical resources for storage and communication. Clearly, too, other matters had to be taken into account in Volume Two, such as the development of publishing and the book trade, changes in legislation, public patronage of the arts, the part played by literature in contemporary society, and the survival of authors as a species. These are just some of the subjects I have tried to consider—in outline and with a minimum of literary value judgements—in this second volume, which is designed to run from 1911 to 1981. Inevitably I have found it necessary here and there to stray into 1982 and even into 1983 when revising the text, but the narrative is concerned essentially with the 70 years since the great Copyright Act of 1911. Moreover this can only be a selective story. The material is too vast and too complex to attempt anything approaching completeness, and has been drawn from numerous sources other than those available in a single organisation. Plenty of other books could be written on specific periods or aspects of authorship during the whole passage of time from the Renaissance to the present day. The bibliography is enormous. But I have never yet found a book devoted to the history of the *business* of writing in Britain, and presented from the authors' point of view.

That being so, and having the good luck to work for two authors' organisations, the Society of Authors and the Royal Literary Fund, and enjoying friendly relations with the Writers' Guild, the National Book League, and a host of agents, publishers, and other members of the book trade, I felt I was uniquely placed to write this book. But I never thought at the outset that it would take me twenty years. Had I known that . . .

Now that I can look back, what are the lessons? Disappointingly, they are the same as those discussed in the Introduction to Volume One. What is an author? Not, in most cases, someone who makes a living by writing, although that would seem the logical answer. The explanation of this anomaly is complex and needs careful analysis. Is writing a real profession as other arts are, and are accepted to be, in the public mind? Is it because most painters, sculptors, composers, and performers have had some formal training, passed an examination, and secured a diploma or degree? As Richard Findlater wrote in *The Book Writers, who are they?* (1966):

> The fact is that writing is an empirical art, which can only be learned by doing it, there is no formal way of graduating in authorship and no way of enumerating its practitioners. For them independence is of the essence, and this includes the freedom to practise without formal qualification, without regimentation, without the pressure of collective action. The price of that independence is the lack of identity in the public mind.

Learning by doing is certainly no reflection on the status of authorship as a profession or as an art, but it does involve every practioner in the classical dilemma: should he take a chance and devote all his time, talent and resources to surviving by his work? or should he rely on another job and treat writing as ancillary, although in his own, and often in the public, mind it comes first?

There is no single straight answer to this question, partly because the abilities and temperaments of individual writers, even their metabolisms, vary; and partly because of practical circumstances. Some have succeeded in the first category, some—by deliberate choice—in the second, although the economics of publication and performance, in the great majority of cases, do dictate that writing must be a part-time occupation. There are plenty of historical precedents. Nonetheless it does seem utterly wrong that an author cannot support himself from the practice of a profession in which he has gained a reputation and a following by talent and hard work. In what other walk of life does that happen? Does a dentist have to run a restaurant to get by?

Oddly there is yet another more dangerous and illogical anomaly, concealed in the fact that writing is *par excellence* our national art. In all our history we can point to plenty of achievements in music, painting, sculpture, architecture, and the crafts. But the record does not compare with that in writing, for there have been battalions of authors of the front rank in every age since Chaucer, and whole armies in the rear ranks, who have helped to make English a world language with a world literature. The paradox is that the very universality of English and its long literary tradition have blinded us as to its value. We take for granted that authors of talent, and a few of genius, will continue to appear, generation after generation; and we assume that, because there are still plenty of writers practising in all the media, almost anybody can write a book, a script, or a play. Sheer abundance depreciates the currency, and familiarity breeds contempt both for the act of creation and the creator; thus we discount the art that has placed Britain in the forefront of literature and language.

I believe that we can no longer afford the luxury of negligence; and that, without proper recognition and adequate reward, authorship as a profession will suffer a serious decline. Unaided, it cannot continue of its own volition. I hope that the history of the past 70 years, outlined in these pages, will help us find the solution.

PART ONE

WRITING FOR PRINT

CHAPTER ONE

From the Copyright Act, 1911,
to the 1920s

The Copyright Act, 1911. The book trade during the First
World War. Methuen prosecuted for publishing *The Rainbow*
by D. H. Lawrence. Rudyard Kipling and 'charity books'.
G. H. Thring, Secretary of the Society of Authors, criticises
publishing contracts. Stanley Unwin's defence in *The Truth
about Publishing*. The row between H. G. Wells, H. P. Vowles
and G. H. Thring. Thring's *The Marketing of Literary
Property*, with foreword by Bernard Shaw. Florence Deeks
versus H. G. Wells.

I closed the first volume of this book at the year 1911—a
seemingly arbitrary date, but chosen for practical reasons. One
was the passage of the Copyright Act that received the Royal
Assent on 16 December 1911, and which represented the greatest
single advance in the protection of authors' rights since copyright
was first established by law in 1709. The previous Copyright Act
of 1842 had fallen so far out of date and had generated so many
problems and anomalies that, already by 1878, the Royal
Commission on Copyright felt obliged to comment:

> The first observation which a study of the existing law suggests
> is that its form, as distinguished from its substance, seems to us
> bad. The law is wholly destitute of any sort of arrangement,
> incomplete, often obscure, and even when it is intelligible upon
> long study, it is in many parts so ill-expressed that no one who
> does not give such study to it can expect to understand it . . .[1]

And that was 43 years before Parliament took the necessary
action in 1911. The reform of domestic copyright was one of the

main objectives of the Society of Authors founded by Walter Besant in 1884. Even so it took the combined and prolonged efforts of the Society, the Copyright Association, the Publishers Association, the music associations and other interests, to see it through; and even then it would not have been possible without the willing assistance of Sydney Buxton, President of the Board of Trade in the Liberal Government of the day.

> The Act repealed 17 Acts absolutely and considerable portions of certain others. It also replaced Common Law in respect of unpublished material . . . Henceforward the copyright owner —be he author, artist, or composer—possessed the sole right to produce or reproduce his work in any form or to authorise others to do so, e.g. by publication, performance, or mechanical recording, including film . . . This right of copyright was his for life, and then belonged to his heirs for 50 years after his death.[2]

Another reason was that 1911 came at the end of the era in which literary communication was restricted to print and the stage. It is true, of course, that both these media continued to play a vital role, and have themselves experienced significant changes since 1911. But it is also true that the Act provided for rights attaching to new media—not only films and mechanical music, which were in their beginnings, but others undreamed of by the legislators of 1911: radio, talkies, television, audio and video recording, and the whole gamut of electronic storage and communication with us today.[3] The Act, I suspect, was far better than its progenitors realised.

If 1911 signalled the end of an era in literary communication, then 1914 played a parallel role in the history of human affairs at large. The First World War accelerated the pace of change in the seemingly solid structure of society associated with the long reign of Queen Victoria, and already weakening during the decade of her son, Edward VII. Almost every important event, political or otherwise, exerted influence outside its immediate range. For instance, the introduction of national primary schooling by the Education Act, 1870, raised the level of literacy and contributed to the explosion of popular journalism during the last quarter of the 19th century—exemplified by the 'penny' publications of

George Newnes, Alfred Harmsworth and Cyril Pearson—which captured the mass market of literate but unintellectual readers. It was the different strata of the periodical press that bred and was exploited by not only well-known journalists such as W. T. Stead and Frederick Greenwood, but also by innovative writers such as Arnold Bennett and H. G. Wells, who combined highly successful journalism with serious fiction and radical ideas. Indeed Bennett, Wells and George Bernard Shaw (the latter operating principally but not solely through the medium of his plays) were three of the leading *literati* who heralded the new age of social thinking and behaviour, outside the strict confines of Parliamentary politics, which the war of 1914–18 hurried into reality.

Literary changes were closely related to, and affected by, movements in the book trade, in which the various interests had been polarised by the formation of trade associations before the end of the century—the authors in 1884, the booksellers in 1895, and the publishers in 1896. In 1899 the Net Book Agreement was introduced with widespread support to control retail prices and inject stability into the marketing of books. Libraries remained an important channel of distribution and communication to the public. The circulating or commercial libraries, such as Mudie's, provided a significant outlet for publishers and were occasionally accused of exerting a form of censorship, moral and economic, upon the length and content of works of fiction because novels relied heavily upon their orders. An agitating development was the so-called 'book war' waged between the Publishers Association and the Times Book Club, 1905–8, whereby the Club sought to buy books at the best trade terms and sell off library copies at cut prices within a few weeks of publication. This form of instant remaindering threatened the very survival of the Net Book Agreement and was fiercely resisted by the publishers, booksellers and most authors—though not by Bernard Shaw who, characteristically, made his own arrangements with the Club. However peace was eventually signed when *The Times* passed into the hands of Lord Northcliffe, who conceded the publishers' case.[4]

Public libraries were still the poor relations among institutional book buyers, and were to remain so until the statutory rate limitation was lifted in 1919.[5] After that date they were free to buy books and periodicals, and generally expand their services, according to the financial resources allotted to them by the local government or other authorities to whom they were responsible; but their extraordinary leap forward as sources of book borrowing, and their emergence as cultural community centres, did not occur until after the Second World War. It was then that they extinguished most of the 'commercials' and, by reason of the vast scale of lending financed by public funds, engendered the campaign that came to be known as Public Lending Right.

In the theatre Shaw led the field in a determined attack upon the censorship of stage plays, compelling the Government to appoint a Select Committee under Herbert Samuel MP in 1909 to inquire into the working of the antiquated Theatres Act, 1843, and the repressive actions of the Lord Chamberlain's office. As Shaw wrote later:

> My objection to censors is that in practice they mean appointing an ordinary official with a salary of a few hundreds a year to exercise powers which have proved too much for Popes and Presidents.[6]

Although stage censorship was not abolished until the Theatres Act, 1968, the 1909 campaign had its effect, and in the intervening years the system was applied with far greater liberality and discretion. Backed by a band of fellow dramatists— among them, A. W. Pinero, R. C. Carton, James Barrie, John Galsworthy, and others—Shaw also worked assiduously for a 'minimum basic agreement' with the West End theatre managers. Again, although no formal document was ever signed, these efforts yielded practical improvements to the content of individual contracts and contributed to the formation of the League of Dramatists (a subsidiary organisation of the Society of Authors) in 1931, described in Part Two.

One other feature deserves reference in outlining the practical aspects of literature immediately before the First World War: and that is the nature and functions of the Society of Authors, the sole organisation representing the business and legal interests of writers,[7] and whose earlier history is related in Volume One. By 1914 the Society had 2,500 members, each paying an annual subscription of a guinea; a Council with Thomas Hardy as President (third in line after Tennyson and Meredith); a Committee of Management chaired by Hesketh Pritchard (successor to a string of hard-worked professional writers, among them Rider Haggard and Anthony Hope Hawkins); an office in Tothill Street, Westminster, manned by a small staff under G. H. Thring, a qualified solicitor specialising in copyright and contracts, a shrewd persistent man, who knew his way about the courts, had little love for publishers or agents, personally dictated and signed a stream of letters week by week (copied, before the age of the typewriter, into old-fashioned letter books), edited *The Author* (the Society's bi-monthly journal), and wrote the minutes of the Council, Committee of Management, and half-a-dozen sub-committees in long hand. How Thring sustained the volume and variety of work of this eccentric organisation, which represented authors of every sort (membership determined by activity not literary merit), playwrights and composers of music, is a mystery. There was no end to what the Society did or was expected to do. It had started a pension fund for members in 1900, a collection bureau in 1912 (to collect royalties for members—an onerous job often requiring recourse to the law—but which Thring was careful to state was 'in no sense a literary or dramatic agency for the placing of books or plays'); it also ran a manuscript reading service, registered play scripts and scenarios, and stamped sheet music to safeguard performance right for composer members. In Edmund Gosse's words, the office resembled a 'firm of solicitors acting solely for literary clients'. It was obviously far more than that, particularly when fresh demands were constantly coming in to set up a co-operative publishing enterprise, act as a clearing house for the book trade (including disposing of members' unwanted remainders), loan money, train beginners, run a register of titles, and take in allied workers such as illustrators and photographers.

Britain entered the First World War on 4 August 1914. The public mood was very different from that at the start of the Second World War 25 years later. In 1939 men and women resigned themselves, without much enthusiasm or any flag-waving, to a long struggle; and, although there were plenty of illusions about the course and nature of hostilities against Hitler, there was none of that hysteria which characterised the opening months of 1914 when 'all over by Christmas' was replaced by the equally misleading 'business as usual', and which in turn wore slowly away as the realities of the struggle bit into daily life.

This casual tempo was reflected at first in the economics of publishing and writing. The total of new titles and new editions issued in 1914 was 11,537 (only 842 less than in 1913), but by the end of 1917 (when the U-boat campaign was causing real shortages in food and materials) it had fallen to 8,131, and a year later to 7,716. Cost of book production rose steadily in the last three years of the war. By April 1916 the price of paper had doubled from 2½d to 5d per lb, and by December 1918 it had risen to 11d. After the ending of paper control in 1919, it went up to 1s 9d. Strawboard for binding had jumped from £4.10s to £35 per ton by April 1917, by which time the use of copper for blockmaking had been prohibited. Type founders lacked lead and, 'as the war advanced, publishers' staffs became increasingly composed of older men, women, and boys below the age of eighteen'.[8] Surprisingly book prices moved slowly. While the quality of production declined (poor paper and fewer pages), by the end of the war the 6s novel (a price first introduced as long ago as 1861) was costing only 7s or 7s 6d, and remained at that level for most of the peace time that followed.

Inevitably taste in reading also changed.

Whole classes of books have disappeared as completely as if floods had passed over them. . . For what was once known to the trade as the 'library biography' we now look almost in vain . . . We do not turn to the romance of remote history for recreation when actual history is being made romantically before our eyes . . .[9]

And so, in the summer 1917 lists, we find a flow of titles about the fighting and home fronts. They included:

Air Power by Claude Grahame-White and Harry Harper
Gallipoli by John Masefield
The First Hundred Thousand by Ian Hay (translated into French)
The Battles of the Somme by Philip Gibbs
The Ruhleben Prison Camp by Israel Cohen

The Eat Less Meat Book by Mrs C. S. Peel
How to pay for the war, edited by Sidney Webb
After-war Problems, edited by William Harbutt Dawson, and a spate of similar titles; while in the sociological section there appeared the problematic *Should Girls be Told?* by W. N. Willis.

As to fiction, H. G. Wells's *Mr Britling sees it through*, first published in 1916, was still heading the bestseller lists in Britain and USA. As often happened, Wells had put into print what so many people were really thinking after two years of war.

> I think I have contrived in that book to give not only the astonishment and the sense of tragic disillusionment in a civilized mind as the cruel facts of war rose steadily to dominate everything else in life, but also the passionate desire to find some immediate reassurance amidst the whirlwind of disaster.[10]

Otherwise a random glance at the new novels of the period reveals the names of E. F. Benson, Algernon Blackwood, Phyllis Bottome, Warwick Deeping, Rider Haggard, Cicely Hamilton, Eden Phillpotts and Horace Vachell. Rupert Brooke was still the most popular of the poets, romanticised by his friends for his physical beauty and early death, whose verses fed the hunger for an idealised past. However, they survived the backlash of those later writers who took the lid off the war—Richard Aldington, Edmund Blunden, Vera Brittain, Robert Graves, Wilfrid Owen, Siegfried Sassoon, Henry Williamson—most of whose work was still a decade away. During the crises of 1917–18 the possibilities of starvation and the casualty lists were all too real for literary pessimism.

At Tothill Street, meanwhile, Thring and a skeleton staff continued to cope with the everyday problems of authorship. Inevitably the membership declined. A number of authors gave up writing altogether, served in the Forces, found work in industry, on the land, in Government offices, or were otherwise lost to literature. *The Author* was punctuated less by references to casualties at the front, than by occasional obituaries recalling the careers of distinguished ghosts of the past: Miss Braddon[11] (1838–1914), author of *Lady Audley's Secret* (bestseller in 1862);

Theodore Watts-Dunton (1832–1914), 'last of the Pre-Raphaelites' and guardian of Algernon Swinburne; and William de Morgan (1839–1917), the potter, who had begun writing successful novels at the age of 62. Although recruitment did not revive with any force until towards the end of the war, the flow of new members never ceased. Some had already made their names, others were on the way to making them. For example:

1915: Norman Angell, Douglas Goldring, Wilfrid Gibson, Logan Pearsall Smith
1916: Max Beerbohm, Erskine Childers, Caradoc Evans, John Oxenham
1917: John Drinkwater, George Moore, J. C. Squire, William Watson
1918: C. E. Bechofer, Arthur Waley, Rebecca West

Two literary events however stood out in the dreary annals of the time. One arose out of the Society's involvement with D. H. Lawrence over the suppression of his novel, *The Rainbow*, in November 1915.

Originally entitled 'The Wedding Ring', Lawrence had completed the manuscript on 2 March. It was then typed out by Viola Meynell and an assistant and passed to Lawrence's agent, J. B. Pinker, who offered it to Methuen. Although they had already rejected an earlier version of the work, the publishers were persuaded on this occasion to move outside the security of their normal (and distinguished) list and venture into the territory of the avant-garde, and to accept the manuscript on Pinker's assurance that any objectionable passages would be removed in proof.

Even so it was a risk. The story was powerful and sensual in both subject and style; but the general 'excess of sex' that Lawrence's friends feared might prove too much for the reader paled before the explicit description, in one chapter called 'Shame', of a Lesbian relationship between a girl and her teacher. Remarkably, although Lawrence did carry out minor alterations at proof stage as promised, this chapter went through untouched. Methuen therefore were fully committed. They paid an advance of £250, printed an edition of 2,500 copies, and published the book on 30 September.

By that time Lawrence and his wife, Frieda, had moved into No. 1, Byron Villas, Vale-of-Health, Hampstead, rented at only £3 a month: '. . . nondescript as a dwelling but redeemed by the natural setting—in this case eight hundred acres of park and woodland that completely surrounded it.'[12]

It was in these sylvan surroundings that Lawrence awaited the reception of *The Rainbow*, fearing trouble. He was not disappointed. On 5 October, Robert Lynd, a respected and intelligent critic, described it in the *Daily News* as 'largely a monotonous wilderness of phallicism'. On 22 October, James Douglas, a popular columnist, published a violent attack in *The Star*, taking a high moral line: 'There is no doubt that this book has no right to exist.' On the following day Clement Shorter denigrated it in *The Sphere*. He could only suppose that the publishers 'failed to read the book in manuscript'—which was substantially true. Prompted by these reviews, and on the authority of the Director of Public Prosecutions, Sir Charles Mathews, the police then moved in. The scene came alive in the dry tone of Methuen's reply of 16 November to an enquiry by G. H. Thring.

On November 3rd, Detective Inspector Draper of the Criminal Investigation Department, New Scotland Yard, brought with him a warrant issued by the chief magistrate at Bow Street Police Court under the 'Obscene Prints Act, 1857', to seize all copies on our premises of 'THE RAINBOW' on the ground that it was an obscene work. The solicitors, in consideration of the reputation of our firm, kindly suggested that we might prefer to hand over the books rather than submit to actual search, and this we did . . .

On Thursday, November 11th, Inspector Draper called with a summons to show cause why 'the said books should not be destroyed and to be further dealt with according to the law'. We understood from Inspector Draper that that was merely a formal matter to obtain our formal consent on the destruction of the book; the impression we received was that it would not be heard in a public court, and we did not therefore obtain legal assistance or arrange to be legally represented.

We asked Inspector Draper if the author could have a voice in the destruction of the books, and understood him to say that the action of the Police was taken against us and the author had no right to appear in the matter.[13]

Neither Pinker nor Lawrence were aware of what had happened until after the seizure of the stock, and neither knew of the court proceedings on 13 November until they read about them in the press. As the sole defendant, Methuen were given a rough time by the police solicitor who described *The Rainbow* as a 'disgusting, detestable and pernicious work', and by the magistrate who ordered them to pay ten guineas costs and confirmed the destruction of the stock. Unprepared for the hearing, Methuen could only offer meek apologies; and in any event they wanted a minimum of fuss, deploring any action by Lawrence's friends that might lead to a public protest.

There had indeed been plans for a letter to be signed by Walter de la Mare, E. M. Forster, John Middleton Murry, J. D. Beresford, Hugh Walpole and Gilbert Cannan; and hopes too that Lady Cynthia Asquith would prevail on her father-in-law, the Prime Minister, to take an interest; but he refused to treat the matter seriously. A similar line was taken by J. C. Squire, literary editor of the *New Statesman*, who thought that the novel was not worth a fight.

Lawrence turned to the Society of Authors, presumably as a last resort. In fact Thring had already been alerted and on 10 November invited him to apply for membership so that the Committee of Management might consider the case. Backed by Philip Morrell, MP (husband of the redoubtable Lady Ottoline), Lawrence duly applied and was accepted, by which time Thring had gathered all the facts he could from Methuen and Pinker, and had also sought legal advice from the Society's solicitors, Field Roscoe and Co. Eventually the Committee met on 6 December and after deliberation decided that 'in the present circumstances they could not take any useful action on the general principles involved'. It is difficult at this distance in time to interpret this brief and dismissive message aright. The Committee included Stanley Leathes (Chairman), Mrs Belloc Lowndes, Arthur Rackham, Bernard Shaw, Walford Davies (the composer), Aylmer Maude, and Charles Garvice—none of them backwoodsmen. But there were other factors to consider.

One was the strict legality or otherwise of the police action, which apparently could not be contested under the 1857 Act. Another was the intense hostility of public opinion generated by the reviewers but—more to the point—which might have been vastly exaggerated and exacerbated by the discovery by some newshound that Lawrence's wife, Frieda (born von Richtofen), was Prussian—and the war was going badly for the Allies at the end of 1915. But the most telling consideration of all was that the case came far too late to the notice of the Society for effective action to be taken before the destruction of the stock.

The other literary event was more protracted and concerned the so-called 'charity books'. This began, one assumes, as a genuinely disinterested effort to raise money for war charities by publishing and selling gift annuals at artificially high prices. Such, for example, was *The Princess Marie José's Charity Book*, but there were many others, several—like this one—sponsored by royalty. The Society's suspicions were aroused as early as April 1915. Not only was the market being surfeited with these books, in competition with the ordinary run of titles, but there was evidence that while printing and the other components of production had to be paid for in the usual way, authors were being expected to contribute for nothing. The situation deteriorated so quickly that in a letter to *The Author* of March 1916, Baroness Orczy (creator of *The Scarlet Pimpernel*) wrote:

> The various 'gift-books' have literally encumbered the book-sellers' shops for the past eighteen months . . . this is nothing better than a hideous undercutting in legitimate labour . . . surely the time has come to cry: Halt!

The Society did so. It sent Charles Garvice and Arthur Rackham to bring in the Publishers Association, and passed a resolution asking all members to refuse to write for any charity book that failed to conform to certain conditions relating to cost of production (including remuneration of those concerned), sale price, size of edition, and distribution. Over 200 members signed this undertaking, together with the whole of the Committee of Management and the majority of the Council. Shaw gave his support in characteristic terms. Galsworthy and Maurice Hewlett grumbled but gave in; but Rudyard Kipling found himself 'unable to subscribe to an undertaking which invests in a committee the right to say what I shall, or shall not do, with my work'. Whereupon he enclosed a cheque for £100 for the benefit of the Pension Fund and resigned from the Society.[14] He was the only writer of eminence who did so. As Wells pointed out, there was nothing to prevent any author subscribing directly to the funds of any charity he or she chose, without acting like a blackleg.

At no time before, during or after the war did Thring allow himself or the Committee of Management to be diverted from what he considered—along with the reform of copyright—to be the main aim and business of the Society: to protect authors from grasping publishers and to make members aware of shoddy clauses in contracts by publishing them in the pages of *The Author*. His practice was to print an agreement in full, and then to analyse the offending paragraphs, arguing the case in detail and spelling out the solution. Nothing roused his ire more than the publisher who tried to invest his agreement with an aura of respectability by using some phrase—and I quote—such as: 'This is my usual *printed* form from which I never vary' or 'the terms of the agreement have been settled by King's Counsel and approved by the Publishers Association'.

Here are a few examples that illustrate practices still common to a number of agreements at the time: the first from John Long[15] (later taken over by Hutchinson), in respect of a novel.

Clause 3. All copies sold of the said work within twelve months of the date of publication shall carry no royalty to the author, but on copies sold, after the expiration of the first twelve months after publication, the publisher agrees to pay to the author and the author agrees to accept a royalty of 15 per cent of the nominal published price on sales of the 6s edition, and a royalty of $7\frac{1}{2}$ per cent . . . on the sales of any cheaper edition.

Thring. All publishers assert that the largest sales of a novel occur either on subscription before publication, or within the first four months after publication . . . Therefore, the effect of this clause would be to give the publisher the book for nothing, except in a minority of cases. If the author desires to give the publisher his work for nothing, there is nothing to prevent him from doing so; but in that case he should execute a deed of gift.

Clause 5 (part). In making up accounts, thirteen copies shall be reckoned as twelve, in accordance with trade usage.

Thring. It means that the author is to allow the publisher 8 per cent discount on the royalties on all copies sold, though the publisher allows this discount to purchasers [booksellers] only when they purchase in quantities of a dozen upwards.

Clauses 10 and 11 (part). The author agrees to give the publisher the first refusal ... of the exclusive right of producing and publishing the author's next three new novels ... and if the publisher accepts all or any of them, he agrees to pay the following royalties: 15 per cent ... on the 6s edition after the sale of the first 750 copies; $7\frac{1}{2}$ per cent on ... any cheaper edition; 50 per cent of the net profits derived from the sale of the American copyright (if any); 50 per cent of the net profits derived from the sale of Foreign rights (if any). The said three novels ... shall be submitted one at a time, and only after the publication of the one previously accepted.

Thring. It is fatal for an author to bind himself to a publisher at fixed rates for subsequent works ... The publisher should not take 50 per cent profits on any of the rights outside, whether they are American or Foreign rights. If any of the outside rights are negotiated for by the publisher. .. then he should take the agency charge of 10 per cent and no more.

And, one asks, what was meant by that misleading term, 'profits'?

The second example,[16] dubbed 'A Sad Agreement' concerned John Lane of The Bodley Head, an adventurous but, on the whole, respected publisher associated with many successful authors. Nevertheless, in several respects, the agreement was as open to criticism as John Long's: e.g. 13 copies as 12, 50 per cent of outside rights, and an option in binding terms on the author's next three works. Thring also noted that Lane committed himself to no date for publication, and that he only offered to pay a royalty (of 10 per cent) after the sale of the first 2,000 copies.

Thring. This method of payment by a deferred royalty is very dangerous for the author. Indeed, examples have been brought to the notice of the Society in which a publisher has printed only the fixed number of copies on which the author is not entitled to a royalty, and has then broken up the type so that it was impossible for the author ever to obtain a return from the sale of his book. . . If, in his ignorance or folly, the author does allow such a large number to be sold free of royalty, then . . . he should be entitled at the very lowest to 30 per cent . . . on the next 2,000 copies and a substantial royalty after 4,000 copies have been disposed of.

In April 1915 Thring published an agreement issued by George Allen and Unwin Ltd, successors to George Allen and Co; and he seized on this succession to draw attention to the dangers inherent in the wording of the preamble in this, and almost all other publishing contracts, whereby the two parties bound themselves to each other, *and their successors and assigns*. For the publisher it was a safeguard. For the author, it might mean the opposite.

Thring. An author may have some important and special reason for publishing with the firm. He might very strongly object that his contract should be assigned to a person about whom he knew nothing, who might be in financial difficulties, or incapable, and ignorant of the book markets and the trade of publication.

In other words, an author should not be treated like a steer in a cattle market, nor should his books be labelled like tins of beans and lumped into the stock which the outgoing publisher— without consultation—sells as part of the assets to the incomer. This was to be a continuing source of trouble and has remained so right up to the present day, when take-overs by conglomerates (for whom publishing is only a subsidiary interest) are relatively common.

Thring's consistent hostility to the majority of publishers (and agents) is explicable in terms of history. He was Secretary of the Society of Authors for nearly 40 years from 1892 to 1930. He began work when publishing was dominated by a handful of respected houses, but in the main crowded with firms of indifferent quality who, in treating with authors, either demanded to buy copyright outright as a matter of course or foisted such one-sided agreements upon them that the result was much the same. That, as already mentioned, was one of the reasons why Walter Besant had founded the Society of Authors in 1884—to combine authors for strength, and to teach them to take as much care of their literary property as they would in buying or selling a house. Thanks to working with Besant, and later with Shaw (who safeguarded his interests by becoming his own agent and publisher), and thanks too to his innate combative nature, Thring became not only a formidable champion of authors' rights but was so inflexible in his attitude that, towards the end of his career—as will be related—he ran into trouble with one of his own members.

Injustices to authors apart, an irritant that sustained Thring in his campaigns was the pretension that publishing was a mystery which only those in the trade could penetrate. For Besant and Thring it was a smoke screen, a cover for shoddy practice and outright robbery that, in the early days, had prompted Besant to issue a series of publications[17] designed to investigate the cost of producing a book, and to explain and evaluate the alternative forms of agreement open to authors and publishers, viz., outright sale, profit-sharing, royalties, and commission. After Besant's death in 1901, Thring used *The Author* as the main medium for explanation and assault. Each issue contained at least one whole page devoted to detailed *Warnings* to authors (and playwrights and composers) on these subjects; and, it must be said, that although for many readers ceaseless repetition of this kind may have weakened its impact, Thring was frequently justified by events.

One such case was that of Galloway Kyle, which I have already described in Volume One, but summarise here for its unusual character. Kyle was associated with the founding of the Poetry Society in 1909 and later edited that Society's journal, *The Poetry Review*; and in doing so there is no doubt that he gave good service both to the Poetry Society and to the cause of poetry at large. But he courted trouble by simultaneously carrying on a publishing business under the name of Erskine MacDonald, and by mixing philanthropy with sharp practice. In short he invited authors who had submitted manuscripts to subscribe for one year

[33]

to *The Poetry Review* and to purchase at least 'four volumes in my shilling series which indicates the quality of matter accepted, and the style of production, facilitating later discussion of terms'. Thring went for him in April 1918. He reported that during 1917 the Society of Authors had taken up no less than 14 cases against him, mostly for non-payment of royalties, and accused him of shady behaviour by using his respectable connection with the Poetry Society to trap authors, anxious for publicity, into having their work published by Erskine MacDonald on highly unsatisfactory terms. Kyle had no recourse but to bring a libel action against the Society of Authors, which he lost, the jury finding for the Society, with costs, without leaving the court room.[18]

For their part, publishers of good standing had already begun to put their house in order, notably by the formation in 1896 of the Publishers Association to promote their collective interests and aspirations, and to co-operate where possible with organisations in the trade, including the Society of Authors. But the PA had no mandatory power over its members, nor has it today. It was unable as a body to insist on acceptable minimum terms in all publishing agreements and so prevent the inclusion of a number of unsatisfactory clauses of the kind that Thring publicised and criticised. Some authors of course enjoyed good terms—probably because they or their agents had fought for them in the first place—but in the generality this was not so; and it was not until 1926, with the appearance of *The Truth about Publishing*, written by Stanley Unwin, that any publisher openly grasped the nettle.

Unwin was a remarkable man. As a youth he had spent 12 months as a 'volunteer' in the German book trade which he greatly admired. He then joined the publishing house of his uncle, T. Fisher Unwin, for whom he worked assiduously for eight years (1904–12). Seeing no prospect of advancement he then resigned, and travelled round the world for a further year to extend his knowledge of the trade and make contacts. In 1914 he launched out on his own by buying up the bankrupt business of George Allen & Co (originally the publishers of Ruskin), and eventually secured sole control of the new company, George Allen & Unwin Ltd. The story of Stanley Unwin's firm and of his own career has been told elsewhere.[19] Suffice it to say that, with all his personal eccentricities, Unwin was not only a highly professional and successful publisher, but a man of vision whose contribution to the cause of literature and the trade of books, domestic and international, was of the first order. But the point of relevance here is that, from the outset, he set himself to learn every detail of the publishing business by personal experience, and for years lived a life of self-denial to achieve his aim. He was thus better equipped than any of his colleagues to state the publishers' case vis-à-vis Thring and the Society of Authors, and to try to dispel the aura of 'mystery' that had attached itself to it. But he made no bones about the quantity and complexity of the problems involved in publishing, and that it required a good business head to deal with them.

This was the purpose of *The Truth about Publishing*, not the first book of its kind but for long the best, which has now (1982) reached its eighth revised edition. The 1926 edition contained eleven chapters, describing the whole sequence of book production, from the arrival and acceptance of the manuscript to its publication, promotion and sale, with some additional matter on contingent aspects of the subject. One chapter was devoted to Agreements, and it was in this that Unwin faced up to Thring (whom he later referred to as 'my old enemy'). It is far too long for detailed analysis, so I will select some salient points.

First of all he accepted the validity of a number of the Society's demands: that the author should retain the copyright of his work, that every book should be covered by a formal agreement embodying all the points at issue, and that—in most instances— the royalty system was fairest to both parties; obvious and uncontroversial points now, but not in 1926. He conceded that an author, or better still a representative who understood bookkeeping, had the undoubted right to inspect his publisher's accounts, and wished that it was exercised more often; further that a royalty statement should always include a clear stock account—how many copies were printed, sold, and remained in stock. He agreed that a book should not be remaindered within two years of first publication, but resisted the claim that no author should allow a publisher an option on his future work. In his semi-Biblical language:

No man would be expected to till virgin soil if he had no certainty of reaping more than the first crop. To suggest that he ought to be satisfied to bid in open competition with those who had done nothing to prepare the soil would be palpably unjust.

Then followed the principal points of contention:

Territory: which areas of the world should be covered by the licence to publish.
Time: how long the licence should last.
Rights: i.e. the 'outside' or subsidiary rights in respect of further exploitation of the book—what share, if any, should be allowed to the original publisher.
Remuneration: assuming a royalty arrangement, how the scale (and advance) should be calculated.

Let it be said at the outset that these points are likely to form the subject of individual negotiation in almost every contract today; and that negotiation—over and above minimum just terms—is the best means of settling them in the light of changing conditions of trade (domestic and world wide), saleability of the subject and the work, pulling power of the author, efficiency of the publisher, and so on. Negotiation does not, of itself—as some seem to think—imply the abandonment of justice for the author, or one side 'winning' at the expense of the other, or even the necessity for aggressive bargaining between the two parties. But, until Unwin issued his book and openly discussed the publishers' case, backed by statistics of production and distribution (however arguable they might be), it was inevitable that men like Thring and Shaw (for the Society of Authors), and leading agents such as A. P. Watt and Curtis Brown, should take a hard line when confronted by terms of the kind handed out by publishers like John Long and John Lane.

To return to the four points above. Unwin claimed that as the publisher had invested his capital and expertise in the enterprise, he was entitled to a fair return. In his view that meant an exclusive licence, lasting for the duration of copyright, to produce a work in volume form in the English language throughout the world, or at least in the home and Commonwealth markets, with a substantial share in the returns from the American and other overseas editions, on the grounds that the work benefited in every sense from the original publication. He also wanted participation in

[36]

other uses, e.g. translation—he was thinking particularly of Germany where he had been trained and had acquired many contacts—arguing that in such cases the publisher could do better business than either the author or his agent acting independently.

Thring replied: The publisher is not the sole investor in the production of a book. The author not only invests his all, but is the primary producer without whom no publisher—or anyone else in the book trade (including many printers)—would be in business at all. The right to participate in further exploitation of a work should indeed be determined by Unwin's own question, 'Who exploits?' or rather, 'Who can exploit to best advantage?' This applied as much to American and overseas sales as to translations, serialisation, cheap editions, and the rest. A number of publishers lacked initiative and the means to exploit, and did little to justify benefiting from anything but the returns from the original publication in volume form. Exploitation and extra sales could just as well come from the popularity of the author, or the activity of the agent, or both. It was fair that the licence to publish should last for the duration of copyright—to give the publisher the chance to recoup and make a profit—but there had to be safeguards. The licence must be terminated, for example, if the book went out of print and the publisher failed to re-issue it promptly, or if he fell seriously behind with the payment of royalties, or if he went bankrupt.

As to the fourth point—royalties—it was the rule before and during the 1920s to draw up a scale of percentages (from 5 to 25 per cent) related to the number of copies sold to booksellers and other distributors, from which the publisher received more than 50 per cent of the published price. Royalties on bulk sales at a higher discount figure, whether to home or overseas buyers, were calculated on the actual amount received by the publisher; and there was a minimum scale for remainders. In essence these arrangements did not differ greatly from present-day practice, except that the advent of modern paperback and book club editions introduced additional sources of income, which not only expanded the market but tested the relations between author and publisher negotiating on the basis of 'Who exploits?' Of that, more later.

Thring retired from his post as Secretary of the Society of Authors at the end of February 1930. Neither a visionary nor a hack, he was a shrewd painstaking solicitor who, by sheer application and persistence, had become an expert in handling authors' problems, primarily their contractual relations with publishers and agents, and their rights before the law, so that those who benefited directly from his efforts during his 37 or so years of service to the Society added up to a very great number. When Thring began work in 1892 the Society was still small and struggling. When he retired, it was strong and respected, and flagrant exploitation was exceptional. But it was Thring's very devotion to the cause of the underdog which caused Stanley Unwin to regard him, unfairly, as 'narrow and litigious', and which, sadly, involved him in a contretemps on the point of his retirement in which his judgement was clearly at fault. In this instance the other party was not a publisher or similar kind of seasoned opponent, but a prominent member of the Society of Authors, one of the leading writers of the day—H. G. Wells.

By August 1929 Wells had completed the second volume of a trilogy designed to give what he called 'the intelligent lower middle classes' a broad and informed understanding of the history and destiny of man. The first volume had appeared in 1920 as *The Outline of History*. The second, due to appear in 1930, was entitled *The Science of Life: A Summary of Contemporary Knowledge and its Possibilities*. For both these works he had required and secured the aid of collaborators—a mixed team of established experts and up-and-coming students—to check the accuracy and fill the omissions of his text. In *The Science of Life* he had depended on his son, G. P. Wells, and the young scientist, Julian Huxley, and he had driven them very hard. Before this second volume was done, he began planning and working on the third, which was concerned with the economic situation and social condition of mankind, and was eventually published in 1932 under the title of *The Work, Wealth and Happiness of Mankind*.

For this volume he had recruited two collaborators, Edward Cressy and Hugh P. Vowles, to whom he had offered the prospect of earning not less than £6,000 each. Quite soon, however, Wells became dissatisfied. The work was going badly, the collaborators were at odds with each other, while Wells himself, naturally volatile and easily depressed, had taken on far too much. So he decided to pay off his helpers and make a fresh start. Cressy accepted a settlement, but Vowles did not, refusing the suggestion that 'he should keep the eight hundred pounds already advanced and, in addition, have the right to publish the material he had prepared'.[20]

So the trouble began. While Wells was on holiday in France during the summer of 1929, Vowles complained to the Society of Authors, where Thring—plainly pre-judging the issue—advised the Committee of Management that Vowles was entitled to damages for breach of contract; and in this sense he wrote to Wells on 8 November. Wells blew up. He denied the existence of any binding contract and personally attacked Thring in the most libellous manner, accusing him of sitting in his office and dictating 'the sort of letter a blackmailing solicitor might have written to a wealthy personal enemy'; all this and more, often in handwritten letters, of which, presumably, he kept no copies—an insane thing to do on every count. From then on things went from bad to worse, and so continued during the winter of 1929–30. As Wells's biographers, Norman and Jeanne Mackenzie, put it: 'All three principals in the dispute behaved so foolishly that a reasonable agreement had become impossible.'[21]

But Wells compounded his part in the affair by persuading Stanley Unwin to issue a privately printed pamphlet on his behalf, entitled *The Problem of the Troublesome Collaborator*, which was circulated to prominent members of the Society, and by lobbying friends in high places to support him and get rid of Thring in an ignominious manner, despite the fact that the latter was about to retire. By this time Thring had appealed to Bernard Shaw for help, which he duly gave, playing the part of Solomon with tremendous gusto and acumen—and ultimate success. He reminded Wells that

> It was like old times. Years ago H.G. had alienated his supporters in the Fabian Society by forcing them to choose between throwing over the Webbs and abandoning him— and had ended by failing to get a single vote in a meeting full of his sympathisers. He was about to repeat that astonishing feat.[22]

Shaw's pressure worked. On 8 April Wells sent Thring (who

[39]

had been threatening to sue for libel) a letter of apology which, after an initial refusal and subsequent revision, was accepted, and the incident was closed with the circulation of another Wells–Unwin pamphlet entitled *Settlement of the Trouble Between Mr Thring and Mr Wells*.[23]

Thring left a legacy: not merely the appreciation of those who had benefited from his efforts, or who valued what he had done for authors at large during his long service or the dry record of achievement concealed in minutes and correspondence, but the publication of a book that is still regarded by fellow professionals with respect. This was *The Marketing of Literary Property*, published by Constable in 1933, with a foreword by Bernard Shaw. The substance and value of the book resided in its clear and compact analysis of copyright, the law of libel, the variety and nature of publishing contracts, subsidiary rights, prizes and competitions, the functions of agents, etc—all such matters presented from the author's point of view. The book was thus a worthy counterpart to Unwin's work and only suffered from one disadvantage: for, unlike *The Truth about Publishing*, its author was never able to revise or reissue it, since Thring died in November 1941 at the age of 81.

Of course what is most readable in Thring's book today, like so many other occasional pieces that Shaw wrote, is the latter's foreword. A handful of brief quotations will show why. On leisure, he wrote:

Leisure is needed to produce art and religion, literature and science, without which we should be happier as birds or beasts than as humans. But it must be a leisure informed, trained, and disciplined by a share in the basic work of the world. If you bring up a class to live exempt from this share and wholly as leisure, you will sterilize them as completely for cultural purposes as if you brought them up to work like slaves to the limit of human endurance without any effective leisure at all.

On authors:

Authors have a very feeble grip of reality, which is a grip that has to be developed by long and intense practice . . . Isolated as they are in a lonely study which their imagination can transfigure into a realm of romance ... they become unreasonable and egocentred to an extent that only you [Thring], who have been all your life up against their petulance, can fully realize.

On publishers:

I take practically no interest in horseracing; but the Derby has forced itself on my attention often enough to give me an impression that the favorites seldom win and that outsiders often do. The same thing happens in publishing; and I would urge authors, especially young authors, to treat publishers not as admiring benefactors who exist disinterestedly for the glory of literature and its heroes, but as punters whose business it is to inspect unpublished books and back their fancy, their stake being the cost of its manufacture and publication, whilst the author is a bookmaker betting against the said fancy, his stake being the work he has put into the writing of it.

Shaw's main point concerned the ownership of copyright as an 'exploitable property' and its value in terms of monopoly.

The blunt truth is that as a man who has no property cannot be robbed, robbers have a strong interest in enabling him to acquire property ... A publisher who has all the works of Shakespeare freely at his disposal will pay me for leave to print my plays, leaving Shakespeare untouched, because I can give him a monopoly and thus enable him to charge a monopoly price whilst Shakespeare can give him nothing ...
It [writing] has the advantage of property rights denied to other professions. A surgeon cannot patent an operation which he is the first to make practicable, nor levy royalties for the rest of his life and fifty years after on all surgeons performing it. A barrister cannot patent an original defence. Einstein has no copyright in relativity ... But the author is a person of property; and as long as his property is worth anything he can live by it if only he has the knowledge and nerve to stick to it and exact its full rent.

We shall see later how well or otherwise this concept of literary property weathered the attacks made upon it, and by the practical difficulties of defence against the inroads of reprography, audio and video recording, and electronic publishing. Meanwhile a notorious case of alleged infringement had already demonstrated the dangers, as opposed to the privileges, of possessing this precious right. Again it concerned H. G. Wells who, in 1925, had been accused by a Canadian feminist, Miss Florence Deeks, of plundering her unpublished manuscript, entitled *The Web of History*, when writing his *The Outline of History*. The action dragged on but was ultimately dismissed, the judge deciding that in all probability both authors had made use of similar sources. In any event, there were no grounds for a legal action as the plaintiff's work had never been published. But Miss Deeks persisted, taking the matter first to the Privy Council, and then petitioning the King to review the Council's findings against her. The case cost Wells a great deal of money—Miss Deeks had none—and was an extreme example of the risks of copyright ownership.[24]

CHAPTER TWO

The 1930s and the Second World War

Thring succeeded in 1930 by Denys Kilham Roberts, who
transforms *The Author*. End of a literary era. Leonard and
Virginia Woolf's earnings as writers. Malcolm Elwin. John
Lehmann, Michael Roberts, and young writers of the Left and
Right. Cecil Day-Lewis proposes affiliation to the Trades Union
Congress. Lord Gorell at the Society. His Libel Bill, 1929.
Succeeded by Ian Hay Beith. Roberts's initiatives. Recollections
of the Society in the 1930s by Elizabeth Barber. Relations with
the Publishers Association. Impact of the Second World War.
Authors' war committees and plans. J. B. Priestley. St. John
Ervine. Collapse of the Pinker agency. Margaret Storm
Jameson's work for refugee writers at PEN.

Thring was succeeded by Denys Kilham Roberts, a young
thrusting barrister of very different mettle. DKR—as he was
known in the office—had literary pretensions of his own[1] and was
on terms of intellectual parity with any agent or publisher and
with most authors whom he had to deal with. He was capable not
only of standing his ground inside and outside the book trade, but
of taking strong initiatives. While Thring had usually been on the
defensive, DKR was always ready to switch to the attack. A man
of strong will, he made enemies, but he handled his chairmen and
members of the Society's Committee of Management (never
without men and women of character and independence) with
tact and decision, and he was careful to keep on good terms with
giants such as Barrie and Shaw.

DKR was at his best during the 1930s. He transformed *The
Author* in content and appearance, enlarging the format, giving it
an attractive cover, adopting a more readable typeface with wide

margins, introducing illustrations (notably portraits of leading writers, by Joseph Simpson), and filling its pages with lively and arresting articles by contributors as varied as Hugh Walpole, Mrs Belloc Lowndes, Gerald Bullett, Clemence Dane, Ernest Raymond, B. N. Langdon-Davies, and R. L. Mégroz (summer issue, 1932); or John Masefield, Luigi Villari, W. J. Turner, Stanley Unwin, and Margaret Kennedy (spring issue, 1939). Although always angled from the attitude of the author, as it had to be, running symposia or series on purely business subjects such as terms for reviewing, translating or broadcasting, discussing the hazards of theatre enterprises (Ashley Dukes) or films (Michael Balcon), or interpreting the law (E. J. MacGillivray), *The Author's* quality rivalled that of any contemporary literary magazine, such as *The London Mercury*, then at the height of (or just past) its reputation under its founder and editor, J. C. Squire. At the same time its record for hard-hitting comment bore comparison with national weeklies such as the *New Statesman*, edited by Kingsley Martin, and the *Weekend Review* (Gerald Barry), and—for getting hold of the facts—with the trade paper, *The Bookseller*, after the latter's rejuvenation by Edmond Segrave.

DKR's arrival coincided with the end of one literary and social era and the start of another. Writers who had been on the make at the turn of the century, or who had stormed the Establishment by the First World War, becoming eminent and established in their turn, were now either dead or dying off, or simply past their prime. Joseph Conrad, Edmund Gosse, Thomas Hardy and W. H. Hudson had died in the 1920s. Robert Bridges and D. H. Lawrence died in 1930, Arnold Bennett in 1931, Lytton Strachey in 1932, John Galsworthy, Anthony Hope Hawkins, and George Moore in 1933, G. K. Chesterton, A. E. Housman and Rudyard Kipling in 1936, John Drinkwater in 1937 when James Barrie also died. Barrie had succeeded Hardy as President of the Society of Authors and was followed by John Masefield. Among the dramatists Henry Arthur Jones had died in 1929, five years before Arthur Wing Pinero. W. B. Yeats died in 1939.

The list is indicative, not of course exhaustive; and the same qualification must apply to that of any *literati* in the 1930s. Among the older writers still high in the firmament were Hilaire Belloc, James Joyce, Somerset Maugham, Bertrand Russell,

Bernard Shaw, Hugh Walpole, and H. G. Wells, all of them proof, for one reason or another, against disaster. Among the younger, but not truly young, we find men and women of talent, writers in all the *genres*, who were facing the problems of survival in a period of world slump and approaching war. Every reader can put together a list of names. I hazard none but prefer to choose, by way of example, one pair, Leonard and Virginia Woolf, not because they belonged to the so-called Bloomsbury group of authors and artists in the 1930s (most of whom have been analysed to the last comma), but because the Woolfs, highly talented professionals, acutely aware of world events, intellectually at the forefront, possessed very little money beyond what they earned. Moreover Leonard Woolf left an exact account of their yearly incomes—derived from writing and the profits of their unique publishing venture, the Hogarth Press—and of how they managed their economy. The following figures therefore are drawn from Leonard's book, *Downhill all the Way* (p.142 et seq), his autobiography of the years 1919–39.

Leonard was primarily a political and literary journalist and editor, who also wrote books. He was literary editor of the *Nation* 1922–30, helped start the *Political Quarterly* in 1930, later editing it, and he contributed regularly to the *New Statesman* and other periodicals. None of his books sold well, with the exception of *Barbarians at the Gate*, a Left Book Club choice for October–November 1939, which reached a captive audience of many thousands. His average yearly income from writing between 1924 and 1939 was £374. Virginia combined literary journalism (mainly the *Times Literary Supplement* and the *Nation*) with writing novels; but it was not until 1928, with the publication of *Orlando*, that she began to earn large sums from her books, so that her average writing income far exceeded that of her husband and worked out at £1,481 per annum.[2] I suppose one must multiply these figures by at least 10 to hit upon a comparable figure for today (1982).

Success came to the Woolfs in their late forties after years of hard work and financial caution, dogged always by Virginia's mental instability which only Leonard's devotion held in check until her suicide in 1941. In the final reckoning however they succeeded because they were gifted and dedicated writers, who made sure of living inside their combined income.

Statistics of earnings by writers of the middle age range during this period are scarce, as no surveys are available of the kind conducted after the war by the Society of Authors. Thanks to the generosity of his widow, who gave me unfettered access to all his private correspondence and accounts, I have been able to trace the economic fortunes of Malcolm Elwin, the literary biographer, critic and editor, whose first full length book was published in 1928 and his last, *Lord Byron's Family* (John Murray), two years after his death in 1973—a span of 45 years during which his literary income rose from *c.* £250 p.a. to *c.* £2,500 p.a., and on which—with occasional supplements—he and his wife managed to live. Like the Woolfs, Elwin was a totally professional writer and man of letters. His career has added interest in that, as a scholar, he survived without any academic appointment or support and without a single grant from the Arts Council. In short, he was a freelance struggling to get by when literary independence, even for a man of his high attainment, was becoming rapidly less viable without a foothold in another medium (e.g. broadcasting) or an alternative bread-winning job.

Although at the heart of literary society before and after the war, the friend of many writers, old and young, and widely respected for his work and judgement, Elwin's reputation never depended upon the sales of his books. Success by size of sales may give a clue to literary taste or even indicate literary value, but it can never reflect the realities of authorship as a whole. It would be misleading, for example, to assess the 1930s solely by reference to the novels of J. B. Priestley or P. G. Wodehouse, to the plays of Frederick Lonsdale or Noël Coward, to the mathematics primers of C. V. Durell, or to the journalism of Arnold Bennett, who was being paid £70 for a weekly article of 800–1,000 words in the *Evening Standard* at the time of his death in 1931. Reality resided rather with the young writers emerging in the 1920s and 1930s, with some of whom the Woolfs had links. One of these was John Lehmann, who worked as Leonard Woolf's assistant at the Hogarth Press from 1931 to 1932, and who returned for a longer spell as partner and general manager from 1938 to 1946. The story of this association has been told by both parties,[3] but the point of relevance here is that Lehmann was one of a band of young writers, who not only set their faces against Georgian complacency (as they saw it), but were in general revolt against the political and social climate of the age—unemployment, poverty and the Means Test, colonialism, and, above all, appeasement of the dictators. As at other times most of them scraped along as best they could and wrote when they could afford to. A few had private means, as Lehmann had; but, as it turned out, his most important role was that of literary midwife.

With Michael Roberts he compiled *New Signatures* (published in 1932 as No. 24 in the Hogarth Living Poets Series) 'which has since been taken to mark the beginning, the formal opening, of the poetic movement of the 1930s'.[4] In 1936 he launched *New Writing*, a 'book-magazine', international in content, appearing twice a year, first with the backing of the Bodley Head,[5] and subsequently with that of the Hogarth Press, and which lasted under different titles (*Folios of New Writing*, then *New Writing and Daylight*) until 1946. In addition, with the support of Allen Lane, he edited for ten years (1940–50) *Penguin New Writing*, a unique venture in literary periodical publishing which at its height attained a circulation of 100,000 copies per issue, the highest in this class of publication since the first number of *Cornhill* which sold 120,000 copies in December 1859.

Young left-wing writers in the 1930s included W. H. Auden, Julian Bell, John Cornford, Christopher Isherwood, Cecil Day-Lewis, Louis MacNeice, Stephen Spender and, towards the end of the decade, George Orwell and Dylan Thomas. Right-wing, or non-partisan writers were John Betjeman, Roy Campbell, Geoffrey Grigson (who edited *New Verse* from 1933 to 1939), Cyril Connolly (who edited *Horizon* from 1940 to 1949), Graham Greene, Anthony Powell, and Evelyn Waugh; but I make no attempt to enumerate or classify precisely, and certainly not to try to compile any comprehensive list. My purpose is to see how some of these writers, in this critical period, solved the daily problem of survival while retaining their essential function as creators or critics. Like their older contemporaries, most of them relied on jobs which might or might not be related to writing, if they did not have private means. For example, Auden and Day-Lewis were schoolmasters, Orwell washed dishes for a time in Paris, Grigson and Greene were journalists, Powell worked for a publisher. The war proved a lifeline for many.

For the left wingers however necessity posed problems of principle. As his son, Sean, records, Day-Lewis was a committed

Communist for two years, from 1936 to 1938, and there was no doubt about his leftist view of society and the place of literature in it.[6]

> It [literature] will become more concerned with the relations between masses and less with relations between individuals: more of a guide to action and less of a commentary on action.[7]

In time he was compelled to temper his view for two reasons. One was that, in order to earn enough money to support himself and his family, he had to come to terms with the capitalist society in which he lived—first as a schoolmaster, then as a journalist and the author of successful detective novels under the pseudonym of 'Nicholas Blake', and during the war as an editor at the Ministry of Information. The other reason was the realisation that, after all, poetry was a purely individual mode of expression, reflecting the thoughts and emotions of individual man, whatever its impact on the 'masses'. Ironically Day-Lewis's own poetry was the least regarded of the leading leftist poets. He suffered much from the implacable hostility of Grigson, an influential critic and, for a time, assistant literary editor of *The Morning Post*. But, for me at any rate, he was the clearest and most level-headed exponent of the social consciousness, and of the aims and attitudes of the new movement, as communicated in poems, articles and broadcasts, and in the way he participated in what might be called 'sub-political activity'.

For example at the AGM of the Society of Authors (which he had joined in 1926), he seconded a motion by Charles King, a translator, to the effect that the Society should revise its rules so as to qualify for affiliation to the Trades Union Congress. He also suggested that 'a popular front of writers should be formed to combat the increasing danger of Fascism'. I quote from Sean:

> Lord Gorell, opposing, said there was no case for him to answer as no reasons for affiliation had been put forward. If there were political implications officers would resign. He was supported by Dorothy L. Sayers and St. John Ervine, and the pro-affiliation speakers included Amabel Williams-Ellis (an editor of *Left Review*) and Raymond Postgate. At the end the chairman, Major Ian Hay Beith, called for a show of hands and

[48]

declared the resolution defeated without a count being necessary.[8]

Two years later Day-Lewis contributed an article to *The Author* (Christmas issue 1938), in which he signed himself as 'Chairman of the Association of Writers for Intellectual Liberty', and described efforts being made by means of meetings and publications to counter Fascist doctrines and oppression, particularly in Nazi Germany. The article generated a lively correspondence, including a vigorous defence of Fascism by Leo Chiozza Money, but it was mainly criticised for omitting any reference to the suppression of freedom in Russia. Day-Lewis was not deterred, and he remained to play a valuable part in the Society's affairs: as a member of the Committee of Management from 1943 to 1946, and later of the Council, as one of the judges of the Somerset Maugham Award (1947–9), and at the memorial service to John Masefield at Westminster Abbey in 1967, when he recited some of the poet's work. Soon after, he succeeded Masefield as Poet Laureate.

Gorell was right in opposing the proposal to affiliate to the TUC in 1936, and so by implication to align the Society with the Labour Party. Forty years later, when for tactical reasons the Society was registered as a trade union, no attempt was made to affiliate. It is likely that any overt move in that direction would split the membership today, as it would have done in 1936, for the 3,000 or so members reflect every shade of political opinion. Gorell had been elected Chairman of the Committee of Management in succession to W. B. Maxwell in 1928 and stayed *in situ* until 1935. Surprisingly he was allowed to combine the post with that of partner in the highly respected publishing house of John Murray; but this was an anachronism, and a rule was made later that, while in office, no member of the Committee might hold a senior position (e.g. as director or partner) in a firm of publishers. Nonetheless Gorell was useful and active, without being an impressive personality, and he had a multitude of contacts in the right places. In 1929 he introduced a Bill in the House of Lords designed to amend the law of libel, so as to give protection against 'blackmailing' actions.[9] He showed tact and forbearance when handling the Wells–Vowles–Thring affairs in 1929–30, despite much provocation by Wells who accused him of being 'scarcely an author'.[10]

In the same period composer members of the Society were deeply worried by the introduction in 1929 of the Musical Copyright Bill, known as the 'Tuppeny Bill', which sought to permit anyone to perform a piece of copyright music on the payment of a fee 'not exceeding 2d per copy'. This was part of a campaign, organised by the International Council of Music Users, representing a mixed cohort of hotels, restaurants, cinemas, gramophone companies and others, against the near-monopoly exercised by the Performing Right Society, and generally sought to weaken the 1911 Copyright Act.

Authors at once sensed the danger, as Gorell explained in a letter to *The Times*:

> The Musical Copyright Bill seeks to establish the principle that it shall be for the users and not for the creators of music to fix the price for its use. If this be established for music, obviously it must be for other things also: book users will ask to fix the price authors are to receive on each copy of their books and motor-car users to fix the price for the use of motor-cars. The principle is not merely so inequitable, but so absurd that it would need no further exposure were it not for the singular fact that the Bill embodying it has actually passed its Second Reading in the House of Commons . . .

In another letter Shaw wrote:

> . . . that it should have passed its Second Reading is explicable only on the quite probable hypothesis that the great majority of members of the present House of Commons are amateur vocalists who have at one time or another been caught out in the act of stealing a performing right . . .[11]

In the event a Select Committee was appointed and, as a result of its deliberations and a continuing blast of ridicule in the press, the Bill was killed.

Gorell was succeeded by Ian Hay Beith, who had served an

earlier term as Chairman and knew the Society's ways. As an author he carried far more weight than Gorell, since he was a popular and prolific novelist and playwright, and had written a war bestseller, *The First Hundred Thousand*. His second term lasted until early in 1939 when he was appointed Director of Public Relations at the War Office and promoted Major-General; but at all times the main burden of administration and initiative fell upon the chief executive, D K R, who on succeeding Thring in March 1930 wasted no time in launching new projects. In 1931 he helped found the League of Dramatists, a semi-autonomous group within the general membership of the Society, and in 1937 The Screenwriters' Association. The work of both these organisations is described in Part Two.

Three other initiatives are of historical interest. The first was an attempt to establish a register of subjects on which authors were working—an idea that came to nothing owing to the opposition of certain publishers, and was only launched by the National Book League in the 1970s. The second, which was successful, was to receive for safe keeping scripts and synopses of plays, scenarios and sketches, written by members, as evidence in cases of alleged infringement of copyright. The third arose out of D K R's dissatisfaction with the quality of *The Writers' and Artists' Year Book*, published annually by A. & C. Black, but which struck him as being 'packed with advertisements from dud and shark concerns'. He therefore compiled a rival volume, *The Authors Handbook*, approved by the Society and issued on his behalf by The Bodley Head in 1935, 1936, 1939 and 1940, and by Nelson in 1937 and 1938. Publication lapsed after 1940, and later Black's so improved the *Year Book* that it gained the formal approval of the Society, which has long since recommended it as a reliable source of information and reference.

In 1936 D K R appointed as his principal assistant a woman of great ability and charm, a qualified barrister, who was to devote the rest of her working life to the Society and who ultimately became General Secretary. Elizabeth Barber recorded some vivid recollections, from which I quote:

I started work in January 1936 at a salary of nothing for the first six weeks, rising to £225 a year for the first year and then to £300 until such time as the Committee decided to review it.

My father thought I had gone mad and said so. I had been working temporarily in his office—he was what was then called County Clerk of Hampshire County Council—on the defence to a claim by the dismissed Superintendent of a mental home for libel, slander, wrongful dismissal, and the 'conversion of a pair of tennis shoes'. I could have had an absolutely secure job there had I wanted it, but I didn't because of the total lack of any sense of fun in almost any member of staff except my father.

The moment I met Denys Kilham Roberts I knew that I had met a kindred spirit at any rate so far as laughing was concerned. Laughter was like strong drink to him, often indulged in when things looked particularly black. So it was to many of the other congenial, brilliant and difficult people I met during my time with the Society. In DKR's case however he would be quite prepared to sacrifice truth to wit and even malice—disconcerting at times if you had to sit silently by and watch some innocent swallowing some unlikely statement.

Shortly after my arrival, DKR was compiling a book of nonsense and surrealist verse and used in his introduction a passage from G. K. Chesterton that he loved to quote:

'So long as we regard a tree as a thing naturally and reasonably created for a giraffe to eat, we cannot possibly wonder at it. It is when we consider it as a prodigious wave of the living soil sprawling up to the skies for no reason in particular that we take off our hats to the astonishment of the park keeper.'

His capacity to take off his hat to the astonishment of the park keeper endeared him to me and to a multitude of other friends, who nevertheless found him—as I did—maddening and almost impossible to work with when the black fit descended on him. I remember W. J. Turner, who had been involved, foolishly and innocently, in a publishing deal which was hard on some of his fellow authors, saying ruefully: 'My dear Denys, just because you don't like the colour of someone's front door, you don't have to pull down every house in the street.'

Combined with the surrealist side of his nature which turned truth inside out or ignored it altogether was a capacity for recognising the true quality of a person or thing. . . It was an education to hear him assess a poem absolutely on its merits, when compiling one of his anthologies, so that many previously unknown poems took precedence over old and familiar favourites. It was the same with pictures . . . and to an extreme degree with wine.

These qualities, combined with the power to charm a bird off a tree or sway a committee made him many friends and, alas, many enemies too. I remember him once saying: 'Why is it that so many authors seem pleased to talk to me and to be seen to be talking to me, but more pleased to say something absolutely beastly behind my back?' I believe it was due to a feeling that there was something phoney about his 'latin' exuberance and enthusiasm; but that when he had gone away and the warmth of his personality was not present, then one wondered whether he had been playing some sort of diabolical game for his own ends. In fact he hardly ever had.

Lord Gorell was a case in point. In early days D K R 'could do no wrong'. But when he compiled *The Author's Handbook*, with entries written by himself instead of by the publishers concerned, Gorell (a partner in John Murray) was far from pleased, and not long after left. Part of the power that D K R exerted was, ridiculous as it may sound, due to the story he put about that he could use the 'evil eye'. Every time that anyone died or was taken inexplicably ill after quarrelling with him, he took credit for it. It was a sinister side to his character that could not be underrated.

Ian Hay, who succeeded Gorell as chairman, was almost the ideal person at the time. He was an established author, with a remarkable gift for handling the most difficult members—and usually only the most difficult appeared—at the Annual General Meetings. As a war-time (1914–18) soldier, re-employed in 1939, he preferred to be known as General Beith rather than Ian Hay. In fact he had been a schoolmaster and, incidentally, had taught Hugh Walpole; nevertheless he looked every inch a soldier, tall, slim, with a trim moustache, and as far as I could make out had no light conversation at all. In those days there was an Annual Dinner and Dance at the Victoria Hotel in Northumberland Avenue and, foxtrotting round that rather pompous ballroom there was absolutely nothing to say. Ian Hay seemed to be made out of cardboard, and you felt that, at the end of the evening, he ought to be folded up and stacked away until he was needed again for some other public function. How different from the wildly waltzing little W. W. Jacobs, with the transparent red nose, who became rather a buddy of mine at the time.

Ian Hay was reliable and had a fund of common sense. I only knew his judgement once to be badly at fault when he said that if ever John Strachey were made chairman, 'it would split the Society from top to bottom'. In fact when John was made chairman some years later, so far from splitting it, he welded the Society together more firmly than ever before—by introducing reforms that infused new blood into the Committee of Management at regular intervals, and let light and air into its deliberations.

In 1939—two years before the expiry of the lease of the Society's crumbling offices at 11, Gower Street, wc2—DKR persuaded the Committee to purchase the freehold (for £3,600) of the present headquarters at 84, Drayton Gardens, sw10. He also bought a house from himself at Mortimer, near Reading, as a refuge for his family and the staff in case of war. The previous move had taken place in 1925 when the Society had transferred from Tothill Street, Westminster, to Gower Street, where in due course DKR installed his wife and child in a flat at the top of the house. It was a curious ménage. Vestiges of the Thring era still clung to the older members of the staff in the persons of Mrs Griffin, the principal secretary, and E. J. Mullett whom Elizabeth Barber described as:

. . . a sort of Dickensian head clerk in a shabby and shiny black suit with celluloid collar, who came to the office when he was 14 and left when he was 60, dying soon after. In 1936 his main job was the Robert Louis Stevenson estate, which had come into the statutory licence period under the 1911 Copyright Act. It was largely a matter of issuing royalty stamps to publishers. I can see Mullett now, surrounded by sheets of these which he rubber-stamped with minute fractions of a penny. From heaps of this strange confetti he would emerge, cracking his finger joints and posing some abstruse copyright or tax problems with which he had floored, no doubt, a City Literary Institute lecturer the night before. In the corner of Mullett's room stood the old letter press used for wet copying before D K R modernised the office equipment shortly before I arrived. So ingrained had previous habits become that, every time the telephone rang, D K R swung round and faced the wall behind his desk. The astonished visitor could not be expected to know that that was where the old-fashioned telephone mouth- and separate earpiece used to hang.

The person who ruled the office in many minor ways was Mrs Barlow, the char, a formidable operator, who always carried her marriage lines in the leg of her bloomers in case anyone should doubt her marital status.

If the staff were late in leaving, she would wash the lavatory seats with soapy water so that no one could sit down on them. John Buchan was always 'Jack Buchanan', and copies of the *Droit d'Auteur* were always the 'Droitwich Papers' which she refused to dust however dusty they got.

Mrs Barlow had also established a pricing system whereby she charged separately for cleaning the office, for making tea, for washing the tea cups, for washing the tea towels, and so on, on top of which she had secured an automatic annual rise of 2s 6d a week. Inevitably the moment arrived when D K R calculated that Mrs B. was earning more than he was, and called a halt. Ever after she referred to D K R, no longer as 'Mr Roberts' but as ''im upstairs', where however she continued to 'do' for Mrs Roberts and feed 'Pewter', the cat, for whom she imported raw liver each day until the poor animal entirely lost its coat. The end was sad. After the war started, Mrs Barlow followed the others to the country but so disliked it that she returned to London and vanished in the Blitz. Bombed to bits, it was said.

Meanwhile the Society retained a nucleus of staff at No. 84 until the intensive bombing began in the late summer of 1940, when the house was shut up. The residue of furniture was stacked in the basement and to keep the damp at bay an anthracite stove was installed in the hall, tended by the father of Caterina Gilardino,[12] who had joined the accounts department in 1936. The keys of the house were left with the nearby A R P post, a wise precaution as the warden and his team were able to deal with an incendiary that penetrated the roof in 1941, otherwise the place would have burned to the ground. The office was re-opened in the autumn of 1945, when everything was found to be in good order with one important exception—dry rot.

Like many major historical events, the outbreak of the Second World War in September 1939 is a convenient moment at which to take stock—in this case of the book trade at large which had been in the doldrums since the betrayal of Czechoslovakia at Munich in September 1938. As it proved, the depression was temporary and was shortly to undergo a remarkable metamorphosis, whereby the greatest problem confronting publishers and booksellers was not lack of sales, but insufficient stock to satisfy the insatiable demand for reading.

During the previous decade, following the Wall Street crash of 1929 and the resultant world slump, the abandonment by Britain of the Gold Standard in 1931, the rise of unemployment to $2\frac{1}{2}$ millions, and the imposition of protective trade barriers by one country after another in a frantic effort to preserve their economies, the British book trade suffered less severely than most. Publishers showed considerable resource in sustaining exports in the face of fierce (especially American) competition, import controls, and outright piracy notably in India and the Far East: but receiving timely aid by the formation in 1935 of the British Council, which regarded the distribution of books abroad as an important and practical means of providing closer cultural and educational relations with other countries.

At home there was a series of experiments and initiatives, as outlined by R. J. L. Kingsford in his history of *The Publishers Association, 1896–1946* (CUP, 1970) from which I quote or draw information for these pages.

These were the years of the 3s 6d cloth-bound reprint series—the Travellers, the Phoenix, the Windmill, the Adelphi Libraries; of Benn's Sixpennies, of the pioneer work of the Phoenix Co., inspired by John Baker with the backing of Hugh Dent, in the sale of books on the instalment plan; and in 1935

Allen Lane produced his first Penguins. Nor should Victor Gollancz's attempt to encourage readers of novels to buy, rather than borrow, go unremembered. In 1930 he formed a new company, Mundanus, with the announced aim of publishing initially at the rate of one a month, and at the price of 3s net, new full-length novels in paper covers. Three were issued in 1930, but the unwillingness of booksellers to put books in soft covers on to their shelves compelled the abandonment of the experiment in the following year. New novels did not get the support of newsagents which enabled the first Penguin reprints five years later to survive the initial opposition from booksellers.

Book clubs also flourished. Their precursor, the Book Society, had been formed by Alan Bott in 1929 and

. . . with Hugh Walpole, Clemence Dane, George Gordon, Sylvia Lynd and J. B. Priestley as its first selection committee undertook to deliver to its members a monthly choice on the day of publication. . . It was doing no more than supply to its members a chosen book at the ordinary published price and was in effect a mail-order bookseller conforming to the Net Book Agreement.

The idea caught on and

. . . the ability to place one order for 3,000, 5,000, 10,000, 15,000 or more books, all of them sold in advance, meant for the book club low distribution costs and for the supplying publisher a considerable reduction in his manufacturing cost.

There were soon eight book clubs, all offering titles at prices substantially lower than the published price, usually at 2s 6d; and it was not long before fears were expressed at the effect which two widely different prices for the same book would have on the public. Discussions between the Publishers Association and the Booksellers' Association (then known as Associated Booksellers) eventually resulted in agreement on a ratio of prices—7s 6d (published) to 2s 6d (book club)—an interval between the appearance of the two editions, and certain other conditions. It is generally accepted that book clubs have contributed materially to the expansion of reading and the growth of trade, although the precise benefits to booksellers and authors have remained in doubt.

Another innovation was the Book Token—a gift token exchangeable by the recipient for a book of his or her choice at a stated price—an idea invented by Harold Raymond of Chatto & Windus and launched in 1932. This has proved itself a great boon to all parties, book producers and purveyors and the public alike, although at the outset its administration was misunderstood by a number of booksellers and so it took time to make its mark.[13] Kingsford suggests that the trouble arose out of confusion with gift coupons offered by firms outside the book trade; initially in 1932 by Messrs Wix and Co, whereby the purchaser of a packet of Kensitas cigarettes exchanged a coupon for a book, out of a list of 450 titles supplied by 15 publishers. The scheme foundered after a year due to the opposition of the booksellers, while similar ones launched in 1933 by the *Daily Mail* and in 1934 by the *Daily Herald*, offering respectively sets of Shakespeare's and Shaw's plays, also died out, despite a characteristically provocative and controversial statement in *The Bookseller* by Shaw.[14]

Sufficient examples have been given to demonstrate that, during the 1930s, publishers were not short of ideas for the improvement of trade and that, in general but not invariably, they were able to agree with the booksellers on collective issues. Relations with the Society of Authors were however less straightforward. An early problem concerned Tauchnitz paperback editions of new British books for sale on the Continent appearing simultaneously with the original edition. The PA wanted the Society to bring pressure on its members, who normally reserved these rights, to insist on an interval of two to three years before the Tauchnitz edition appeared. After canvassing the membership, the Society was unable to meet the PA's request. Most authors refused to prohibit the appearance of Tauchnitz even for a few months.

Another dispute arose over the broadcasting of published material in copyright. Ever since 1923 the Society had made its own terms with the BBC, rates being revised and raised at regular intervals. The publishers wished to take a hand in order, first, to prevent the use of such material within a minimum interval after publication, secondly to participate in the fees paid, and thirdly to ensure that the BBC made full acknowledgements as to publisher and price as well as to the author. This last request was reasonable enough, and it seems strange nowadays that there was any difficulty over it; but the Society resolutely refused the first two requests, and only later gave ground as regards the transmission of straight readings from a book.

These exchanges led to broader discussions about subsidiary rights as a whole, and ultimately about 'all rights, markets and obligations to be assumed by the publisher in an agreement with an author'. This resulted in the PA issuing its first *Guide to Royalty Agreements* in which 'it laid down the principles (with specimen clauses and notes and alternatives to meet a variety of circumstances) which were necessary to protect publishers against ill-informed or unreasonable authors and agents and to protect authors against rapacious publishers'.[15] This of course was a collection of recommendations only, as neither the PA nor the Society had mandatory powers over their members. However, the *Guide* was a beginning from the publishers' point of view and served as a basis for future revision and discussion between the two organisations. At the same time the Society continued—and this remains one of its principal services to individual members today—to vet contracts clause by clause if necessary and, in addition to the issue of its detailed 'Quick Guide' to *Publishing Contracts*,[16] to advise on any business problem arising between author and publisher.

The Second World War was to force far-reaching changes on the book trade, notably the need for collective action in the face of shortages of paper, binding materials, metal for printing, labour and bomb damage. The notorious raid of 29 December 1940 destroyed virtually all the publishers' premises and stocks in Paternoster Row, and destruction was continued by further raids at least until May 1941. Earlier in 1940 the Government had proposed to levy purchase tax on books, a move that roused a united and superhuman effort by authors, publishers and booksellers, acting together with public figures such as the Archbishop of Canterbury, Kenneth Lindsay and Harry Strauss,

[59]

tabled an amendment in the House of Commons to exempt books from the tax, so that, confronted by a barrage of public meetings and private representations and a powerful speech in Parliament on 25 July 1941 by A. P. Herbert, the Chancellor of the Exchequer, Sir Kingsley Wood, was persuaded to withdraw the proposal.

Perhaps the severest difficulty encountered by authors at the start of the war was that of official indifference: in particular, reluctance on the part of the Government to work out any scheme, well in advance of hostilities, to harness their talents. In May 1939—thanks to an informal agreement with Humbert Wolfe, minor poet, man of letters, and civil servant in the Ministry of Labour—DKR had circulated a questionnaire to a large number of authors, inviting them to state their qualifications and preferences for work in the event of war. The final question on the paper had inquired after the respondent's attitude to military service, conscription, etc—probably in all innocence—but it caused a flutter in the House of Commons when, on 25 May, a Mr Mander pressed the Minister on the legality, not only of the question, but of a professional organisation such as the Society of Authors undertaking such an enquiry at all. The Minister pleaded ignorance and the matter was not raised again. By that time however a large number of questionnaires had been completed and returned to the Society's office—and they made interesting reading.

On 28 July, barely six weeks before the invasion of Poland, the Ministry of Information set up an Authors' Planning Committee: Chairman, Raymond Needham, KC; Secretary, A. D. Peters, the literary agent. The Committee included R. H. S. Crossman, A. P. Herbert, Professor John Hilton, Dorothy Sayers, L. A. G. Strong, and Denys Kilham Roberts. The objects generally conformed to those of the May questionnaire, but progress was very slow. DKR and Peters kept in close touch and tried to maintain momentum. Fresh lists of authors were assembled, annotated and classified, while Dorothy Sayers produced the best draft plans. That nothing positive emerged was due, possibly, to the lulling effect of the phoney war which lasted seven months, to the fact that individual authors were beginning to find their own niches in industry, the Services, and Government departments (including the Ministry of Information), to the ludicrous but real problem of translating the general objects of the war ('stopping Hitler', 'liberating Europe', etc.) into effective subjects for writing other than more or less crude propaganda, and lastly to the apparent lack of unanimity among authors themselves, as demonstrated in a symposium published in the spring and summer issues of *The Author* in 1940.

For example, Osbert Sitwell wanted a Minister of Fine Arts for whom he considered Samuel Hoare 'the perfect choice . . . with his overwhelming passion for literature'. John Strachey stated, 'The best thing that the Government can do for authors in wartime is to leave them alone.' E. M. Forster wanted the BBC to give more time to literature. He calculated that the Home Service was devoting only one and a quarter hours out of 120 a week to the subject, while broadcasting to the Forces rendered a nil return out of 84 hours. St. John Ervine pointed out that, in the absence of contemporary alternatives, readers were turning back to Trollope and Maria Edgeworth. Ernest Raymond thought that the Ministry of Information was potentially more important than any Service Ministry, that paper was the most vital munition of war, and that writers had always won more battles than soldiers.

The most positive contributions amounted to warnings—variously advanced by J. B. Priestley, Henry Nevinson, Anthony Armstrong, V. S. Pritchett, Bernard Shaw, and others—to the effect that authors should resist any pressure to accept lower fees and royalties, on the grounds of false patriotism, or because publishing was in temporary difficulties and production costs were rising (but being paid for in the ordinary way). A. D. Peters contributed some facts and figures. In peacetime ten per cent had been a common royalty on cheap editions, although Penguins had originally offered seven and a half per cent on their sixpennies, latterly reduced to five per cent. He cautioned authors to beware of a cash figure, e.g. 2d per copy offered by a book club, instead of a royalty rate, and he rejected the argument that large print-runs justified lower royalties—just the opposite.

By this time Hitler had intervened; and soon after Duff Cooper became Minister of Information in May 1940, the Authors' Planning Committee was dissolved. A letter from John Masefield, President of the Society, had no effect. Initiative then passed into the hands of J. B. Priestley, whose radio talks were having a powerful impact upon public opinion. Thanks to him a new group was formed, called the Authors' National Committee, with an impressive list of names at the head of the notepaper, supported by DKR as Secretary. The Committee's object was familiar, 'to ensure a fuller and better directed use of the services of our best authors in connexion with the war effort'; and in February 1941 DKR canvassed nearly 100 leading writers, most of whom responded favourably. The same problem then arose—how best to make use of all this goodwill and offers of service? Priestley's first idea was to ask Walter Monckton, who had succeeded Duff Cooper, to attach authors to the various Services, like artists or war correspondents of a superior grade. 'For example', he wrote, 'a first-class writer could do something imperishable about this desert campaign of Wavell's if he were on the spot.' But Monckton rejected the idea, and the next move was to ask William Collins, the publisher, if he or a group of publishers would undertake the publication of a series of short books dealing with the problems of reconstruction after the war, each book to cover a specific subject, all under the aegis of the Authors' National Committee. Collins was enthusiastic, brought in Dwye Evans of Heinemann (Priestley's publisher), and signed an agreement with Priestley himself to write the first title, *Out of the People*, which duly appeared (at 2s 6d) and by February 1942 had sold 41,000 copies out of a print-run of 50,000. As it proved, this was the only title in the series for, by the time of publication, various factors combined to bring the project to an end: a fresh paper crisis, Priestley's own over-crowded programme of writing, broadcasting, lecturing and travelling, and—behind it all perhaps—his growing concern with the reform of society on socialist lines, a partisan commitment not shared by his colleagues on the editorial board of the Committee (Margaret Storm Jameson, Professor John Macmurray, and DKR), nor by the publishers.

Meanwhile DKR had been carrying on the ordinary business of the Society which, after the initial shock of the war and a drop in membership (which surprisingly soon recovered), was conducted in collaboration with the current chairman, St. John Ervine. Ervine was primarily a dramatist and critic, and an Ulster Protestant of volcanic temperament, given to violent thoughts and statements that needed tactful handling. As a recruiting officer, he was first class: pleading eloquently with members to pay their overdue subscriptions and stay with the Society, and attracting new members, young unknowns and old eminents alike. But when it came to asking Beverly Baxter, former editor of the *Daily Express*, to join, his wrath overflowed.

Nothing on earth will induce me to write to this man, even uncivilly. If I were to hear that he had just been removed to Hell, I should send a note of sympathy to Satan.

Pinker was his agent. However the agency—founded and raised to a successful and respected level by James B. Pinker, the friend (and private banker) of writers like Joseph Conrad and Arnold Bennett—declined after J.B.'s death in 1922 and finally came to grief in the hands of his two sons. The New York office under Eric collapsed in 1939, the London office under Ralph in 1940, both brothers being declared bankrupt and convicted of fraud. Ervine was owed money, but remarkably subdued his feelings.

I have no rancour towards Ralph. I'm sorry for the fool. I'm willing to let the money due to me remain unpaid until the debts due to necessitous authors are all discharged. . . which probably means that I must say good-bye to it for ever.[17]

It was probably with a sense of relief that DKR turned in 1942 to Ervine's successor, Margaret Storm Jameson, no less respected as a professional writer and novelist, who happened to be living in Mortimer nearby. But there was another reason. Margaret and her husband, Guy Chapman—writer, academic and publisher—were particularly well equipped to cope with the crises of the time. Both were 'Europeans', primarily Francophiles, while Margaret had additionally a close knowledge of central European writers—anti-Nazi Germans and Austrians, Poles and Czechs—for whom she as President from 1938 to 1944, and Herman Ould as Secretary, of the English Centre of PEN, performed prodigies of service. In her autobiography[18] she searingly described her experiences, recalling with startling power the day-to-day desperations of the late 1930s and early 1940s, when Hitler was overrunning Europe. After 1938 the clamour for help was deafening.

There were too many of them.

We answered every letter, we tried to get the visas needed, an effort involving us in hundreds of letters to the Home Office and visits to overworked refugee organisations. For one person we got out, ten, fifty, a hundred sank. . .

'There is only one way to help people,' A. R. Orage once said to me, 'and that is to give them money.'

Herman looked at me wearily. 'Where on earth do you imagine it can come from?'

'We can try'. . .

From one source and another we raised almost three thousand pounds, not a great sum. . . After a time I knew that I would rather go out scrubbing than write any more begging letters.

But this remarkably *large* sum helped salve the destitute; and, thanks to further efforts, most refugee writers were retrieved relatively quickly from internment in the Isle of Man, where all had been banished in a panic—geriatrics and healthy young students alike—in the summer of 1940.

They even managed to hold a PEN Congress in London in 1941, and shamed the Government into supporting them by securing the patronage of

> . . . four heads of governments in exile, thirteen ambassadors and ministers, six High Commissioners, a round dozen eminent Englishmen, and Denis Saurat, who was lending us the French Institute.
>
> We were not in a position to refuse alms. The Free French, who ought to have been our guests, invited the Congress, the whole of it, to a reception at Dorchester House. For the rest, we wrung from the Government a small cocktail party in Lancaster House, for the fifty or sixty delegates only, and the use of an aeroplane to bring over two American writers [Thornton Wilder and John Dos Passos].

None of these achievements were publicly recognised; nor, I suspect, are they even remembered—except in PEN minutes—today. Margaret Storm Jameson's successors at the Society of Authors were John Strachey and Osbert Sitwell, who alternated—with one break, from 1949 to 1951, when Arthur Bryant took the chair—over the next decade, until Margaret came back again in 1954. During their terms of office a great deal of work was undertaken both by members and by officers of the Society to combat the economic problems of authorship post-war.

CHAPTER THREE

Post-war Prospects

Composers form own Guild in 1944. Authors writing for
Government departments. Outlook in 1945. Shaw appoints the
Society to act as his agent. Agents discussed. Elizabeth Barber
succeeds D. K. Roberts as Secretary of the Society, 1963–71.
Her successors, 1971–81. The Society's Collection Bureau.
Association of Authors' Agents, 1975. Post-war taxation and
authorship. Authors and social security.

With the invasion of Normandy in June 1944 came the growing
conviction that the war was all but won. However unjustified, this
feeling was reflected in a flood of articles, leaflets, books and
broadcasts about peacetime plans for reconstruction and in many
other manifestations. At the Society it took the form of a revival of
membership, and the decision—heartily encouraged by the
Committee of Management and Secretariat—of the composers to
set up on their own. Musician members had always been
something of an anomaly. They had belonged on and off since
before the First World War, basically because they were not
numerous or active enough to go it alone, and so had turned to the
Society *faute de mieux*. By the autumn of 1944 it had been agreed
to form the Composers' Guild, with Ralph Vaughan Williams as
the first President. Although still 'under the auspices and within
the membership of the Society', it was not long before the Guild
found its feet and became totally independent: and has so
remained to this day.

The war however was not won in 1944, and the problem of
authors' contribution to the war effort—as authors—was revived
in an interesting exchange of letters in the winter issue of *The
Author*. Hugh Shearman opened the subject by referring to the

employment of authors by public departments in order to popularise particular services and seek the co-operation of the public.

> It seems to me that a completely new class of professional relationship is coming into being . . . between the author and some public department which will give him a fairly free hand, will have very little notion as to how he ought to be paid, will not employ authors often enough to acquire guiding experience and will be most accustomed to doing business on semi-contract terms with specifications. . .
>
> I feel it is not so much a problem of exact definition of rates of pay, but rather of inventing some sort of way in which it can be conveyed in a general sense to people who have no experience of the matter, that literary work really is as slow and laborious and highly specialised as it is, that fairly high rates of payment for the produce of such work, when surrendered outright, are no swindle, and that the author is a much rarer kind of specialist than the surgeon or barrister and should not be paid less generously.

The novelist, H. E. Bates, by then a squadron-leader in the RAF, replied:

> What is new of course is the tendency of the armed services, and also of such temporary services as Civil Defence, WVS, Womens' Land Army and the NFS, to enlist writers as writers purely and not as washers up of dishes or scrubbers of floors. . .
>
> In 1941 I walked into the Air Ministry and asked with great scepticism if they could use a writer and was staggered and delighted to be told Yes. The Air Ministry of those days went one further, and said they could use a short story writer. I was accordingly commissioned, given my training in the regulation way, and have never been quite the same man since. I was in fact the first State short story writer, if that isn't too pompous a name, and my job for the better part of two years was to live with and write about the crews of the RAF. In these two years I wrote enough stories to fill two volumes, each of which subsequently sold, in English alone, something like a quarter of a million copies. From the proceeds of these works, both

serially and in volume form, I got nothing in the shape of fees or royalties and of course did not expect anything.

Bates was not however recommending his RAF experience as providing the right solution. Indeed in ordinary circumstances, at war or not, he abhorred the idea of any organisation having an author on the staff. A salary implied—ultimately necessitated— toeing the line. 'The author is a casual specialist, not a regular. He should be called in and then, in good time, be kicked out.'

Bates was supported by Hilary St George Saunders who was, perhaps, the best-known and most successful staff writer of the war.

Any author who may be employed by a public or private corporation should fix his own terms and, if he feels unable to do so, then he should employ a competent agent.[1]

With the end of the Second World War and the Labour landslide at the 1945 General Election the race for reconstruction was on. In a review of the book trade, Edmond Segrave, editor of *The Bookseller*, reported that the output of titles (new books and reprints) had fallen from 14,904 in 1939 to 6,705 in 1943 (the low point) but had since risen to 6,747 in 1945. In the same period publishers' turnover had doubled from £10 millions to £20 millions, including a healthy export business despite the war. The potential of post-war publishing was enormous, with the inevitable abolition of controls on paper and other materials, and the apparently limitless demand for English language books in liberated Europe and all those countries soon to be known collectively as the Third World. In short, prospects were excellent.

What of the authors? In general, relations with publishers had clearly emerged from the era of crass exploitation, although in most cases it remained true that 'as the capitalist who financed the deal, the publisher was in a commanding position', and on occasions took unfair advantage of it. Collectively the relationship between the Society of Authors and the Publishers Association was one of watchfulness, at times erupting into hostility; in other words the normal attitude of any representative organisation whose members are engaged in commercial and professional survival. Experience shows that however close the common interests of 'partners' in a trade may be—in this case publishers and authors, but no less true of publishers and booksellers—uncritical collaboration does actual disservice to both sides and leads to disillusion. Thus most of the euphoria generated at this time about 'partnership' and post-war prosperity had soon to be discounted.

1945 was a stimulating year for the Society: the sense of liberation at the end of the war, the return to offices in London, the continuing rise in membership, and the celebration of the Society's Diamond Jubilee[2]—60 years since the foundation by Walter Besant in 1884–5. The financial outlook however looked less rosy with most of the income coming from membership dues of only 30 shillings a year. Before the end of 1945 however prospects were transformed by the receipt of a postcard from Bernard Shaw, now nearly 90 years old, inviting the Society to take over the management of all his literary and theatre business.

DKR had of course been preparing the way for this electrifying communication and others that followed, elaborating the terms, all on the basis of a flat rate commission of seven and a half per cent for the Society. As is well known, Shaw had always handled most of his own authorship business. Constable acted as his publisher on commission, R. & R. Clark of Edinburgh were his printers, a handful of translators and foreign agents played their parts on licence, all deferring to the author and his faithful secretary, Blanche Patch, operating from the flat in Whitehall Court or the house at Ayot St. Lawrence with whom Elizabeth Barber, as the Society's Assistant Secretary, kept in close touch.[3]

Shaw's decision to appoint the Society as his agent sprang from his lifelong distrust of the ordinary run of literary agents. He had stated his views at length in the December 1911 issue of *The Author*, in which he alleged that if a publisher accepted a book, there was no great difficulty in securing the standard royalty of ten per cent, and that it paid an agent to sell as many books as he could on this basis rather than fight for better terms both as to the royalty scale and as to subsidiary rights:

. . . it must be taken as a fact that it is the agent's interest to have a low rate of profit on many books, and the author's to stand out for the highest attainable rate of profit on his single book.

Shaw went on to argue that it was more important for an agent to be on friendly terms with editors, publishers and managers than with any individual author, so that

> Finally he settles down into an agent whose real business is to procure books for publishers, articles for editors, and plays for managers, though his ostensible business is to procure publishers for books, editors for articles, and managers for plays.

Shaw's remarks were coloured by the conditions of the trade immediately before the First World War, when it was not unusual for a popular author to receive royalties of 25 per cent, while even a starting rate of 15 per cent was quite common. At that time too the number of reliable and successful agents was small, in contrast to the crowd of applicants for authors' business, whose names appear in the Society's records. Some of these simply went bankrupt; others trod the rocky path of literary consultancy, writing tuition, reading fees, and vanity publishing, singly or in combination. Galloway Kyle, as already mentioned, was a notorious example, A. M. Burghes another. Burghes, convicted of fraudulent conversion in 1912, had begun business in the 1880s, shortly after A. P. Watt (1875), who is generally regarded as the first literary agent proper, and whose firm still stands at the forefront today. Watt was followed by J. B. Pinker in 1896, Curtis Brown in 1899, and Christy and Moore and Hughes Massie, both in 1912. These firms led the field almost on their own until after 1918, with one important exception, William Morris Colles, who was closely connected with the Society at and after its foundation, and was a personal friend of Walter Besant.

Colles acted for a time as legal consultant to the Society and had an office in the same building at 4, Portugal Street, off the Strand. He conducted an enquiry into the Civil List, published as a Society pamphlet in 1889 under the title of *Literature and the Civil List*, and in the same year started the Authors' Syndicate which duly developed into a full-scale agency. In effect, owing to the Society's need to concentrate on the definition and defence of literary property in all its forms, and on the reform of copyright, Colles became the Society's agent, 'concluding agreements, collecting royalties, examining and passing accounts, and generally relieving members of the trouble of managing business details'. I quote from Volume One of this book:

> Professionally however Colles proved a disappointment. Although he acted for a time for several successful writers, including Arnold Bennett, Eden Phillpotts, A. E. W. Mason and Somerset Maugham, he failed to keep their custom, the relationship usually ending in ill humour. The Society too became increasingly dissatisfied. Early in the 1900s it ceased to advertise the Syndicate in *The Author* and then severed the business connection altogether. Late in 1909 it supported Maugham in a court case brought by Colles over a claim for commission. The jury found for the plaintiff . . . a judgement of which the Committee of Management was at pains to express its public disapproval.
>
> Colles's comparative failure at a time when literary agency was a pioneer industry had a dual effect, for it lost both Colles himself and the Society a unique opportunity to establish a highly profitable business when other agents were making their names and fortunes. In fact the Society made a fresh start when, in 1912, it set up its Collection Bureau—following the adoption of the statutory licence period (of 50 years after the author's death) in the Copyright Act 1911. Since that date the Society has acted for a number of literary estates, not in open competition as a placing agent for the work of living writers, but usually in response to a request by an author nearing the end of his life, or by his executors and heirs. An early example was the estate of R. L. Stevenson. . .[4]

The Society's other main agency activity before Shaw's action in 1945 was the work done by the League of Dramatists, the subsidiary organisation set up in 1931 to negotiate agreements and collect fees and royalties on behalf of dramatist members, for which Harold Rubinstein (partner in the firm of solicitors, Rubinstein Nash) acted as Secretary for a number of years.

Between the wars the number of reliable agents increased,[5] in response to the expansion of the book and periodical markets and the growth of two new media, films and broadcasting. Even so the great majority of authors dispensed with agents, either because they preferred to handle their own business (backed by the Society if they were members), or because there were not sufficient agents equipped to meet the potential demand. In any event, then as now, the pros and cons of employing an agent were nicely balanced, depending as much on the particular circumstances of the author as on the efficacy of the agent.

The situation has been fairly presented in a pamphlet[6] recently re-issued by the Society, the main points of which are as follows:

A good agent should:

a) Sell your work, exploiting all potential outlets and helping to project your image. He should know the market intimately: what subjects are needed, by whom, in what form, in which media and, no less important, what subjects are not needed. He should have effective access, both at home and abroad, to publishers, editors, producers, managers and others who control the outlet for a writer's work.

b) Negotiate all business contracts in accordance with your instructions.

c) Offer you a degree of editorial and literary advice—or procure it for you.

d) Account to you as soon as possible for all monies received.

On the other hand

An indifferent agent will be of little value. He will simply allow you to make contacts and sell the ideas, while taking commission for drawing up routine contracts. . . Even after the termination of an agent's authority, he remains legally entitled to commission on money accruing under contracts negotiated in the past.

Once therefore an author has authorised an agent to handle a book (he need not commit any other title or portion of his output), he may—to his chagrin—find himself tied for life in respect of that work. This has obvious disadvantages if only because most

[72]

agencies are highly sensitive to change in terms of ordinary business efficiency and of the personalities of the principals. It accounts for the relative frequency with which partnerships have been dissolved and fresh agencies set up by promising associates who take their authors with them. Inevitably the personal element colours relationships all through, no less between agent and author than between agent and publisher and author and publisher: hence, as already stated, the need for wariness in order to sustain the health of all parties, and for an occasional confrontation to clear the air.

Like the publisher William Heinemann, Thring never lost his distrust of agents and issued frequent warnings in *The Author*. Both he and Shaw pointed out that whereas a client was reasonably protected by the law and regulations of the Law Society against the malpractices of a solicitor, no such safeguard existed against an agent, for whom no formal qualification was required and who belonged to no professional or trade association. Indeed in the 1920s the Society 'repeatedly urged the formation of an association of agents so that a general code of conduct could be enforced'.

In the late twenties one of the agents, Raymond Savage, made the attempt and failed. He reported that the three biggest agencies refused to support such an organisation, others were suspicious of it, and too many of the remainder were the incompetent and unscrupulous agents who had everything to lose by joining. In 1937 he tried again, and met with the same refusal by the big three; but he joined with two other firms to form the Society of Literary Agents, and hoped for success. The Society failed . . .[7]

Relations with the Society of Authors improved marginally after DKR succeeded Thring as General Secretary in 1930; but basic suspicions remained, punctuated at intervals by explosive incidents. In 1937, for example, DKR gave—it must be fairly stated—undue prominence to the following action by Curtis Brown.

On 7 June the Curtis Brown agency wrote to Harper's in America, for whom Curtis Brown was the English agent, asking if the writer Leo Huberman would be interested in doing a history of America for Gollancz. . . Harper's cabled that Huberman was interested, and supplied his English address. Curtis Brown then wrote to Huberman, saying that Harper's had indicated he was interested and explaining that they were Harper's agent. They asked him to come in and discuss the matter. The meeting took place, and the question arose as to whether Huberman should employ Curtis Brown as his agent. He decided to defer his decision until he had spoken to Victor Gollancz. When he saw Gollancz, he learned that Curtis Brown had not been instrumental in getting the offer from Gollancz but that Gollancz had written directly to him, care of Curtis Brown, whom Gollancz knew to be the English agents of Huberman's American publisher. Curtis Brown had opened the letter, and then written their own letter to Harper's. Huberman thereupon wrote to Curtis Brown asking (1) why they had not forwarded the letter, (2) why they had opened it, (3) why, once they opened it, they did not inform him of its existence and full contents, and (4) why they communicated some of the contents to a third party. Curtis Brown replied that they always attended to all business on an author's behalf so as not to trouble him unnecessarily. Huberman went to his solicitor, who suggested that the Publishers' Association or the Society of Authors should arbitrate. Curtis Brown refused to consider either possibility: they had explained themselves fully and satisfactorily. There the matter rested . . .[8]

David Higham who, with Nancy Pearn and Laurence Pollinger, broke off from Curtis Brown in 1935 and established a successful agency on his own, criticised the Society on the grounds of the General Secretary always being a lawyer: 'Lawyers are people you use to tell you what you can or can't do, not, usually, what you should and ought to do.'[9]

However valid or otherwise that may be as a generalisation, not even the bare facts were true of the Society; for while Thring was a solicitor, and D K R and Elizabeth Barber barristers, and while the present incumbent, Mark Le Fanu, is a solicitor, there was a period of ten years (1971–81) when the administration was controlled by 'laymen'. But, first, a word about the background. During the 1950s D K R relied increasingly upon the support of

Elizabeth Barber to run the office. In short he did less and less work, spent a large part of every day at the Savile Club, and helped himself to a generous allowance of holidays. At the same time he did not relax his authoritarian attitude towards the staff, most of whom were overworked and underpaid, and female. Elizabeth therefore needed all her powers and, fortunately for the Society, she played the part superbly. Indeed, for many people, she *was* the Society. Philippa MacLiesh, formerly secretary to the publisher, Michael Joseph, who was appointed Elizabeth's assistant in 1954, paid her this tribute—among others published in *The Author* after Elizabeth's death in 1979.

When I first met Elizabeth Barber in 1954, she seemed to me just what I imagined a woman barrister should be. Tall, with classical features and (then in her early forties) already elegantly grey, she was remarkably handsome and, when she bothered about her looks—she often didn't—could be beautiful. She had a good voice and natural authority. Many found her formidable as, on occasion, she needed to be. But it was her great charm and warmth of personality one remembered most. She would go to endless trouble to avoid damage to the sensibilities of a thin-skinned author, and would give sympathy and practical help to anyone down on their luck, often over-taxing her own strength in the process.

As her assistant, I would go to her with some problem, often a daunting file of correspondence between author and publisher ending in dispute and, as it seemed to me, total deadlock. We would talk it over, she would probe out the essentials of the problem and, miraculously, a solution would emerge.

Sadly, when the time came for Elizabeth to succeed DKR in 1963, her long and punishing stint as *de facto* chief executive began to tell, and she suffered a deterioration of health that led to retirement in 1971. The problem of succession—for long one of her chief worries—then had to be solved and in a novel fashion for, at that time, the Society could not afford to appoint and pay a lawyer or other person of Elizabeth's calibre. The solution eventually reached was indeed original—namely a triumvirate consisting of three senior members of the staff: Philippa

MacLiesh, head of the advisory service; George Astley, who had joined the Society in 1956, registrar and secretary of the Translators Association; and myself, a comparative newcomer, in charge of publicity and publications. In fact each of us, as Joint Secretaries, had a multiplicity of jobs, as did most senior members of the staff, some of whom are referred to in the Notes.[10] Our reign lasted seven years and survived the usual frictions of a *troika* with remarkable success, but by 1978 we felt the need to re-appoint a single executive as the head of administration, and we were fortunate to find David Machin, then deputy managing director of the publishers Jonathan Cape, and earlier a literary agent and partner of A. P. Watt & Son. Thanks to his invaluable experience and drive, David created a forceful new image for the organisation during his three years of service as General Secretary, particularly necessary shortly after the Society had been registered as a trade union. In 1981 he returned to publishing as joint (later sole) managing director of The Bodley Head, and was succeeded after a few months by Mark Le Fanu, formerly a solicitor with McKenna and Co., who had joined the Society as Assistant General Secretary in 1979.

When David Higham implied that the appointment of a lawyer as General Secretary inhibited effective action, he went on to quote some questionable examples by way of illustration, one of them being the Society's confrontation with the BBC in 1946–7, when it mobilised its big guns and forced the Corporation to concede a much improved rate of minimum fees which, Higham averred, 'soon became the maximum. It applied to all contributors to programmes, whether they were professional authors or not.'

In fact the BBC soon introduced graduated scales, paying more to those who could command better terms. This made the point that Higham missed. It is not the primary function of a professional organisation or trade union to bargain solely for members in the market place. It does of course advise them of the range of rates and conditions they might obtain, and act for them individually when required; but its prime duty in this area is to establish minima (regularly reviewed and revised) below which—in this case—no author should accept payment, and above which he or his agent are free to secure the best possible terms.

On the other hand the Society's Collection Bureau, acting for

Shaw and about 50 other literary estates, has always operated as an agency and conducted negotiations on behalf of clients, but it is an agency of a special kind. As explained earlier it is not in open competition as a placing agent, but since it came into existence in response to requests by certain authors or their executors or heirs, and since—as an arm of the Society—it reflects the rights of authors as a whole, there is a specific obligation to license publication or performance only on the best possible terms, or not at all.

Inevitably the activities of the Bureau raised the ire of certain other agents. This surfaced for example in correspondence between A. D. Peters and DKR during the summer of 1962. Peters accused the Society of letting the agents down when they tried to make a stand against the publishers' insistence on a fixed 50 per cent share of royalties on paperback editions of hardback titles. He wrote:

> The Society will never be in a position to take a resolute stand about anything, so long as it acts as a literary agency. It cannot, as a Society, be resolute, while, as an agency, it has to accept terms which the Society is pledged to discount.

DKR riposted:

> You are evidently unaware the Society will in no circumstances associate itself with any publishing contract which it regards as falling short of what it considers equitable. And this includes, of course, all subsidiary and sub-lease arrangements.

As to the 50:50 division:

> It was not the Society that let the side down in 1957—nor, indeed, on any other occasion. The onus rests squarely on you and your friends for failing to consult the Society in the first instance and for creating such a climate of ill-will among the members of the Council of the Publishers Association before you belatedly asked the Society to come to your aid. Despite the hours Ian Parsons [then PA President] spent with me trying to work out what might have been a mutually acceptable

formula, the situation was so irretrievable that Parsons wrote: 'I hope you will agree that the wise thing now is to let matters rest, allow for exacerbated feelings to subside, and hope that some degree of flexibility will return of its own accord.'

After the 1960s relations with agents gradually improved, an important step forward being the long overdue formation in 1975 of the Association of Authors' Agents under the initial chairmanship of Mark Hamilton of A. M. Heath, although even then the largest firm, Curtis Brown, held out. There is now therefore a representative organisation for agents which, though it has no mandatory powers over its members, provides a forum for advice among the majority of 90 or so agents listed in *The Writers' and Artists' Yearbook*, and is a body which other trade organisations can consult.

As to the future, there is an undoubted need for agents to handle the complex and multifarious rights arising out of all the outlets now available to an author's work—films, broadcasting, audio and video cassettes, etc.—all additional to print. Few authors have the time or ability to handle such business once they have become successful. On the other hand good but less popular authors, not to mention young ones making a start, find it difficult to interest any agent at all in their work. And whereas if, as some claim, a manuscript has a better chance of publication when offered by an agent, on the grounds that it has been selected and screened from a mass of submissions, then publishers are limiting the market and endangering the free flow of original work in whatever *genre*.

It is a matter of history that the Second World War generated a series of radical reforms that altered the pattern of society, these being planned, if not actually begun, before the return of peace. Taxation was one example, for long a contentious subject among authors who felt aggrieved at being assessed for income tax on a strictly annual basis, however wide the fluctuations of their income, and because—for the purposes of tax—sales of copyright were treated as income.

As early as 1909 the Chancellor of the Exchequer refused a

request by Robert Harcourt, MP, a member of the Society, to treat 'monies received from the sale of copyright or performing right as capital, and as such not subject to income tax'.[11] In November 1915 Bernard Shaw and Charles Garvice[12] took the matter up again. They compared an author to an inventor, whose sale of a patent was treated as capital, but discovered that, in tax parlance, invention was regarded not as a profession, but as a 'scarce and happy accident', while authorship was a continuing chore.

In 1919 a Royal Commission consulted various professional people whose incomes were taxed on different bases. At that time authors were pleased to be assessed on a three-year basis. However, among others to give evidence was John Galsworthy who—to the chagrin of most of his colleagues—plumped for the substitution of one year in place of three, a recommendation adopted by the Inland Revenue. At the same time repeated pleas that expenses incurred in the creation of a literary work should be deducted before tax were turned down.[13]

In 1944 battle was joined again. Two author-members of the House of Commons, Harold Nicholson and E. P. Smith (Edward Percy, the playwright), aided by Charles Morgan, the novelist, confronted the Chancellor with two complaints: first, annual assessment of income tax; and, secondly, the imposition of US tax on gross and then UK tax on net sums received on the sale of work by British authors in the States.

Despite his great age, Shaw could not resist taking part in the dialogue. Surprisingly he paid scant attention to the double taxation issue; but, in a long letter to *The Times* (1 February 1944), he supported the restoration of the three-year average, although in the public eye he weakened his general case by demanding exemption from surtax for 'all legitimately earned incomes exceeding £20,000'. In an earlier letter to DKR (15 January) he had written:

Our real grievance is that an author who makes £20,000 plus one penny once in his lifetime is taxed at the same rate as a landlord-capitalist who has a settled permanent £20,000 a year without doing a stroke of work for it, and bequeaths it to his widow and children without making any other provision or sacrifice for them.[14]

In the event the Chancellor did concede the three-year spreadback, though—illogically—only in respect of a *lump* sum received for a work; and so it took more time and sustained effort—a deputation in 1949 led by J. J. Lawson, MP, Osbert Sitwell, and Rosamond Lehmann, and subsequent manoeuvres involving, principally, Woodrow Wyatt, MP, and members of a taxation sub-committee[15] set up by the Society in 1952—to remove the anomaly: so that, under the Finance Act, 1953, spreadback was applied also to *royalties* receivable during a period of two years from the date of first publication or performance of a work.

As to double taxation, this campaign had been won by the signing of a convention in 1945 between the UK and USA. Not only was it of great importance in itself on grounds of equity and a practical incentive to the export of contemporary work, but it formed the pattern on which double taxation treaties with other countries were modelled in succeeding years.

In 1950 the Government appointed the Millard Tucker Committee to investigate two tax matters. One was the taxation of trading profits (settled for authors, as explained, in 1953, despite an adverse report by this Committee). The other concerned provisions for retirement. The Society pointed out that there was no superannuation scheme open to an author, and urged tax relief on contributions to any such scheme designed to protect him and his dependants in old age. This concession was eventually granted in the Finance Act, 1956, which enabled the Society, in the following year, to arrange group endowment insurance—known as the Retirement Benefits Scheme—permitting an author to contribute varying amounts at irregular intervals according to his ability to pay, thus ideally suited to the fluctuations of his earnings. The scheme was an immediate success—over £50,000 was contributed in the first five years.

The taxation sub-committee set up by the Society in 1952 derived, in part, from a test case conducted personally by Compton Mackenzie before the Court of Appeal, at which the Solicitor-General (Manningham-Buller) appeared for the Crown. Although of obvious importance to Mackenzie, it was not less so to all authors since it revived the familiar issue of sales of copyright. In this instance the author had sold the copyright in twenty of his books to his publisher, Macdonald, for the sum of

£10,000, contending that, as a capital transaction, it was not subject to income tax. However, despite much wit and eloquence on the appellant's part, the Court upheld an earlier ruling to the contrary by Mr Justice Danckwerts. Costly as the exercise was to Mackenzie, the case bore fruit for others. For one thing the proceedings gained a great deal of publicity, and drew attention to this and other tax injustices suffered by authors, as well as to the parlous situation of authorship in general. Ultimately, thanks to the intervention of Lord Goodman and Sir Edward Boyle, a clause was introduced into the Finance Act, 1967, which, in certain circumstances, made it possible to spread *forward* over six years any lump sum received for the sale of copyright. The original point was therefore substantially met, and enabled an author, who in his later years found himself with a declining income, to raise a tax-free lump sum to meet the costs, for example, of buying a house or an annuity for retirement.

Taxation has always been, directly or indirectly, an important part of the everyday business of the Society, which has therefore accumulated a fund of knowledge and experience, in addition to that provided by outside tax consultants retained for the purpose. It would therefore be wearisome to refer to more than a handful of cases, by way of illustrating the variety of problems affecting the practice of authorship.[16]

In 1958 the House of Lords upheld a decision, handed down the previous year by the Court of Appeal, to the effect that royalties accruing from the marketing of the works of Peter Cheyney after his death, but contracted during his lifetime, were not liable to tax in the hands of his executors. This ruling sounded too good to last, and no one at the Society had any illusions but that this 'hole in the tax net' would be closed by legislation: as indeed it was by the Finance Act, 1960.

In 1967 the novelist, Ralph Hammond Innes, won a dramatic victory over the Inland Revenue. What had happened was that in April 1960 he had presented his father, as a gift, with the copyright in his then unpublished book, *The Doomed Oasis*, its market value being assessed at £15,425. The tax inspector had decided that this figure should be included in the author's tax return for 1960–1, despite the fact that his father paid tax on the book's earnings. Hammond Innes immediately appealed to the Special Commissioners who duly upheld him: whereupon the tax authorities took the case twice further—to the Chancery Division of the High Court where Mr Justice Goff ruled against them on the grounds that income tax was 'a tax on what has been received or earned, not on what might have been'; and then to the Court of Appeal which again found for the author. At that point, although given leave to appeal to the House of Lords, the Revenue called a halt.[17] In this instance the Society, of which Hammond Innes was a prominent member, had offered substantial financial support, but in the event was not called upon to contribute.

In 1968 the Society persuaded the Chancellor, Roy Jenkins, to exclude from the special charge upon unearned income royalties or other sums accruing from copyright in a deceased author's work. As A. P. Herbert, the Society's President, pointed out, he was sure that an author's widow was not the kind of 'quarry' the Chancellor had in mind since, 'if considered as "wealth", her husband's royalties must always be a dwindling asset, unlike the wealth which is firmly founded on stocks and shares'. Happily the Chancellor himself tabled the necessary amendment to the Finance Bill.

Value Added Tax was introduced on 1 April 1973. Both before and after that date the Society—in association with the Writers' Guild, Publishers Association, British Copyright Council, and others—made repeated representations to HM Customs and Excise to alleviate, if not eliminate, regulations that bore unfairly on self-employed authors required to register under the statute.

Representations were also made in 1974, and through the British Copyright Council in 1975, to exclude authors' and other copyrights from the proposed Wealth Tax, on the grounds that copyright was already subject to taxation in one form or another, and because it was impossible to arrive at a fair valuation 'on an open market basis'. As it happened the Bill was abandoned; but by then it seemed likely that, as a result of these pressures, copyright would have been excluded had the legislation materialised.

The replacement of Estate Duty by Capital Transfer Tax in 1975 attracted similar problems of copyright valuation. While the new tax exempted transfers between spouses—a great relief—inflation and other considerations may at any time produce distorted calculations when CTT eventually has to be paid. Normally the Revenue proposes a figure based on two to three years' past royalties, but this can only be a starting point. To quote A. P. Kernon, FCA, writing in the autumn issue 1979 of *The Author*:

> If a book is running out of print, or if as in the case of educational books, it may need revision at the next reprint, these factors must be taken into account. In many cases the fact that the author is no longer alive and able to make personal appearances, or provide publicity, or write further works, will result in lower or slower sales. Obviously this is an area in which help can be given by the publishers, and in particular one needs to know what their future intentions are, what stocks of the books remain, and what likelihood there will be of reprinting. Copyrights are by their nature wasting assets, and it is often quite misleading to base the future value on past performance.

Perhaps the most publicised case in recent years arose out of the uncertain attitude of the Inland Revenue towards literary prizes. This had long been a grey area, but in 1978 Andrew Boyle, a member of the Society, appealed to the Special Commissioners against the Revenue's decision to tax the £1,000 Whitbread Award, which he had won in 1974 for his biography of Brendan Bracken, *Poor Dear Brendan*. The Society supported the appeal, briefing leading Counsel on his behalf, with promises of financial contributions from the publisher, Hutchinson, the National Book League, and the Royal Society of Literature. The hearing took place at the end of November when the Commissioners found for the author, holding that the Award was a voluntary one and did not represent the proceeds of exploitation of the book either by Boyle personally or by his publisher acting as agent on his behalf. The Revenue did not take the case further. However, splendid as the victory was, it did not resolve the problems of Arts Council grants and awards, a very important area for authors and other artists. Eventually the Revenue and the Arts Council came to an agreement whereby awards in respect of training schemes, or to enable creative artists to devote time to research and development, would not be taxed; whereas grants offered for non-training projects would be. This meant that, for example, grants offered to writers for specific projects (e.g. writing or completing a particular book) were taxable—a decision that may have influenced the literature panel of the Arts Council when it virtually abandoned its Writers' Grants scheme in 1981.

Experience has shown that public opinion in Britain is inherently philistine in its attitude towards the arts, and that it is very ready to suspect claims by creative artists or their representatives for anything that smacks of 'special treatment'. Writing is particularly vulnerable in this regard. A full-time author does not attend an office every day or work in a factory doing a 'real' job; nor does he get paid on a regular weekly or monthly basis. On the contrary he sits at home staring at a blank sheet of paper, and if that produces nothing, or if once in a while it does yield a handsome return, then he must expect to meet all kinds of obstacles when seeking to adjust the rules to his peculiar situation.

I have illustrated the point as regards taxation and retirement insurance, but that is not the end of the matter. Philistinism surfaces in other ways. For example, to enter your occupation as 'author' is to put yourself at an immediate disadvantage when applying for a house mortgage or a bank loan or even a passport. Social security is also a pitfall. In common with other self-employed people, authors are not entitled to unemployment benefit. So when they need state assistance, they must have recourse to supplementary benefit, which involves a rigorous examination of assets and living conditions, and a visit by an official which many applicants would do anything to avoid. Moreover the Department of Health and Social Security (DHSS) classifies authorship as a 'remunerative occupation' irrespective of its returns. Thus if, say, a biographer engaged in lengthy research has used up the publisher's advance and run out of funds, he is not entitled to benefit if he works 30 or more hours a week. He therefore has to play out a fiction by asserting that he devotes no more than $29\frac{1}{2}$ hours weekly to an all-consuming task, which in fact involves every waking moment of his time.

Likewise in claiming state retirement pension (women at 60, men at 65), the author has to sign a statement to the effect that he has actually 'retired', i.e. given up writing, which few authors can ever do, or be expected to do: since—for them—writing, like eating, drinking and sleeping, is an essential part of existence. Furthermore it is an unnecessary requirement because, if an author is already in receipt of a state pension (towards which he has duly paid contributions), he may not keep any net earnings (e.g. from articles or royalties) in excess of £57.10 per week (1982); so the matter is automatically regulated without having to tell lies about 'retirement'; moreover, five years later (woman 65, man 70) the restriction is removed. An additional irritation is the rule that any excess over the £57.10 has to be related to the week in which it arises or when the work was done. Since most authors' earnings arrive irregularly and at long intervals, they may well exceed £57.10 in any one week. It has taken strenuous efforts by both the Society of Authors and the Royal Literary Fund to have this rule eased, so that earnings can now be averaged over a period. Under supplementary benefit, the normal limit of income permitted without penalty, or 'disregarded', is £4 per week or £208 per year (1982).

Having myself worked as an administrator at both the Society and the Fund for nearly 20 years, I have come to realise that the sheer size and complexity of national insurance and state welfare has imposed an impossibly high degree of rigidity upon the system, coupled with the official assumption that, since most people in work are paid weekly wages or monthly salaries, regulations have to be couched accordingly. Self-employed people exist, but they are a nuisance, while authors are a particular nuisance.

CHAPTER FOUR

Authors' earnings and Public Lending Right

Authors resist publishers' post-war attempts to reduce royalty
rates. Royalties on overseas sales. Full-time or part-time
writing. Walter Allen's *Critical Times for Authors*, 1953.
Surveys of authors' earnings and contracts, 1955–82.
Comments by Richard Findlater. Public Lending Right,
1951–82.

When—as mentioned—the Second World War came to an end
and controls upon trade began to go, the outlook for publishing
looked unnaturally bright. Moreover the continuing currency
crisis intensified the drive for exports, in which books played an
important part, to the extent that, by the end of the financial year
1950–1, books exported had reached 31.06 per cent of the total
publishing trade turnover of £37,514,972. Both these sets of
figures were to rise much higher in future years. However, danger
signs were already in evidence. First, people were beginning to
spend money on other sources of entertainment and on objects
other than books—sport, travel and holidays, better housing and
home equipment, television sets, etc. Secondly, the rise in the cost
of producing and distributing books was reckoned at over 133 per
cent above the corresponding figure for 1939. Besides this,
publishers had failed to raise the retail price of books early enough
to offset these higher costs and accustom the public to paying
more than half-a-guinea for a novel or 15s for a serious
biography.

When the Publishers Association woke up to realities, it fell
prey to panic. Unable to avoid paying printers' and suppliers'
bills, or to persuade booksellers to accept a general book discount
of less than 33⅓ per cent, its executive turned against the least

entrenched party in the business of book production—the authors. Using specious arguments about 'partnership' and the 'sharing of burdens', it proposed early in 1951 that all royalty rates in excess of the initial 10 per cent be reduced by $2\frac{1}{2}$ per cent across the board. This manoeuvre was stoutly resisted by the Society of Authors and intelligently discussed in the leading article of the autumn issue of *The Author*, which concluded that a reduction of royalties of $2\frac{1}{2}$ per cent or even 5 per cent would not 'so decrease the price of the finished book that the public will buy more copies of it'. In the event no concerted move was sustained by the Publishers Association, and the matter was dropped.

Three years later the Publishers Association recommended its members to insist on a larger share of the income deriving from a book's subsidiary rights when drawing up contracts with all 'new unknown authors whether through agents or direct', and to introduce specific minima in *all* contracts on the grounds that this would ensure that the publisher's share would represent 'the reward to which he is entitled for his part in creating or adding to the value of the named rights'. The minima included a rigid 50:50 split of royalties from paperback editions of hard bound books, irrespective of sales, and similar demands in respect of other reprints, book club editions, and so on. None of these demands had been discussed beforehand with either the Society of Authors or the agents, and so they roused a storm. A letter published on 14 April 1954 in *The Times*, signed by John Masefield and 18 other leading members of the Society, accused the Publishers Association of trying to set up a cartel or monopoly which would

strike at the root of the author's freedom of contracting. . . if the present officers of the Publishers' Association have their way, a publisher will refuse to print his work at all unless he agrees to surrender a share in the earnings only remotely derived—and often not derived at all—from book publication.

In short, as D K R pointed out repeatedly in correspondence, it was far better—in view of the variety of terms and conditions attaching to different classes of books—to negotiate contract by contract, although always in the knowledge that equitable minima had already been established in the principal clauses, without having to embody every item in a formal document which, by its nature, could only be very generalised in order that everyone could accept it.

The accusation of monopoly—also raised at this time in the House of Commons—came at a bad moment; for, following the Board of Trade enquiry into re-sale price maintenance in 1948 and the subsequent passage of the Restrictive Trade Practices Act, 1957, the Net Book Agreement was clearly under threat. This Agreement, revised in 1957, had been in force for over fifty years and, as the great majority of publishers, booksellers and authors agreed, was essential to the survival of viable and effective bookselling. Without it books would, like groceries, be open to cut-price and loss-leader devices; stockholding bookshops dependent on selling books at published prices would disappear, and all would suffer as a result. In the event the danger came to a head in 1962, when the Agreement was successfully defended before Mr Justice Buckley in court.

Meanwhile the Publishers Association's campaign for a larger share in subsidiary rights income rumbled on, alienating authors and agents alike. Unfortunately the latter, led by A. D. Peters, waged a fight on their own, and this led to the exchange of discourtesies with the Society quoted earlier and weakened a collaborative effort that should have operated from the start. In the event the dispute (specifically the 50:50 split of paperback royalties) was watered down, as so often happens, by 'natural forces' and the fact that the PA exercised no mandatory powers over its members. Quite soon individual publishers were making their own terms with authors and agents (with partial or no reference to the PA resolution), so that in the end the heat was taken out of the original 50:50 ultimatum.[1]

A parallel process characterised a counter-offensive conducted by the authors about royalties on overseas sales—a matter of growing importance since book exports were now approaching 45 per cent of the total publishing turnover. Complaints had begun in 1952 when J. L. Hodson exchanged letters with Geoffrey Faber through the correspondence columns of *Time and Tide*, subsequently continued in *The Author*. Hodson asked how it was that, whereas the author received far less on books sold abroad, the publisher's return—despite high discounts granted to distributors—remained about the same as from home sales. Next year the Society of Authors appointed Hodson to chair a sub-committee and seek a formal solution to the problem. This had its effect and agreement was reached whereby the author would receive either the home royalty scale on the net sums received by the publisher, or about half that scale on the UK published price, dependent always on the size of the discount (45 per cent or more) which the publisher had to offer his overseas distributor. This has remained the general practice ever since, although in a few cases publishers are prepared to pay the same royalty on export and home sales, both based on the UK published price.

Although for obvious reasons writing was difficult during the war, it was never inhibited by lack of demand for reading. With the return of peace and normal conditions of trade, it was hoped that opportunities for writers—especially new ones—would increase. Indeed the number of new titles and reprints rose steadily year by year, and so did sales, especially overseas, of most categories of publication; yet the serious young novelist found himself no better off than before.

Late in 1950, Denys Val Baker, a youngish but experienced and enterprising man of letters wrote:

> During the war years and up to 1947, almost any first novel would subscribe up to publication about 2,000 copies, and provided that reviews and publicity were forthcoming, subsequent sales would probably exceed 3,000 altogether. At present the demand has hardened considerably. . . Unless a first novel has something special to recommend it, subscription sales may be around 1,000 copies or a little higher, and the probable run on sales up to publication may not bring the total up to more than 2,000 copies sold. . . From the publisher's point of view he knows that even on a first novel he must nowadays achieve a sale of about 3,000 copies to break even.[2]

He referred also to the contraction of the literary periodical market, which represented a vital supporting source of income for writers like himself in the area of criticism, poetry, essays, and especially short stories.

> As I write I have before me the fortieth and final number of *Penguin New Writing*, one of the last of a positive avalanche of casualties which include *Horizon, Welsh Review, Wales,*

London Forum, Writing Today, Windmill, Modern Reading, Life and Letters Today, and *Our Time.*

Other outlets apart, e.g. radio, he concluded that the young novelist was 'quite powerless'.

> He can only write novels and look for a publisher. . . He can also take a job—in a bank, in the BBC, in a bookshop, in the Army. But that is merely solving the problem by evading it altogether. A violinist is unlikely to develop his career by putting aside his violin and working in a shop or a factory, and anyone who admits that must admit that the same applies to a novelist.

Val Baker was stating the classic dilemma that confronts all young, and many older, seemingly established, authors; a dilemma rarely solved in the whole history of literature.[3] His statement roused a response from a namesake, John Baker, who had made a reputation as a forceful pioneering publisher with a large heart for struggling authors. He wrote:

> Literature, with a capital L, unless preserved by Time, has always been in a bad way, but books considered as merchandise have not. You can act upon this truth in two ways. You can either decide that you will be a writer of Literature. . . or you can blend your creative abilities with a certain amount of merchandising.
>
> The best publishing houses try to keep a balance between literature and scholarship and some merchandising of an innocuous or even useful kind. I think that it is possible to produce works of information, or the more popular kind of merchandising novel, to make a contribution to creative writing, and to survive both as a publisher and an author.
>
> This, it seems to me, is the point of view that young authors must adopt, if they wish to survive. . . For nearly every member of the public is engaged in some compromise with his desires, and will finally resent the notion that only authors shall do exactly as they please: enjoy themselves and expect to be paid for it, too.[4]

The subject was discussed further by Walter Allen, critic, novelist, and literary historian, who pointed out that originally *all* writers combined their craft with other forms of employment and were, in effect, the 'literary equivalent of what today we call a Sunday painter'.[5]

> The professional writer was the product of a revolution in the dissemination of the printed word, of the discovery, first exploited on a large scale in the eighteenth century, that books could be marketed as consumers' goods in competition with other, diverse kinds of commodity.

Out of this development arose the concept, if not the reality, of the 'professional writer' and the false notions, to which even John Baker, in his otherwise percipient remarks, subscribed in the last sentence quoted above, that such a person

> . . . is a free man; he makes his own hours of work; he takes a holiday when he feels like it; above all he has no boss. Merely by virtue of being a writer, it is assumed that he knows all other writers, that they are as wonderful as their works, and that his life, when he is not writing, is spent in perpetual hobnobbing with the fashionable and the great.
>
> To the outside world, then, the professional writer's life spells freedom of a kind that cannot possibly exist; what is seen is a dream life.

Allen went on to consider not only the means of survival open to a writer unable to live by the exercise of his truly creative powers, but the effect of such means upon the quality (let alone the quantity) of his output. He might, if he was lucky, as John Baker suggested, make up the deficit by engaging in 'merchandising', if necessary under another name—as did Cecil Day-Lewis, poet and Poet Laureate, who—as mentioned—wrote successful detective stories under the pseudonym of 'Nicholas Blake'. Or he might spend five days a week in an office concerned either with related occupations, such as publishing, broadcasting, journalism, teaching, or librarianship; or with unrelated ones within the whole field of banking, commerce and industry. Many examples could be quoted throughout history, but I confine myself in this instance to the names of a handful of poets of the first quality familiar today: T. S. Eliot (director of a publishing house), Louis MacNeice (BBC producer), Charles Causley (county school teacher), Roy Fuller (lawyer), and Philip Larkin (university librarian). These examples, and there are many others, inhibit any conclusive reply to the question as to whether a creative writer is invariably deterred by having to earn his living outside literature; or whether, economics apart, he gains greater insight into life by being involved in an everyday occupation. In contrast, there is undoubted truth in the fact that any writer engaged in the difficult and demanding task of serious fiction, be it a novel or a play, or an historical study depending on intensive research, or a textbook, or a translation, or an imaginative children's book, relies on one prime requisite for the proper pursuit of his work. I mean *continuity*, so that the flow of effort can develop and sustain a momentum which is otherwise lost if the writer can work only in his spare time. Without it there is also the danger that a daily job will exhaust the mental energy and imaginative reserves necessary for writing, which was the substance of Val Baker's statement.

Most of the material contained in this dialogue between publishers and authors was viewed in a pamphlet, commissioned by the Society of Authors from Walter Allen and issued in 1953 under the title *Critical Times for Authors*, in which Allen discussed contemporary trends in publishing, book buying, library lending, the position of the author, the incidence of income tax, and means of assisting writing, including the formation of a fund 'established from a royalty on works falling into the public domain when the statutory period of copyright expires fifty years after the author's death'. The pamphlet received wide and generally favourable publicity, but the main criticism was that, incisive as Allen's remarks were, they remained speculative.

This challenge induced the Society to institute a series of surveys, essentially statistical, over the next twenty years, and which went far towards converting estimation into fact.

The first survey was launched in 1954–5. It was directed by a sub-committee[6] chaired by J. B. Priestley, and administered by the British Market Research Bureau Ltd. Its object was

to investigate the existing financial relations between author and publisher, with special reference to home royalties, overseas sales, book club and paperback reprint sales, and various ancillary rights.

It took the form of a confidential postal questionnaire, circulated to members of the Society for 'completion anonymously by any member who has had at least one book published during recent years'. The results, published in 1957, were quantitively disappointing, only 607 replying out of a membership in excess of 3,000, i.e. about 20 per cent. Nevertheless it was considered reasonably representative of all ages and income levels, and revealed that a quarter of the respondents were full-time writers living off their work, while the remainder were part-time in varying degrees. Nearly everyone reported a deterioration in terms offered by publishers (smaller advances, lower percentage rates, the lowest extended to cover a larger number of copies sold). Returns from book club and cheap editions remained the same, but unremunerative, while most publishers showed an aggressive interest in a share of ancillary or subsidiary rights.

Five years elapsed before the next move, a longish interval because the Society was heavily engaged in two other campaigns under the dynamic leadership of A. P. Herbert: Obscene Publications and Public Lending Right, of which more later. In 1962 however came the chance to commission Richard Findlater, a professional journalist on the staff of *The Observer* and lately appointed editor of *The Author*, to write a sequel to *Critical Times*. This he did in greater scope and depth than had been possible in 1953, backed by his own investigations at the heart of the trade, by the results of the 1957 survey and other Society findings, and by information from two leading literary agents.

His 32-page booklet, *What Are Writers Worth?*, published by the Society in 1963, explored the same general territory as *Critical Times* with two important additions. One was an attempt to assess the number of *bona fide* authors by reference to the official census, Whitaker's *Reference Catalogue of Current Literature*, and other sources, from which Findlater estimated that 'professional authors, in the sense that they had written full-length books and would be eligible for full membership of the Society of Authors', totalled between 6,500 and 7,000. The other was a significant section devoted to 'Paperbacks and authors', in which he quoted Tony Godwin, then of Penguin Books:

Paperbacks were still no more than a minor sideline in 1948, a promising trend in 1954. By 1960 they had come to be recognised as the most dynamic factor in the publishing world.

Findlater added that the number of paperback titles on sale in Britain had risen by 65 per cent in two years—from 5,886 listed in May 1960 to 9,578 in June 1962, and that the non-fiction categories (fast overtaking fiction) now ranged over a great variety of subjects, selling at prices up to 15s each. Aside from the flood of American imports (many of them remainders), the annual output of UK published paperbacks was of the order of 75 million copies, and the principal share of the business was in the hands of nine firms specialising in the market, some of them US controlled. In publishing terms paperbacks were indeed a fast-growing and highly profitable development, whose success was largely, though not entirely due to price.

. . . paperbacks are cheaper than hardbacks not because their covers are softer but because their runs are longer. While other economies count—the standardisation of format, for instance, reduces costs in production, storage and transport, and the lower rate of royalty paid to the author is not unhelpful—the main reason for the gap between the softcover and hardcover prices of any book lies in the size of the print-order.

Perhaps the most striking sign of success was the fact that you could find a paperback anywhere, not only in bookshops proper.

. . . in supermarkets, tobacconists' and department stores, on the shelves of newsagents and public libraries, and in thousands of homes where—less than ten years ago—a book was another name for a magazine or was, at best, something which was borrowed but never, never *bought*.

How had this revolution benefited the author?

At present the general royalty rate normally paid by paperback publishers is $7\frac{1}{2}$ per cent, which the author may or may not have to share with his hardback publisher: this compares with the usual 10 per cent minimum in hardbacks and with 5 per cent in US paperbacks (on which the author gets a bigger advance). Only a few big names, in the 'leader' class, get $12\frac{1}{2}$ per cent. Authors should, in time, take 10 per cent as a virtual minimum rate.

Three years later, in 1966, Findlater wrote a second booklet as an extension of the first, entitled *The Book Writers: who are they?*, and founded statistically on a full-scale survey conducted among the membership of the Society of Authors by Research Services Ltd (chairman Dr Mark Abrams). By any standard—but especially among authors, generally renowned for their resistance to form filling—this survey roused a remarkably high return: 1,587 replies out of 3,240 authors living in the UK and Europe, or 48.9 per cent, far the most telling response to date.

Broadly four main questions were asked: the type and number of books written; income from books and subsidiary rights, 1963–5; income from other kinds of literary work; information about the status and conditions of authorship. It was upon the replies to these questions that Findlater based his case, beginning with:

The book industry is booming . . . over 20,000 titles and around 300 million volumes by British authors are published annually in the UK . . . £50 millions worth are now exported annually . . . about 100 million British paperbacks are sold every year . . . Millions of hardbacks are bought by local authorities for schools or public libraries, which now hold over 80 million copies, borrowed without charge nearly 500 million times a year . . .

Book writing is not booming. In plain terms, it doesn't pay enough. It doesn't pay as much as it *ought* to, in a country with a growing appetite for books. The British public wants, increasingly, to read: it does not, on the whole, want to *pay* for reading . . . A golden nucleus of book authors, not necessarily the best, build up small fortunes in ways denied to the pop novelists of the past. But hundreds more—and these by no means flops or failures—squeeze only a miserable dole from their work. Britain is getting its books at the expense of its authors and on the cheap . . .

In order to interpret the survey more clearly he divided authors into two types:

1. A *primary* author was one who put writing first, however well or badly he did out of it, and whether he lived by it or not;

2. A *secondary* author was one who treated writing as a by-product or alternative source of income, additional to a bread-and-butter job, irrespective of the financial results.

On this basis the figures were clear and stark. Primaries constituted 56 per cent of the respondents. Most of them had published four or more books altogether, over half at least one book between 1963 and 1965. In terms of income however, taking into account all sources of literary income (books plus journalism, scriptwriting, etc.), only just over half (another figure of 56 per cent) of the primaries earned £500 a year or more from writing—£500 then being about half the national average wage. 44 per cent earned less than that figure.[7] Secondaries constituted 44 per cent of the respondents; one quarter of them earned £500 a year or more, three-quarters less.

Taking the two classes—primaries and secondaries—altogether, the survey showed that one-sixth[8] earned £1,050 or more per year from writing, one tenth £550 to £1,050, while two-thirds earned less than £6 a week, and many of those as little as 30s.

Two further points were thrown up by these figures. First, how important was income from subsidiary rights, often assumed to compensate the author for the slender rewards of his volume sales?

If you break down the survey figures, you find that this is true for some authors, who may earn more from subsidiary rights than from sales. But it applies only to authors in the top income bracket—i.e. the sixth who earn over £1,050 a year—who, in this context, rank as a rich *élite* . . . For the majority of authors no such harvest is in view. Nearly three quarters (71 per cent) of those who had published books had earned *nothing at all* from their subsidiary rights.

Secondly, how important was income from 'other literary sources', i.e. journalism, broadcasting, lecturing, etc.?

Just under a quarter received no more than £60 to £70 a year from this supplementary source, and just over a quarter earned *nothing at all* . . . it is a common fallacy that *all* media are open to a really good writer, that if you can write a book you can succeed in any other form. Many kinds of book writing— valuable and necessary kinds—are unmarketable outside hard and even paper covers, and only a handful of professionals are all-purpose performers . . .

At the top end of the scale, the Lucky Sixth—those who did best out of volume sales and subsidiary rights—also enjoyed a good income of £1,000 a year upwards from 'other literary earnings'. Their financial felicity suggests that in the writing game, as in others, the old adage that 'nothing succeeds like success' applies with increasing and alarming effect—alarming because the test of failure often has little to do with merit or value, while the penalty of non-success is growing steadily more severe.

What of value came out of this survey?

In so far as it aimed to replace speculation with facts and figures about economic and other conditions of writing, it succeeded all too well, providing a solid base for Findlater's findings. It added force to the continuing campaign for improved terms from publishers; specifically for a fairer division of royalties from books sold by hardback to paperback houses, and for higher payments to authors on books sold abroad. It also highlighted the scandal of massive public lending of copyright works without remuneration of any kind to the author beyond the royalties deriving from the purchase of copies required for library use. And it did rekindle the proposal to accumulate a fund out of royalties to be paid on out-of-copyright books, which in time might serve as a rich source of literary patronage.

These conclusions were reinforced and expanded over the next sixteen years, 1966–82. In 1972 the Society revised and repeated its 1966 survey among its members, yielding returns upon which Findlater commented in the winter issue of *The Author*:

In the past six years the annual total of titles has risen from 26,000 to nearly 33,000; the value of the export trade has increased by nearly 50 per cent; the number of borrowings from public libraries is up by around 120 million annually; about 25 million more paperbacks are said to be sold every year; book prices have rocketed, together with the profits of many publishers. *Everything* has gone up: surely the author's income from his books has gone up too? . . . On the contrary: this year's survey reveals that the situation is *worse*. After six years the national scandal persists. Our society has more reason than ever to be ashamed of the way in which it rewards most living authors of its books.

By 1980 publishers' output was choking the market with a record number of 48,000 new titles and reprints. At the same time the industry was running into a recession and beginning to take it out upon authors—the primary producers—by such manoeuvres as delays in publication and payments, and here and there by outright reneging on contracts. It was a situation savouring of anarchy and thus a suitable moment at which to conduct another investigation. In fact there were three more. The first was the work of David Caute, literary editor of the *New Statesman*, who with the help of the Society of Authors and the Writers' Guild, examined the standard printed contracts of 60 British publishers. His report, *Publish and be damned*, appeared in the *New Statesman* on 13 June 1980 and revealed an extraordinary range of variations, some of them highly discreditable to the publishers concerned, including respected houses.

For example, if an author failed to meet the deadline, he forfeited the advance; or he had to pay the cost of proof corrections in full; or accept changes in the text without prior consultation; or give options on future work; or expect payment only once a year; or concede far too much in the whole spectrum of subsidiary rights. All these and other points had been battled over for years but, like weeds in a garden, they regularly reappeared in one corner or another. In essence, as Caute pointed out, they sprang from the fundamental fact that, in nine cases out of ten, the publisher dictated the terms, while the author, unless protected by his agent or his union, allowed himself to be driven by necessity or was so mesmerised by the prospect of even a paltry advance that he overlooked the rest of the contract and signed regardless.

Commenting in *The Author*, David Machin, General Secretary of the Society of Authors 1978–81, wanted 'realistic agreements about *basic* terms and conditions, which could still leave plenty of room for individual negotiation and for the development of the all-important personal relationship, for which no document can make provision'. This pointed the way towards a minimum terms agreement on which both the Society and the Writers' Guild were already at work, and indicated by two more joint investigations conducted in 1980 and 1981. The first consisted of a questionnaire, based upon the period 1975–80, designed 'to measure the opinions of authors about the performance of their publishers'. 1,760 replies were received, covering 253 publishers who were assessed on a points system as to the degree of editorial interest, efficiency of copy and proof reading, quality of design and art work, consultation over the jacket, promptness of publication, performance as to promotion and distribution, success in selling subsidiary rights, behaviour over remaindering, and overall record. The aim of the exercise was not solely confined to fact finding, but to tell authors about the merits or otherwise of the different publishers and remind them of what they had the right to expect; and, not least, to bring pressure to bear upon errant publishers to put their own houses in order. The outcome of the exercise, together with a league table, was duly made public.

The next enquiry sought information about authorship earnings over the two years 1979–81 and confirmed the downward trend revealed in the earlier surveys. Analysing the results in 1982 Findlater concluded that, whereas in 1966 *c.* 16 per cent of all full-time and part-time authors, lumped together, were earning more than £1,000 p.a. (then the national average wage), and that about half regarded writing as their principal occupation, the latter figure had dropped to less than a third by 1972, and to less than a sixth by 1982. In other words, the great majority wrote books in their spare time and paid the household bills out of other sources of income.

Writing in *The Sunday Times* of 13 June 1982, Norman Lebrecht quoted the example of Robert Gittings, author of biographies of Hardy and Keats, who had been a professional writer for more than thirty years.

Gittings, now 71, earns £2,000 to £2,500 a year from seven books currently in print. 'That money ought to support me while researching and writing my next book,' he said. Instead, he supplements his income by staging dramatised recitals of Hardy readings, and, ultimately, falling back on lifetime savings and investments.

Fiction, on the other hand, had been faring both better and worse. Whereas twenty novelists out of the sample earned very high incomes comparable to those of star footballers, 118 averaged £1,600 a year, some as little as £150, and that was the realistic test of the *genre*.

Mark Le Fanu, David Machin's successor at the Society, said bluntly that the professional writer as a species was threatened with extinction.

It is a terrible waste of creative talent, and puts at risk the future of British publishing, its exports and thousands of jobs.

I now turn to Public Lending Right (PLR), referred to by Findlater, and widely recognised as one of the sources of income that should be available to authors *as of right*. In view of the length and complexity of the historic campaign that lasted in effect from 1951 to 1982 (when Parliament authorised payments to be made as from the financial year 1983–4), I have recorded the main facts and arguments in detail elsewhere.[9] Here I will confine myself to a brief outline.

The campaign proper began in 1951 when John Brophy, the novelist, wrote an 'Open Letter' published in the summer issue of *The Author*, in which he contended that:

since books provided a living for everyone concerned in their production and sale—except for the great majority of authors without whom the book trade would not exist,

since it was in the national interest that contemporary literature should be encouraged and sustained, and

since most books were borrowed, not bought

charging for the use of in-copyright books by libraries was a legitimate and hitherto untapped source of income which would do much to correct the anomaly whereby the primary producers (the authors) were forced to make ends meet by pursuing vocations other than writing.

In practice he suggested that each reader should pay one penny (1d) per volume each time he borrowed it from the library; and that the libraries should collect the pennies, deduct 10 per cent for administration, and pass the net sum collected to the authors via their publishers.

This proposal ran almost at once into furious resistance, mainly from public librarians, who objected initially on two grounds: the sanctity of the 'free' public library service, and the support given to literature by public library buying of books, especially new novels, and 'difficult' books without strong commercial appeal.

Such were the opening shots in a campaign complicated during its long and tortuous course by muddled thinking on both sides. For example, at one stage, the librarians advanced the argument that, having bought an in-copyright book, any institution committed to lending could do what it liked with it, without any further obligation to the author or copyright owner who had already received a royalty on the copy purchased. On their side, some authors weakened their case simply by pleading poverty, whereas that was just one of the issues arising out of the larger question of the economics of writing, and therefore not the prime justification for PLR.

The definitive argument emerged as the campaign developed and can be plainly summarised as follows:

Under copyright, all transactions involving use of a work are conditional. When an author writes a book, he creates a piece of artistic/intellectual property which is protected by law; so that when a copy is sold, the buyer does not automatically acquire the right 'to do what he likes with it'. He cannot convert it into a play or a film, read it over the radio, publish a translation, and so on, without formal agreement and specific payment, otherwise he would be infringing copyright. What was claimed was that lending to the public (whether by public or commercial libraries) constituted an ancillary use of an author's property which, for historical reasons, had been omitted from copyright legislation, but which in natural justice copyright had been designed to protect. How could it be right that a single copy of a book be lent out several hundred times to members of the public, without the author receiving a penny for such use?

In due course the copyright issue was recognised as the core of the authors' case, which in its essence led to its acceptance by Parliament—that the law should be amended to include public lending as one of the acts restricted by copyright, and that this should be done as a matter of justice and for no other reason. The fact that, in the end, legislation giving effect to PLR was not passed by way of amendment to the Copyright Act, but as a separate statute, did not invalidate the point, for this was due to another factor—reciprocity. Under international copyright agreements, all signatory countries are obliged to honour copyright commitments in full. This would have meant that foreign authors, who had in-copyright books in British libraries, would have been able to claim PLR payments, while British authors with books in foreign libraries were unable to do so—either because in certain countries (e.g. Sweden and Denmark) PLR was reserved under domestic (not copyright) legislation for nationals only or because, as in most other countries, PLR did not exist at all. This imbalance applied with particular force to American authors, with works plentifully available in British libraries, and would have resulted in a heavy outflow of sterling payments without any possibility of a cent in return, since PLR was hardly a topical issue in USA. The outstanding exception was West Germany, where PLR had been duly legislated for under copyright, and contributed considerable PLR income to British authors as from 1981.

To return to the campaign. The Society of Authors adopted Brophy's proposals and converted them into a full-scale crusade but, after preliminary skirmishes, decided to await the findings of the Roberts Committee appointed by the Government in 1957 to investigate the public library service and recommend reforms. When it appeared in February 1959, the Committee's report yielded useful and significant statistics about library stock and borrowings (392 million copies of books lent in 1958, soon to rise to 500+ million), but insisted that public libraries should remain 'free' and never considered PLR, no authors having been invited to serve on the Committee or consulted in any way.

The Society of Authors then prepared for serious battle by providing all the administration for the campaign, and persuading Sir Alan Herbert (APH) to take command. At 70, and tired after his success in helping to force through the Obscene Publications Act, 1959, he was naturally reluctant to accept, but 'that very autumn got out the logarithms and was soon deep in a swamp of sums and plans'. His first move was to recruit his publisher, Alan White, chairman of Methuen, and together they prepared a memorandum published by the Society in March 1960. This document, reasonably and forcefully argued, was nonetheless a declaration of war.

[It] designated authors and publishers as the 'book producers', i.e. the two parties with the right to benefit from PLR, because they provided the life blood of the library system.

[It] stated that public libraries no longer fulfilled their original purpose as 'engines of education' for the benefit of the poor; but offered entertainment in reading and all sorts of services additional to the lending of books—for enjoyment by everybody, irrespective of income, rich and poor alike; and all made possible by public money. Therefore a new concept was needed to cope with the new situation—in short a public lending right, analogous to public performing right, and authorised by Parliament.

[It] discussed various methods of operating and financing a PLR scheme [though later APH reverted to the Brophy proposal to charge the borrower].

Two alternative Bills were then drafted—one to amend the Copyright Act, 1956, the other to amend the Public Libraries Act, 1892. On 23 November 1960 the second Bill was presented to the House of Commons by William Teeling, MP, supported by six Conservative and five Labour MPs, and on 9 December given a second reading when it was talked out.

Thus began the first phase of lobbying, publicity and pressure, lasting approximately five years, led by APH, Alan White, and their supporters inside and outside the Society of Authors. In 1964, APH stood down. He had not achieved PLR, but he had conducted a vigorous and exhausting campaign with consummate skill and wit, and—most important—had set the cause ablaze. Thanks to him, the public was now aware of PLR as an issue, even if confused by details. In a 'farewell' speech at the Royal Society of Arts on 10 December, he said:

> We want recognition . . . *of the principle of a repeated fee for repeated exploitation, repeated enjoyment.* [my italics]
> This is, after all, the active principle of copyright.
> Sir, as you know, I do not give up, and I shall be in battle order still.

The second phase of the campaign, in which I was closely involved, lasted seven years, from 1965 to 1972. It began in effect in February 1965 with the publication of the Government White Paper, *A Policy for the Arts*, which was inspired by Jennie Lee, the first Minister for the Arts under the recently elected Labour administration, and was followed soon after by the appointment of Arnold (Lord) Goodman as chairman of the Arts Council of Great Britain. Both were determined to increase public patronage of the arts, and they secured the necessary finance to do so.

The Arts Council at last gave writers and publishers of books and periodicals the recognition they deserved by expanding the existing poetry panel into the literature panel, with Cecil Day-Lewis as chairman, while a working party was appointed to pick up the threads of PLR and initiate fresh action. Alan White and Eric Walter White, the Literature Director, were sent to Scandinavia to report on the Swedish and Danish variants of PLR. On their return an entirely new plan was drafted, based on the Danish system of annual stock sampling instead of the Swedish one of book loans—to be conducted in representative libraries all over the country, and financed not by charging the borrower but by a central Government grant calculated as a percentage of total library book funds. This change of policy as regards finance was due to advice from Jennie Lee, who made it clear that no Government in power—of whatever party—would be likely to abandon the 'freedom' of the public library service, and that the writers and their friends were butting their heads against a brick wall unless they changed course.

The new plan, mainly the work of Alan White, was forwarded to Jennie Lee at the Department of Education and Science in April 1967 and, at her request, shortened and revised, and formally resubmitted in October. Nothing happened for a year. However, as early as the end of 1967, it was becoming clear that any action to approve, or even discuss, the plan was being opposed by senior civil servants in the Department, and that some fresh move would have to be made to prompt a positive reply. In the meantime the campaign was sustained by letters to the press, broadcasting, the publication of a *Pocket Brief for PLR*, and talks up and down the country to librarians, library students, lunch clubs, and many other gatherings—a chore that largely fell to me. Not even a blistering attack on Miss Lee in an article by Michael Holroyd in *The Times Saturday Review* of 15 February 1969, nor two subsequent deputations to Ministers, nor a debate in the House of Lords, nor a round table conference of interested parties (the first ever), produced any tangible result. However, valuable information was coming in all during 1969 about the mechanics of PLR thanks to test runs, organised—with the help of sympathetic librarians—at Hove, Cheshire County, and Southwark GLC, using a prime list of in-copyright works drawn up by William Taylor, city librarian of Birmingham and a member of the literature panel, whose support for PLR was invaluable at this stage. This exercise revealed beyond all doubt that the manual checking of stock in card indexes was impracticable and that PLR could only be operated in libraries equipped with computers, programmed to record the stock of qualifying titles and their use. At that time only a handful of library authorities were so equipped, and it seemed likely that at least a decade would have to elapse before there would be enough of them, representative of different regions and interests, to make PLR a practicable undertaking.

In the meantime the fight for the principle continued. In the summer and autumn of 1970, on a hint from the Department of Education and Science a fresh plan was worked out by Ronald Barker, Secretary of the Publishers Association; namely calculating PLR by reference to the statistics of library sales available from publishers, booksellers and library suppliers. This had the advantage of by-passing librarians altogether, but it did mean that PLR could only relate to books purchased as from the start of the scheme, which would be unfair to older authors no longer producing fresh work or whose titles did not justify reprinting. It was further suggested that payment might take the form of a 'lending' royalty (calculated as a percentage of the published price), additional to the royalty received on the sale of a book. The author thus stood to receive two royalties on all copies of his books sold to public libraries, but no continuing payment for use.

The Barker plan was submitted in October 1970 to Lord Eccles, who had succeeded Jennie Lee with the change of Government, and eventually rejected by him, though with the promise that he would look at the whole subject again. In the ensuing months, his memory was repeatedly refreshed—by the publication of APH's autobiography, which devoted a whole chapter to 'Battles about Books', by the joint publication by André Deutsch and Penguin Books of a symposium on PLR edited by Richard Findlater, and by notice of a Private Member's Motion on PLR for debate in the House of Commons, put forward by David James, MP. On 16 February 1971 the entire prospect was transformed by Lord Eccles's admission that 'there was some justice in the original claim that authors' rights in their books were not adequately covered by law', and by his consequent decision to set up a Department of Education and Science working party 'to consider an amendment to the Copyright Act, 1956, which would add lending to the public to the acts restricted by copyright'. The PLR lobby was of course delighted but reminded the Minister (Eccles had been Minister of Education in 1960) that it had taken him eleven years to reach the logical solution contained in APH's first Bill of July 1960, to the effect that, since library lending was no different in principle to other ways of using authors' property already protected by copyright, the omission should be made good by amending the copyright law.

The new working party, composed of representatives of all the relevant interests, deliberated for a year and published its unanimous report in May 1972. Within its terms of reference it was a masterly piece of work. It was not required to offer any solution; nonetheless it advised against both the Swedish system of loan sampling and the Danish one of stock sampling on grounds of accuracy and practicability as applied to the immensely larger and more complex library system of the UK. Instead it discussed two alternatives, both related to library purchases:

1. Surcharging, i.e. adding a uniform sum or percentage to the published price of a book, or

2. Blanket Licensing, whereby libraries would be licensed to lend books in return for an annual fee,

The money in either case to be collected and distributed by a Lending Right Society, analogous to the Performing Right Society, to which all qualifying authors would assign their PLR interests.

The publication of the Department of Education and Science report was followed a month later by the issue of a joint statement by the Society of Authors and the Publishers Association, who plumped for Blanket Licensing and offered to set up the Lending Right Society, backed by an independent tribunal to handle arbitration and safeguard the public interest. It was estimated that PLR would cost £4 million p.a.—of which £½ million would be absorbed by administration, the balance to be allotted 75 per cent to authors, 25 per cent to publishers, calculated on sales to, or purchases by, libraries as explained. It was a far from perfect scheme, but one which could be made to work, and at the time there seemed no practicable alternative.

This statement was immediately subjected to a blistering attack by five writers: Brigid Brophy, her husband Michael Levey, Maureen Duffy, Francis King, and Lettice Cooper—all members of the Society—who adopted the title Writers' Action Group (WAG). They advanced three principal objections:

1. Basing PLR on library purchases of books, not on actual lending. This therefore was a 'purchase price' scheme, and not related to continued use.
2. Calculating the payment on the published price was not a fair method of assessing the true value of any book.
3. Excluding books held by libraries before the scheme started was unjust to many authors.

So began the third phase of the PLR campaign, from 1972 to 1982.

WAG's objections were undoubtedly valid, but they offered no practicable solution to the problems of implementation, which—after years of effort—had caused the Society and the Publishers Association to recommend Blanket Licensing, *faute de mieux*. Unhappily WAG's action was not confined to PLR, but developed into a protracted assault on the personnel and constitution of the Society which, though successfully defended, left a legacy of bitterness and distrust. At the time great fear was felt lest the conflict should not only confuse the public, but present the Minister with a ready-made excuse to drop PLR altogether. In fact he did not do so, but neither did he act on the Department of Education and Science report which was left in limbo. Meanwhile PLR was kept alive, partly by the publicity generated by WAG, and partly by the Society's decision to go all out for the recognition of the principle, leaving implementation till later. All this bore fruit. An Early Day Motion of 21 February 1973 attracted no less than 269 signatures of MPs of all parties in the House of Commons; while Denis de Freitas, legal adviser to the Performing Right Society (which had had long experience of administration in the related field of music performance rights) who personally worked assiduously to heal the rift between the authors, drafted a fresh Bill solely to establish the right and capitalise on the support expressed in Parliament.

These preliminaries—wearisomely familiar—were not wasted however. Late in 1973 Ernle Money, MP, promised to introduce PLR by way of a Private Member's Bill, but gave way to Norman St John Stevas who, on replacing Lord Eccles as Minister of the Arts in December, immediately declared his support. A similar statement was made by the Labour spokesman for the arts, Hugh Jenkins. Parliament was dissolved on 7 February 1974, by which time St. John Stevas had committed himself to a Government Bill, to finding the necessary finance from the Treasury, and to setting up a panel of experts, the Technical Investigation Group (TIG), that aimed to solve the problems of implementation once and for all.

This was the breakthrough that both the Society and WAG—now nearing agreement—had long awaited; moreover their hopes were sustained by the return of Labour in the March General Election and by the appointment of Hugh Jenkins as Minister. A second Election in October, when Labour was again returned to power and Jenkins confirmed in his appointment, was followed by the promise of PLR in the Queen's Speech (an historic event after 23 years' campaigning), and raised hopes higher than ever. However the optimism generated by these moves anticipated too much too quickly. For one thing the investigations instituted by the Technical Investigation Group, with the library tests that followed, were inevitably protracted; and it was not until March 1976 that the Government—prodded repeatedly by Lord Willis—introduced its long-awaited Bill in the House of Lords, and that TIG published its final report, which demonstrated that, with the progress of data processing in public libraries, loan sampling was not only feasible, but fairer and less expensive than the purchase price scheme.

But this was not the end and the next obstacle was as depressing as it was unexpected. The Bill was handled badly in the Commons. The pace was dilatory, attendance at the debates was sparse and, since Jenkins had been replaced in April by Lord Donaldson, business was conducted in the Commons by a junior Minister, who seemed unable to cope with the implacable opposition of three MPs (two Conservative, one Labour) who, for reasons of their own, were determined to defeat the measure. They were successful. In the early hours of 17 November time ran out, and the Bill died.

Yet another start had to be made, and it was not until two and a half years later that victory was won—thanks to sustained pressure in and out of Parliament by the PLR lobby led by Brigid Brophy and Maureen Duffy who exhibited great skill and determination, and to the Labour Government's insistence on seeing the business through shortly before it went out of office. After completion of the Third Reading in the Commons on 31 January 1979, and approval in the Lords on 6 March, the Bill received the Royal Assent on 22 March, nearly 28 years after John Brophy published his first proposals in *The Author*, in the summer issue of 1951. However further administrative action was necessary, involving a delay of five more years, before any author received his first PLR cheque.

CHAPTER FIVE

Writing and the Law

A. P. Herbert. Obscene Publications Acts, 1959, 1964.
Professor Bernard Williams's Report, 1979. Censorship and
obscenity discussed. Defamation Act, 1952. P.Q. 17 case.
Faulks Report, 1975. Official secrets and access to Government
records. Closed shop legislation. Press charter enquiry, 1976–7.
The Society of Authors becomes a trade union in 1978.

The sheer length of the PLR campaign, the complexity of the
subject, and the involvement of so many individuals and
institutions, in addition to Parliament, make it clear that PLR
was hammered out and won, not by one, two or half-a-dozen
people, but by at least a hundred, all of whom played important
roles in the drama. Even so it is right to state that had it not been
for A. P. Herbert the campaign would never have caught fire as it
did when he was in charge in the early 1960s, and that his efforts
were the essential preliminary to all that followed, right up to the
end. Indeed it was his wit and his flair for communicating a
difficult subject in clear, humorous and forceful terms that made
the reading public aware of, and interested in, PLR.

PLR however was only one of APH's many services to
authors, let alone to society as a whole. He was the natural
successor of Besant and Shaw in regard to the campaigns he led
and the results he achieved for authorship as a profession. The law
of Obscene Publications was another example.

It will be recalled that the Society had waited until 1960 before
asking APH to take over PLR, owing to his concern with the
Obscene Publications Act, 1959. This business had started several
years earlier. Shortly after the war, it was becoming clear that
existing legislation—stemming from Lord Campbell's Act passed

in 1857 to suppress the trade in pornographic books, and the pronouncement of Chief Justice Cockburn in the Hicklin case of 1868—could not last much longer. Cockburn had said:

> The test of obscenity is whether the tendency of the matter charged as obscene is to deprave and corrupt those whose minds are open to such immoral influences and into whose hands a publication of this sort may fall.

This definition of obscene libel had been widely adopted in the courts of law in the English-speaking world, and had weathered a number of literary *causes célèbres* including the prosecution of D. H. Lawrence's novel, *The Rainbow*, in 1915, Radclyffe Hall's *The Well of Loneliness* in 1928, James Hanley's *Boy* in 1934 (three years after publication), and the confiscation by Customs of numerous copies of James Joyce's *Ulysses*, first published in Paris in 1922.

Writing in the spring 1937 issue of *The Author*, Edmond Segrave, editor of *The Bookseller*, concluded caustically:

> There is, of course, no censorship of books in this country. Everyone keeps saying so ... The Director of Public Prosecutions ... says so categorically ... if there is no censorship there are plenty of willing censors ... When every man is his own censor and can control the circulation of a book because of a single word in it, a state censorship of books is either a superfluity or a necessity according to how you look at it.

Segrave was referring to the activities of private informers, policemen, magistrates, *et al.*, or more obliquely to printers who refused to print, or booksellers and librarians who avoided stocking certain books, for fear of prosecution under the obscenity laws.

In 1949 Sir Hartley Shawcross, the Attorney-General, answering questions in the House of Commons about Norman Mailer's *The Naked and the Dead*, indicated a new line when he said: 'Looking at it as a whole I do not think its *intent* is to corrupt and deprave—or that it is likely to lead to any other result than disgust.'

This shift in attitude was tested in 1954 when five prosecutions were brought against publishers, only one of which succeeded. Furthermore, in the case of *The Philanderer* by Stanley Kaufmann, published by Secker & Warburg, Mr Justice Stable made history with his summing-up, in which he said: 'Are we going to say in England that our contemporary literature is to be measured by what is suitable for the fourteen-year-old schoolgirl to read?'

The jury acquitted, and this was the signal to the Society of Authors to set up an action committee, chaired by APH 'to examine the law and recommend reforms'. Although the Publishers Association stood aside officially, several publishers joined the committee as individuals and lent it powerful support.[1]

A Bill was then drafted, the essence of which was to require a court to consider 'the general character and dominant effect' of any book in question, and to listen to expert evidence about its literary or artistic merit. The Bill was introduced by Roy Jenkins, MP, in March 1955 under the Ten-Minute Rule and defeated, and so was a modified version presented by Hugh Fraser, MP, in November. Further moves were complicated by the action taken by the Home Office to control the imports of American 'horror comics', and enacted in the Children and Young Persons (Harmful Publications) Act, 1955, which covered some of the same ground as the Herbert Committee's Bill, and was criticised for attempting to solve the problem piecemeal. However the subject was revived by a Private Member's Bill in March 1957, which secured a Second Reading and was referred to a Select Committee whose report, issued in March 1958, conceded '80 per cent of the authors' claims'. APH wrote later:

Now, we thought, the Government, having interfered so much, would take the job over. But seven months of silence made plain that it would not.

After four years we were thrown back into the hazards of Private Members' time. None of our champions won a place in the ballot, and no other Member would tackle the ticklish thing. Mr Jenkins, quite properly, after four years of discussion, tried to get a Second Reading 'on the nod'—without formal debate. But two or three Members, twice, cried 'Object', and we were stuck. [28 November 1958.]

... it was at this point that, seeing red, I announced my intention to stand as an Independent at the East Harrow by-election. It was not 'blackmail'. I had every intention of getting in, if I could, and seeing what I could do.[2]

This was a typically daring move by APH who—backed by friends and the entire staff of the Society of Authors who addressed envelopes in their spare time—issued a pamphlet, *I Object* (Bodley Head), sub-titled 'Letter to the Electors of East Harrow: with some proposals for the reform of the machinery of government', and prepared to do battle. The seriousness of his intentions, and the ridicule he continued to pour on the Government, had its effect.

No one was more surprised than I, on Dec 16, when I was told that a special debate on our Bill had been arranged by the Government.

The debate was useful but inconclusive. Not one of our main points had been firmly conceded in the Home Secretary's speech. But then Mr Butler sent for Mr Jenkins and agreement gradually began, though not with the Law Offices of the Crown. One day the Members stopped saying 'object' and we got our Second Reading 'on the nod'. I followed suit and withdrew from East Harrow, where the selection of an official Conservative candidate had made my prospects of election nil.[3]

In the end, after much bargaining in Committee, the Bill was enacted in attenuated form in July 1959. C. R. Hewitt commented that the new test of obscenity was at first sight 'no great advance on *Hicklin*'. 'Tend to deprave and corrupt' stayed in, while the move to make the Attorney-General or the Director of Public Prosecutions solely responsible for prosecutions was defeated. However, important gains included the requirement that any offending 'article' (print, tape or film) should be 'taken as a whole', thus making sense of the context in any one case; also the vital concession that expert evidence could be called as to literary and artistic merit, and that it was open to prove justification as being 'for the public good' in these terms.

Within a year the Act was being tested at the Central Criminal

Court, when Penguin Books Ltd were prosecuted for publishing a paperback edition of D. H. Lawrence's *Lady Chatterley's Lover*. No less than 35 expert witnesses gave evidence, and Penguin won the case, though they had to pay costs of £13,000. This was a resounding victory for the Act; even so its inadequacies soon became apparent and some of these—notably display (not sale) of offending material, and the immunity of wholesalers of 'bulk pornography'—were corrected in an amending Act passed in 1964, which created a new offence, viz., *'having* an obscene article for publication for gain'. This clause was applied in 1967 when a London bookseller was convicted—the experts disagreeing as to literary merit—for stocking *Last Exit to Brooklyn* by Hubert Selby Jr. and published by Calder and Boyars. Since this was a local destruction order, the bookseller's three copies were solemnly burned, but the publishers decided to force the whole issue into the open by announcing that they were going ahead with the production and distribution of the book, and were duly summonsed. The case was tried in November 1967 before an Old Bailey jury which, after nine days, returned a verdict of Guilty. John Calder's subsequent complaint about the lack of qualifications, educational and otherwise, of jurors expected to reach a fair and informed decision about a complex literary case of this kind merely high-lighted the central problem of devising laws and procedures in order to control what is ultimately a subjective issue. The whole question of obscenity was, in other words, a Hydra-headed monster. When one head was cut off, at least one, more often several new heads appeared.

In 1968 the Theatres Act abolished the censor and the Lord Chamberlain's office and, technical problems of licensing apart, placed the play on parity with the book, at any rate in principle. In fact the 'liberation' of the theatre generated fresh problems for those concerned with legislating for obscenity. APH wrote:

'Obscenity' is a difficult word, made unnecessarily obscure by the law. 'Indecency' is comparatively clear, and is seldom likely to baffle a jury for long. But the law, in its efforts to ease the position of those accused of obscenity, has banished the conception of indecency from the stage. Many citizens must have been surprised to learn that actors may now display or dangle their private parts over the footlights, whether for art or saleable excitement, without the law officers of the Crown or the police being able to interfere.[4]

That was written in 1970, one year before APH died,[5] since when a number of explicitly erotic or otherwise controversial shows have been put on which would have strained even his tolerant mind to snapping point—for example, the simulation of buggery in *The Romans in Britain* performed at the National Theatre in 1982.

By 1968 APH was having his doubts about the efficacy of legislation although he did not want to abandon it altogether; and so when the Arts Council set up a working party (which finally recommended that both the 1959 and 1964 Acts be abolished for an experimental period of five years),[6] he re-stated—in a Note on the Working Party report—views he had earlier expressed in the run-up to the 1959 Act, and which deserve repetition for their patent common sense. There were two alternatives, he said:

(A) The honest writer, the serious artist, says to himself: 'I must tell my story as well as I can, and communicate at every point the emotions of my character to my readers. If there are love or sex scenes I must be sincere and truthful there as well. I must use artistic restraint, and, with the law looking over my shoulder, reasonable care: but, if my work demands it, I am entitled, in the present age, to be more outspoken than, shall we say, Jane Austen.'

(B) The obscene, or, as I prefer it, 'pornographic' writer, says to himself (if a good old English word may be used): 'I am going to make my readers randy as often as I can—and this will be the main attraction.'

One (A) writes a story, or a treatise, in which any sexual effect is incidental, and any shock may be accidental. The other (B) deliberately trades in lust. He does not care if he 'corrupts' or not: he markets something that he knows will sell . . . (B) debases the coinage, exposes honest literature to unfair competition, and discourages honest work.

At one time I wanted to call our Bill, *The Protection of Literature Bill* . . . Literature requires protection
(a) from unfair persecution by the law
(b) from unfair competition from 'adulteration', i.e. by the

'dirt for dirt's sake' writers . . . who seek to enjoy the 'freedom of literature' without deserving it.

The controversy continued. In 1971 two obscenity trials took place: one of *The Little Red School Book*, the other of the *Oz Schoolkids Issue*, both publications being explicit about sex, drugs, and generally anti-Establishment on these and other sensitive subjects. Discussing them in the summer 1972 issue of *The Author*, John Montgomerie[7] commented:

> *The Little Red School Book* was intended for consumption by schoolchildren. The *Oz Schoolkids Issue* was to a considerable degree written by schoolchildren. There is undoubtedly a strong feeling among the public that juveniles should not be involved in this obscenity business.

In the same issue of *The Author*, Toby David referred to the continuing confusion of the law. For example, if a prosecution failed under the Obscene Publication Acts 1959/1964, it was still possible to convict under, say, the Post Office Act, 1953 (sending offensive matter through the post), the Sexual Offences Act, 1956, and so on.

No consideration of the subject can omit the name of David Holbrook, champion of the anti-permissive party among authors, who actually resigned from the Society on this issue. He wrote:

> I am myself deeply concerned about the increasing tendency to thrust pornography on children and the harm that this may cause . . . I am myself assembling serious essays which argue that pornography is a threat to psychic well-being, human values, and to democratic society. There is experimental evidence that exposure to pornography causes young men to become more deviant, and that sexual depiction on the screen leads to increased sexual activity, largely of a masturbatory kind, and greater feelings of violence. This confirms the results of my own ten years' study of psychology and culture, which convinces me that pornography can damage people's emotional lives.[8]

Holbrook's symposium, *The Case against Pornography* (Stacey, 1972), appeared on the same day as another, the

Longford Report (Coronet Books, 1972), both containing contributions by eminent writers. Among them, Kingsley Amis and Elizabeth Jane Howard made the telling point that pornography was partly responsible for 'the degeneration of literature'. Explicitness about sexuality was just bad writing: 'It is simply easier work retailing a series of bedroom tussles than trying to emulate Hardy, Tolstoy or Richardson': while George Steiner defended restraint on the ground that human privacy was at stake.

In the ensuing decade the activities of Sir Cyril Black, MP, and Mrs Mary Whitehouse on one side of the fence, and the Defence of Literature and Art Society on the other, made sure that the subject was never allowed to lie low for long. Moreover it was a period in which the temperature of public opinion was undoubtedly sustained by the frequency with which scenes of violence (often associated with sex) were shown on television, by the daily reporting of crimes of robbery and rape in the cities, and by the horrors of civil war in South-East Asia and Northern Ireland. It was probably the combination of these factors that induced the Home Office in 1978 to appoint a committee, under the chairmanship of Professor Bernard Williams, to make a fresh enquiry, this time into obscenity and film censorship. After receiving a host of submissions,[9] the Committee published its report in November 1979. It recommended *inter alia*:

The abolition of all censorship of the written word.

A ban on the sale of pornography, not merely on display, in shops which children and unsuspecting adults are liable to enter.

A ban on pornography exploiting children or involving the physical injury of others.

A ban on live shows which include any real sexual activity that is 'offensive'.

and

Provision for specially designated cinemas to be allowed to show films which fail to obtain a censor's certificate.

The *Guardian* commented on 27 November:

. . . what is offensive to reasonable people should not be thrust in front of them—but that people who are not offended by the material concerned should not be denied access to it.

The report substitutes the objective test of what people find offensive for the subjective test of what is obscene or what is likely to corrupt.

To conclude. The Williams Report confronted yet again some of the problems scouted, but not solved, by the Acts of 1959 and 1964. By 1982, however, its findings had not yet been expressed in any fresh legislation.

A related subject to which authors have always been vulnerable is libel, in its connotation of defamation which may be defined as a statement 'concerning any living person which exposes him to hatred, ridicule or contempt or which causes him to be shunned or avoided or which tends to injure him in his profession, vocation or trade'.

One aspect of libel of which authors long complained was 'unintentional defamation' against which, for many years, there was no defence, following the case of *Hulton v. Jones* in 1910. In that instance a barrister, named Artemus Jones, succeeded in suing for libel a newspaper which had reported that one Artemus Jones, a churchwarden, was living in sin with a mistress in Dieppe. Thereafter it was widely assumed that any person whose name was taken in vain, however unwittingly, could win a case against, say, the author of a novel, even if that author was genuinely unaware that any real person of the name existed.

It was this situation that Lord Gorell tried, without success, to correct with his Bill in 1929. Nine years later APH and Sir Stanley Reed introduced another Bill in the House of Commons, but agreed to its withdrawal on the assurance that the Government would appoint a committee to examine the whole law of defamation. The Committee began work in April 1939, was interrupted by the war, but resumed in May 1945. Its report was published in 1948 and led to the passage of the Defamation Act in 1952. For authors the main point of interest concerned Section 4 which provided that any author or other person, who had 'innocently' libelled someone else, could make an 'offer of amends'. If the offer was accepted, the author would usually only have to publish an apology and pay costs. If not, and the author made the offer as soon as practicable, exercised all reasonable care, and acted without malice, then that would provide a good defence.

It is not proposed to pursue the legal aspects of libel in detail here, such as the defences of justification, fair comment, and so on, but rather to consider briefly its impact on the relations between an author and his publisher. Since most publishing agreements contain a clause in which the author indemnifies the publisher against the risk of libel and infringement of copyright, potential loss can be substantial. There is not only the matter of damages and costs, but if the book has to be withdrawn, consequent loss of sales and royalty income as well. However, to protect the author, the Society recommended the insertion of a phrase to the effect that the author is only solely responsible if these risks are *unknown to the publisher*. This has had important consequences, notably in one outstanding instance, the case arising out of the publication in 1968 by Cassell of *The Destruction of Convoy PQ 17* by David Irving, in which Captain Jack Broome, RN, the naval officer in command of the convoy, sued for libel and was awarded compensatory damages of £15,000 plus punitive damages of £25,000. Since it was established that the publisher was indeed aware of the libellous nature of the book, but decided to publish on the grounds that 'any threatened action is first class publicity', judgement was entered against both defendants. But the case did not end there, and by the time it had reached the House of Lords, the total sum incurred by damages and costs exceeded £100,000.[10]

In May 1971 the Government appointed a committee of inquiry under the chairmanship of Mr Justice Faulks to consider what changes, if any, should be made to the Defamation Act, 1952. A large number of submissions were received from organisations representing authors, publishers, and others, yielding a bulky 300-page report in 1975. For authors the main points included protection for the translator who had written a straightforward unbiased translation of an original text that turned out to be defamatory; familiar doubts about the ability of a jury to reach a fair decision in an emotive issue, or even to understand the complexities of a case; measures to reduce costs; and the right of certain near-relatives to bring an action where the deceased had been libelled.[11] No changes were recommended regarding unintentional defamation, and nothing has yet been done (1982) to give effect to any of the Faulks recommendations.

Libel (or defamation) is not the only source of danger to those authors who search for facts and seek to write honestly about them. Another vulnerable area, often exposed after the Second World War, was 'official secrets'. Even today the whole subject remains shrouded not merely in mystery but in illogicality—as the historian, Professor M. R. D. Foot,[12] has made clear on several occasions, notably in *The Author* (summer 1970 and winter 1971). The Official Secrets Act was first introduced during the Agadir crisis of 1911, and was subsequently added to and reinforced. In its essence it sought laudably to protect sensitive state information, but its application was discredited by the post-war publication of politicians' memoirs, and by the activities of journalists and others writing up, for example, the careers of the spies Philby, Burgess and MacLean. A second but related fact is that the mere passage of time usually renders publication innocuous, so that the events in question are transmuted into items of history. Some of the confusion was cleared up in 1966, when the rule regulating access to public records was, with certain exceptions, reduced from 50 to 30 years,[13] but the difficulties over publication have not been solved, and remain an occupational hazard for historians.

So much for some of the *exterior* dangers. Of no less importance were some of the *interior* ones, for example the implications of the Trade Union and Labour Relations Acts of 1974 and 1976, which made the 'closed shop' legal throughout British industry. It was their application to the press and the attitude of the National Union of Journalists (NUJ) that aroused fears among authors. During the debates preceding the 1976 Act, Antonia Fraser and Michael Holroyd[14] wrote to *The Times* on 4 March 1975:

> Many members of the Society of Authors contribute to newspapers and periodicals, and broadcast as well, since work of this kind is a natural and necessary adjunct to their activity as writers of books and other works.
> Some are members of the NUJ, but the great majority are not and cannot be, because their output as journalists is not

sufficient to qualify them for membership of the union. They are anxious on two grounds: first, that such outlets shall not be denied to them or to anyone who has something worthwhile to communicate, as this endangers a fundamental human freedom; secondly, that such denial might altogether exclude certain types of contribution (e.g. an article requiring specialised knowledge), and it would certainly depress standards of criticism and reviewing.

In the event Michael Foot, then Secretary of State for Employment (and a former editor himself), while refusing to alter the labour relations legislation, promised to enact a charter of press freedom, and invited representatives of the press unions and proprietors to hammer out the details. If they failed, the Government would itself put the charter together and impose it by law.

In this way a press charter committee came into being, composed of representatives of most, but not all, of the interested parties. Michael Scammell, representing the Society of Authors and, as editor of *Index*[15] a front runner for freedom of expression, doubted—as indeed did others—whether freedom needed to be defined in detail.

Our freedoms and rights exist to the extent that they are not encroached upon by legislation to protect other rights. 'Freedom from', not 'freedom to' is the essence of common law; a press charter would inevitably have the opposite effect of that intended, for to define is in itself to limit.

As to the Committee:

It rapidly became clear that our presence was superfluous to the main business of the meetings, for battle lines had already been drawn up between the Newspaper Proprietors' Association (NPA), representing Fleet Street, and the Newspaper Society (NS), representing the provincial newspapers, on the one hand, and the NUJ on the other. ... When questioned about the possible effects of a union monopoly on freedom of the press, the NUJ representatives asserted that there was no conflict whatsoever, that the freedom of the press was in fact limited and hindered by the unfettered freedom of the proprietors, with their well defined class interests, to print (or suppress) what they liked, and that press freedom would gain, not lose, from an NUJ closed shop.

The proprietors, for their part, took an exactly opposite view. Freedom of the press was guaranteed above all by multiplicity of ownership and the ultimate sanction of the public to give or withhold its custom . . .

What we had, therefore, was a classic industrial confrontation between unions and employers . . . But it is hard to resist the conclusion that neither employers, nor journalists, when the chips are down, are particularly prepared to put press freedom before their sectional interests.[16]

As expected the Committee was unable to agree on the terms of a press charter, and the Government went out of office before it could draft its own Bill. In the meantime, for a variety of reasons—among them the continued existence of a rival union, the Institute of Journalists (IOJ)—the NUJ was unable to enforce the closed shop except where it had separate agreements with owners to that effect. At the same time writers were only exceptionally refused publication on the grounds that they did not belong to the union, but the threat did not disappear.

When the press charter was being discussed in 1976–7, the Society of Authors still regarded itself as a professional association, or the nearest equivalent. Constitutionally it had always been a company limited by shares (all allotted to members of the Council) and non-profit making. Revisions in 1893 and 1908 had not altered this basic concept formulated at its incorporation in 1884, when the Society was founded. A fresh attempt to modernise the Articles and Memorandum of Association, involving lengthy consultation with counsel and the Board of Trade, began in 1963 and petered out through sheer exhaustion in 1968. Then in 1973 a working party was appointed to examine the subject once again. Its report was published in 1974 when the Electoral Reform Society was commissioned to organise a postal referendum among members, requiring them to vote on four recommendations, including one that the Society should become a trade union. This was voted down; even so all the alternatives and all the work done after the referendum was over failed to resolve one immovable problem: that, in order to effect any *radical* change, the Society would have to be wound up as a company, and would have to make a fresh start—an action that might well result in its demise. It was decided not to take the risk and so, by 1975, this attempt too had come to nothing.

Nonetheless, the general feeling remained that *something* ought to be done to bring the constitution up to date and strengthen the Society's standing as a negotiating body, and to this end political forces were already at work. Already in 1971 it had been placed on the special register of companies, in order to conform to the Industrial Relations Act passed by the Conservative Government of the day. Had this not been done, the Society might have forfeited its legal existence. Although special registration ceased under the Trade Union and Labour Relations Act, 1974, the Society was allowed to retain its company status with all its obligations to members, administration of trusts, and other duties. Furthermore, as mentioned, it was this Act that legalised the principle of the closed shop and encouraged the formation of trade unions in order to facilitate collective bargaining and negotiation in industry—a policy that applied as much to organisations, such as the Society, representing self-employed authors, as to those representing salary and wage earners.

This legislation began to make itself felt quite soon, and a clear hint was received from contacts inside the BBC (with whom the Society had long conducted business on behalf of radiowriters) that, in the future, the Corporation might have no recourse but to negotiate solely with unions that, wholly or partially, represented authors . Besides this, the Society was continually under pressure 'to come into line' from unions with whom it co-operated in matters involving publication or performance; and the risk was steadily mounting of losing members in disputes with unions, or where union support was essential to the interests of solidarity.[17] Finally when it was realised that the Society would no longer be compelled to abandon its company status in the event of becoming a trade union, the implications were obvious.

In 1977 therefore soundings were taken at the Certification Office for Trade Unions and Employers' Associations to find out how the Society stood. The reply was that, subject to a small addition to the Memorandum of Association to clarify aims, the

Society would be eligible for listing as a trade union; and provided that it could prove its complete independence of 'employers' (e.g. publishers) and could show that in no way could it be construed as a 'company union', then it stood to receive a Certificate of Independence under the Employment Protection Act, 1975. By this process it would be registered as an independent trade union, while remaining a limited company. Neither of these steps, it should be added, involved affiliation to the Trades Union Congress.

To conclude. During 1977 and 1978 all the necessary moves were made to obtain the approval of the Council and Committee of Management, and to consult the membership in this matter. In February 1978 a ballot was conducted among the membership by the Electoral Reform Society, which returned a 2:1 vote in favour of the Society applying to become a union; and so the process of listing and certification was completed by the end of the year. After 94 years the Society had fulfilled Bernard Shaw's dictum expressed at the Annual Dinner in 1906 when he said:

> Literature is . . . unfortunately a sweated trade . . .
>
> Without union and collective action we are helpless. When we begin working, we are so poor and so busy that we have neither the time nor the means to defend ourselves against the commercial organisations which exploit us. When we become famous, we become famous suddenly, passing at one bound from the state in which we are, as I have said, too poor to fight our own battles, to a state in which our time is so valuable that it is not worth our while wasting any of it on lawsuits and bad debts. We all, eminent and obscure alike, need the Authors' Society. We all owe it a share of our time, our means, our influence.[18]

Shaw never actually advocated taking the steps that were taken in 1977–8, as others did at other dates. The reason was that the majority of members always resisted it

> . . . partly because they disliked the face of trade unionism as displayed in industrial action; partly because they considered it impracticable in that any attempt to enforce a closed shop (as the ultimate sanction) would fail, since a number of writers

would always disregard the ban; but at heart because they felt that to regiment writers was tantamount to dictatorship over the mind . . .[19]

In 1977–8 these objections were neither overlooked nor evaded. The referendum notice sent to members specifically rejected any idea of a closed shop for writers, both in principle and in practice; but it recommended joining the trade union movement on other positive grounds—as a measure of self-defence and corporate strength, for the right of access to ACAS (the Government's Advisory, Conciliation and Arbitration Service) in disputes, and for the right to disclosure by 'employers' of information necessary for collective bargaining. Over all, it was better to operate inside rather than outside the trade union movement, without losing essential freedoms.

However, as expected, a certain number of members who had voted against the proposal in the referendum decided to resign, some of them giving publicity to their decision in the press.[20] Although the final total was less than feared (fewer than 100), it did include some eminent writers whose loss was deeply regretted. They included Laurens van der Post, Harold Pinter, Lady Antonia Fraser[21] (a former Chairman), Professor Hugh Thomas, and the President herself, Dame Veronica Wedgwood. Whereas writers of this calibre were, and always are, in a position 'to go it alone', not so the rank and file who are the very ones most in need of a representative organisation.

CHAPTER SIX

Copyright

The Writers' Guild and the Society of Authors. Breakaway and rapprochement. Authors' Lending and Copyright Society. Copyright Act, 1956. Copyright reform. British Copyright Council. Whitford Report, 1977. Government green paper, 1981. ALCS constitution. Piracy and reprography. The new technology—video and microform. Electronic publishing and authorship.

The question of writers joining trade unions was not of course confined to members of the Society of Authors. Apart from the book section of the NUJ, catering for journalist-authors, an organisation then called the British Screen and Television Writers' Association (BSTWA) had, on the initiative of Ted (later Lord) Willis, been registered as a trade union in 1956. BSTWA was the title adopted by the Screenwriters' Association (SWA) set up in 1937 as a semi-autonomous section of the Society of Authors, on similar lines to the League of Dramatists (1931), the Radio-writers' Association (1947), and other groups of specialist writers formed in later years.[1]

The career of the SWA is detailed elsewhere[2]: suffice it to say here that, soon after the war, the SWA severed its practical connection with the Society and, with the advent of commercial television in 1954, competed actively with it for the representation of TV writers, although both sides managed to collaborate as members of the Television Writers' Council and of the Radio and Television Safeguards Committee. Eventually a truce was arranged. The Radiowriters' Association (RWA) retained radio, the BSTWA films and TV, and to this end changed its title to the Screenwriters' Guild in 1961 and the Writers' Guild of Great

Britain in 1965, in which year it became affiliated to the Trades Union Congress. At the same time the Society continued—as it does today—to advise individual members with regard to contracts and other business involving films and television, as well as book and subsidiary rights in general; and to administer the Broadcasting Group (successor to the RWA) consisting of members concerned with all aspects of the medium.

Relations however remained strained and were exacerbated by the Guild's evident desire to replace the Society in every field of writing. Thus in 1965 it set up a radiowriters' section of its own and eventually secured recognition by the BBC for joint representation (with RWA) for radio drama. Finally in 1974 it added books, poetry and stage plays to its list. This latter move was the direct outcome of pressure by the Writers' Action Group, some of whose members wished to attach WAG to an existing trade union. After approaching the NUJ and certain other unions, it was eventually accepted by the Guild, thanks principally to the advocacy of the then chairman, Gerald Kelsey, and of Lord Willis, the president.

Plans to push the Society off the map failed, however. For one thing the Guild's membership remained at about half the Society's, with the book section representing only a small proportion of the total. For another, the Society was too strong, since, collective representation apart, the wide range of services established during its many years of existence was difficult to emulate—especially the advice service available to every individual member on publishing contracts and all other authorship business, including litigating on matters of importance to all authors; the publication of *The Author* and Quick Guides; and the administration of welfare funds, trusts, and literary estates. In addition, as explained, the Society itself became a trade union, though not affiliated to the TUC. Furthermore, as time passed, much was done by personalities[3] on both sides to bring the two parties together. So that finally it proved—while remaining to a certain extent in competition—more profitable to collaborate, especially over major campaigns such as PLR, authorship surveys, and the preparation of a minimum terms book agreement between authors and publishers.

Perhaps the most important exercise in collaboration between the Society and the Guild concerned the development of the

Authors' Lending and Copyright Society (ALCS), the purpose of which was to collect income for the use of material which the copyright owner was unable to do on his own or by normal channels—in short, a literary collecting society analogous to the Performing Right Society in music, which had been founded in 1914 and had, ever since, collected millions of pounds for its members. But, first, a look at copyright in general.

So far (1982) the 1956 Copyright Act is the only comprehensive piece of copyright legislation passed since 1911. It was a belated move to ratify the Brussels Convention, 1948, of the International Copyright Union of Berne and the Universal Copyright Convention, 1952, the latter designed to bring into the copyright fold 'developing' countries and the USA on somewhat easier terms than those required by the Berne Union. It also aimed to update the 1911 Act in certain particulars, following the recommendations of the Gregory Committee (which reported in 1952) and those of the British Copyright Council, founded by the Performing Right Society and the Society of Authors in 1953.

In the opinion of many authors and publishers, the new Act did not go far enough. Although it removed the 1911 qualification whereby 25 years after the author's death anyone had the right to re-publish a copyright work on payment of a statutory royalty of 10 per cent, it was hesitant about the copyright in work commissioned by newspapers and periodicals, and it very shortly became outdated in that it made virtually no provision for the new and rapidly growing technologies, in particular reprography (i.e. photocopying in all its forms), sound and (later) video recording.[4]

It was not long before pressure began building up for a new Bill and—in response to this pressure—the appointment in 1973 of a Committee, under the chairmanship of Mr Justice Whitford—to consider afresh the law on copyright and designs. In the autumn 1974 issue of *The Author*, Denis de Freitas, then legal adviser to the PRS and responsible for drafting the British Copyright Council's submissions to the Whitford Committee, wrote:

> Authors and publishers believe that authors' rights should not be exercised so as to prevent society enjoying the benefits of technology, and that the solution must lie in devising means whereby the public may enjoy greater access to, or make greater use of, authors' works under a system which will ensure

that the authors receive fair remuneration. It is proposed, therefore, that the making of copies by photocopying and allied equipment should be covered by a system of blanket licensing. This means that, on the one hand, any institution, such as a school, using photocopying equipment will, having obtained a blanket licence, be freed from the necessity to seek out and obtain permission from the copyright owner of each individual work copied. Such licences would be issued by a central licensing body.

The above is quoted as one example only within a formidable list of additions and revisions submitted by the BCC for incorporation in a new Copyright Act, which was in any event needed to enable the UK to ratify the 1971 Paris text of the Berne Convention. When the Whitford report was published in March 1977, it grappled with most of these items. Philippa MacLiesh commented in *The Author*:[5]

There is ample evidence of the [Whitford] Committee's desire to protect the integrity of copyright, in the face of the problems created by technical developments in the last 20 years, coupled with the more recently apparent threat—to both the international copyright conventions and to national copyright laws—of the competition laws of the EEC [European Economic Community] ... It goes on to warn that the European Commission, in pursuing its principal aim—the free flow of goods within the Community—may make serious inroads on the profitable exercise of these authors' rights.

And she referred to the publication in 1976 of the report, *Copyright in the European Community*, by Dr Adolph Dietz, commissioned by the EEC, 'which contains specific recommendations for phased harmonisation of the copyright laws of the EEC countries'.

Of special interest was the emphasis laid on the necessity to amend UK law so as to grant the author certain 'moral' rights, which he would retain even if he had sold his copyright, and to comply with article 6 *bis* of the Berne Convention:

... the right to claim authorship of the work (the right of

[129]

'paternity'), and the right to object to any distortion or modification of the work if this would prejudice the author's honour or reputation (the right of 'integrity'). The UK law contains no equivalent provisions.

As to ownership, Whitford recommended that Crown copyright be brought to an end. There had long been complaint, against the arbitrary assumption of copyright in articles and other works written for Government departments and agencies, such as national museums, galleries, and so on. It also generally, though not entirely, supported the claim that in cases of doubt, notably in commissioned work, copyright should be presumed to belong to the author.

Finally Whitford did not accept the view that the term of copyright should be extended, without qualification from 50 to 70 years after the author's death. This had been the subject of varying opinions inside the Society of Authors, whose Committee of Management decided in the end to disagree, on this one point, with the BCC. Of the variants only a few voted for perpetual copyright, or for leaving the rule as it stood (at 50 years). Henry Cecil[6] favoured a scheme whereby, at the end of the 50 years, an author's copyright would pass for ever into the ownership of the state, which would then administer it for cultural purposes. Antonia Fraser, herself an eminent biographer, was aware that authors like herself were users as well as owners of copyright material, voted for the view that, after 50 years, the copyrights should be passed into a 'public paying domain' for 20 years, during which time there would be no restriction on the use of such works, provided that set royalties were paid on any title re-published or performed in any medium.[7] In this view she was supported by Piers Paul Read and the majority of the Committee of Management.

Following the customary pattern in the way it acted over copyright, Public Lending Right, and other authors' rights, the Government took four years to react to Whitford. Eventually, in July 1981, there appeared a green paper, *Reform of the Law relating to Copyright Design and Performers' Protection—a Consultative Document*. It was received with deep disappointment. While commentators applauded the proposal to take action over moral rights and to limit perpetual copyright in unpublished works, they found little else over which to rejoice. For instance, the paper barely scraped the surface of reprography in that it either rejected outright or responded half-heartedly to the BCC's recommendations for blanket licensing and fair dealing. It dismissed any idea of a levy on tapes and tape recording equipment (introduced in West Germany in 1965); and it weakened and confused the issue over commissioned work, relying, whenever a difficulty had to be faced, on 'further discussion'.

> The general impression the green paper gives is that the Government intends no more than minimal tinkering with the law to enable the UK to comply with its international obligations, rather than a comprehensive overhaul of the kind envisaged by the Whitford report, which is so urgently needed.[8]

The BCC and both the authors' organisations—the Society and the Guild—were at one in their condemnation of the green paper; but it did not discourage them in their efforts to establish collective licensing. The idea was by no means new for literature. In 1964 A. P. Herbert and Alan White had proposed a licensing body known as the Authors' and Publishers' Lending Association (APLA), while in 1972 Michael Gilbert had prepared a scheme for a similar organisation called the Authors' and Publishers' Copyright Association (APCA), both to act on behalf of authors and publishers of works qualifying for PLR. When the Writers' Action Group (WAG) took its own line about PLR, it formed a licensing company for authors alone, but had to put it into cold store when the Government decided to institute a statutory agency for PLR on the grounds that all the income would be provided by the Treasury. This duly took place with the appointment of Mr John Sumsion as the first Registrar of Public Lending Right for a period of five years starting on 1 September 1981, with an office at Stockton-on-Tees.

In 1976 however the WAG company was revived and incorporated in April 1977 as the Authors' Lending and Copyright Society Ltd. (ALCS) with the general object of providing a collection and distribution service for authors and others in respect of rights that could only be effectively administered on a collective basis. There was no doubt that such a service was needed, if not for PLR, then for reprography and the other purposes as recommended by Whitford. But the promoters of ALCS were precipitate and acted without adequate consultation, to the extent that the Society of Authors had to warn members, and some agents their clients, against joining ALCS until the constitution, as first published, had been amended. In the end a working party of representatives of the ALCS and the Society examined the matter together over a period of 18 months, reaching agreement by the autumn of 1980. A year later a further move was made whereby both the Society and the Guild were awarded corporate representation, together with elected members, on the ALCS Council of Management. By that time over 1,000 writers had joined the new organisation and membership was growing fast. Its efficacy had early been demonstrated by an agreement with the West German collecting society, V.G.WORT, whereby monies accruing to British authors under the German PLR scheme (in respect of British copyright books in German libraries) were paid to ALCS for distribution. The first payment, for the years 1973–9, amounted to about £57,000.[9]

Meanwhile work had been going forward in two committees. One, under Denis de Freitas, was concerned with forming a licensing authority, to be known as the Copyright Licensing Authority (CLA), whose function would be to issue licences to users and to pay over royalties received to the organisations representing copyright owners, e.g. the ALCS for authors, and the Publishers' Licensing Society (PLS) for publishers. The other, under Lord Wolfenden, concentrated on devising a form of licence, adaptable to all types of users. At the time of writing, the work of both these committees was well advanced, and seemed to offer a framework within which workable solutions might be found.

Even so, it is clear that the problems faced by authors and publishers in trying to protect their properties under copyright are immense, even in sophisticated countries which belong to one or other of the international copyright conventions and where, for example, illegal copying by members of the public is due more to ignorance than to any desire to defraud. In these countries, where educational and other kinds of institutions are likely to co-operate in licensing schemes, and where levies on equipment may be imposed, there does seem a fair chance of success. Prospects are poor in countries that do not observe copyright law at all, or where enforcement is lax, or where governments and pirates combine to legalise piracy, for example, by legislating for a 'statutory' royalty of say 2 per cent. Writing in *The Bookseller* of 6 September 1980, Malcolm Rowland, international secretary of the Publishers Association, estimated that piracy (in print alone) was costing about £500 million annually worldwide. Taiwan had long been regarded as 'the cradle of piracy', but the practice had now spread throughout South America and Asia and was due partly to the desperate shortage of books and to their high cost when imported from Europe or America, and partly of course to the desire to make quick profits. Whether the motive for piracy, had any element of respectability in it or not, the long-term effect was bound to be damaging—if only to native authors and publishers who were trying to get established.

Unhappily piracy of the grosser sort has not been eliminated even now from a copyright conscious country such as the USA. In *The Bookseller* of 1 December 1979, David Machin wrote:[10]

In 20 previous years as a literary agent and publisher, I never had cause to believe that widespread unauthorised publishing of British writers' work in the United States was anything but part of transatlantic publishing history. It was with a sense of amazement and growing anger that I found that one of the first priorities in my new position was to investigate complaints of the contemporary version of the practices against which Charles Dickens and other Victorian authors battled for decades.

Machin then went on to describe the activities of four American publishers engaged in the business, one of whom had issued a 48-page catalogue.

. . . mainly printed in three close columns, containing critical and biographical works by hundreds of American and British and some European authors, but with a particularly strong emphasis on British writers active in the late 19th to mid-20th centuries . . .

A director of this firm, reported to be the third largest library supplier in the United States, had been quoted as saying:

> Who is Dame Wedgwood, and what's she fussing about? It's unproductive to search out every author to send them a royalty. How the hell does one find out where this guy Priestley lives? Don't you realise that these days it costs 10 bucks to write a letter?

Machin concluded:

> Why . . . have we not encouraged one of our members to take legal action which will expose its activities in the courts once and for all? It may come to that, but the simple answer is that we do not see why a British author should have to go to the very considerable expense and trouble of bringing an action in a foreign court. Surely it is fair to ask the Americans to put their own house in order?

However this did not inhibit the bringing of actions wherever feasible in the UK and elsewhere. In 1981 the Society of Authors and the Writers Guild, acting together, succeeded in an action against the BBC and its former Head of Features, Desmond Wilcox, following the issue by BBC Publications in 1975 of a book entitled, *The Explorers*, infringing the rights of eight writers who had contributed to the award-winning television series of that title.[11] Another important case was won in the High Court in 1982 when the Coles Notes Company of Canada, publishers of examination study aids, were found to have infringed the copyright in works of three writers: Alan Sillitoe, Laurie Lee, and George Bernard Shaw (estate). The author plaintiffs were all members of the Society of Authors, which backed the proceedings together with more than ten publishing houses.[12]

So far I have been referring to attacks upon authors' and publishers' rights through piracy *in* print, and piracy *of* print by means of unauthorised reprography. However even greater threats have arisen, due to other advances in technology. I mean the replacement of the printed word in books and periodicals by various devices involving cassettes and the use of the visual screen, be it the domestic television set or what is known as the visual display unit (VDU).

First, the cassette. The idea of listening to the spoken word on gramophone disc, sound tape or cassette—rather than reading—has long been familiar. The conclusion, after several years' marketing experience, is that authors and book publishers have nothing to fear from this source. On the contrary, plays, poetry, children's and other stories, novels, etc., recorded in this way, especially when done by contemporary authors or well-known actors, actually enlarge the market, and either whet the appetite for books or attract buyers who would normally never buy a book at all.

The video cassette is at first sight another matter. Most of those on ordinary commercial sale reproduce—legitimately or otherwise—films, plays, features, events, etc., which have already appeared on the screen. In other words they are 'canned' versions of original presentations in a medium other than print; and extend enjoyment and use by their availability just as a sound disc deepens understanding of a symphony or other musical work. There are, in addition, novel opportunities for video equipment, now being pursued, for example, in education. Audio-visual teaching by means of study courses, integrating books and cassettes, linked to the Open University, ILEA, or other institutions—in other words enriched correspondence courses— hold great possiblities; and so it is likely that, overall, the use of video cassettes, and of video discs now coming on the market, will expand, rather than replace, 'further reading'.

Thus far there does not seem to be any fundamental conflict between screen and print, because the two media either complement one another, or are not comparable at all. There are however radical developments whereby the one actually penetrates the technique of the other: in other words, ways in which the screen can replace the book page and whole volumes of pages, allied to the revolution in information storage and retrieval. Here is a brief outline of the situation at the time of writing (1982).

A modified television set can reproduce the teletext systems developed by the BBC and IBA (Ceefax and Oracle respectively).

The amount of information available for transmission is limited in subject and quantity, as is the spare capacity of the screen itself, but it is free to anyone who has a set and has paid for a licence. A viewer can however obtain a far greater range and quantity of information from Prestel, the viewdata system operated by the Post Office, whereby the television receiver is linked by telephone and a key-pad or channel selector to a central computer; in this case the information must be paid for. Virtually all the information supplied by these systems is factual—'informatics' is the jargon—and offers immense potential in the provision of news, business data, scientific and other research. It is not expected that anyone will want to read a novel, a biography, or belles lettres in this way, but 'informatics' will clearly compete with encyclopaedias, directories, dictionaries, guide books, reference books, etc., and even newspapers, whose present publishers are bound to feel the draught if they do not move into the business of supplying material to the central computers or 'databases' and become information providers.

The role of the computer is obviously vital, specifically because of its ability to compress material, a process by no means new in publishing. Microfilm publication (the reproduction of print in microfilm or microfiche, readable on a scanner) is well established.[13] It has been successfully applied to the accumulated issues of newspapers, periodicals, specialised documentation, and all sorts of archives, and offers great advantages in terms of cost, access, and storage space, and also counteracts loss of the original through physical decay. However the process of compression is being taken much further by the computer, according to Christopher Evans who, in his book, *The Mighty Micro* (Gollancz, 1979), forecast that the entire contents of a book could be contained in a single silicon chip and read in a portable viewer. *The Bookseller* of 11 August 1979 commented:

> The read-out terminals of the late '80s will be about the size of the average book today, and of course, you will only need one of them. The screens on which the text is displayed will vary in size depending on what one wants—page-size for the hand-held book, wrist-size for quick reference and portability, a ceiling projection for reading in bed in absolute comfort (at last!).

It is evident from this and from what is happening already that, in certain areas of the book and periodical trades, there may be no future for printers, and not much future for some kinds of publishers and booksellers as we know them. Authors however cannot be metamorphosed or dispensed with. Thoughts have to be thought and stories conceived and—by whatever gadget—written down before anything else happens. Nor in theory should the new technology generate insurmountable problems with regard to copyright protection or remuneration, which will be a prime concern of the organisations now being set up to represent copyright owners. Piracy remains the greatest threat, facilitated by invention and operated on an international scale by black market recording. There can be no relaxation in the campaign against it if creative authorship is to survive.

There is yet another aspect of electronic or 'paperless' publishing, not primarily concerned with copyright or money, but which will create a whole new set of hazards for the writer. To quote Gordon Graham, chairman of Butterworths, writing in *The Author*, spring 1981:

> Some authors already are composing their texts on word processors with visual screens. They can alter at will as they compose, or after they compose. When they are satisfied, what used to be called their manuscripts, automatically stored in the computer, can be called up on screens by editors whom the authors have never met. The editors can make their suggestions or amendments, which the authors can then review, on their respective screens, which may be hundreds of miles apart. When they are agreed, the work will be 'published', i.e. made available to 'readers' who, like the authors and editors, will be users of the databases. Work so composed will never appear on paper. They may never be tactile, except when users press their buttons to command 'print-outs'.
>
> Paperless publishing calls up questions of motivation and reward deeper than monetary. Today, the measurement of the impact of a book or journal is the number of copies taken into the hands of readers, whether they buy or borrow, and indeed whether, having bought or borrowed, they actually read. Electronic publishing, on the other hand, will be measured by the number of times a page is summoned to a screen. While it is

sales—ironical because, unless a book is *written* in the first place, nothing else follows. Furthermore there are few alternative sources of income open to book writers. I do not refer to the media of performance—films, stage plays, broadcasting—nor to those who are first and foremost dramatists and scriptwriters, nor to staff journalists. I am thinking rather of freelance journalism which historically has often provided a useful and natural outlet for those who write for print in the broad sense of the term.

What in reality are the opportunities?

History tells the tale. By the early 1900s the explosion of popular journalism, detonated a generation earlier by men like George Newnes, Alfred Harmsworth, and Cyril Pearson, had transformed the whole of periodical publishing. So far from driving out the quality publications in the manner of Gresham's Law, it vastly expanded the market for reading, so that between 1870 and 1900 the number of newspapers rose from 1,390 to 2,448, and magazines from 626 to 2,446. In contrast to George Gissing who thought that mass media lowered standards, other highly talented writers revelled in the openings offered by the 'new journalism'. Arnold Bennett, for example, began by winning a *Tit-Bits* competition for £20, became assistant editor of *Woman* in 1893, and learned the trade of journalist, writing a mass of miscellanea at all literary levels. He went on to become not only a highly successful novelist but the most influential book reviewer of his day, earning £5,000 a year with a regular column in the *Evening Standard* at the time of his death in 1931. In 1895 H. G. Wells was paid £100 by W. E. Henley for the series rights of *The Time Machine* (then called *The Time Travellers*) for publication in *The New Review*. From then on his immensely successful career as a journalist and book writer is a matter of history, in part due to the popularity of his science and social fiction, in part to the hard bargains he managed to drive with publishers as a matter of business policy. Bernard Shaw broke into regular journalism as music critic of *The Dramatic Review* in 1885, and subsequently wrote reviews and critiques for *The Pall Mall Gazette*, *The World*, *The Star*, and *The Saturday Review*, the latter edited by Frank Harris. Shaw of course made his reputation primarily as a playwright, but he remained an electrifying freelance journalist to the end of his life, and was an excellent man of business, respected for his acumen by editors and theatre managers alike.

These were some of the stars, and therefore exceptional cases; for then as now rewards in journalism ranged from the heights to the depths. Grub Street has never vanished from the geography of journalism, nor have some of the grubbier practices in high places. In 1920 the Society of Authors' Committee of Management circulated to 422 editors of periodicals of all kinds a series of propositions concerning copyright, payment, and other business affecting the treatment of freelance contributions, the object being

> to obtain for the authors a generally adopted practice, which will be fair to both parties, and one which, in the absence of any express contract, will be universally recognised as embodying and protecting the rights of the author and the editor with equal justice to both.[1]

It was proposed for example that:

> 1. If no special terms are made before publication, it will be understood that the editor receives a licence for the first (British) serial use only. For his part, the author undertakes not to republish in serial form within six months.

> 2. The editor shall not demand by endorsement of a cheque, or otherwise, the copyright of a work.

> 3. All contributions shall be paid for on publication or within six weeks of acceptance, unless author and editor have agreed other arrangements.

Only 170 replies were received, of which 71 were generally or partially favourable, 10 gave no clear answers, and 80 refused outright. Typical refusals were:

> My acceptance would upset the whole system of book-keeping in this office. *Ideas*

> If we purchase the article, it becomes our property. *The Aeroplane*

> We have our own arrangements, which have answered well for the past fifty years, and we see no reason for departing from them. *The Graphic, The Bystander*

Reasonable replies were received from the editors of *The Yorkshire Post* and *Sunday at Home*: 'The pith of the matter is that the editor, in accepting a contribution, shall be explicit in his statement of price and conditions.'

The editor of the *London Mail* said that the practice of securing copyright by the endorsement of a cheque 'is a dirty business'.

Another source of grievance, familiar today, arose out of delay in publication (thus of payment), where an editor kept an article for weeks or months on end and left the author in limbo, the latter fearful of losing the chance of publication or of getting into the editor's bad books by demanding an answer. J. St Loe Strachey, respected editor and proprietor of the *Spectator*, wrote:

> I have always tried to pay for outside articles at once, but the difficulty is to say what is acceptance. One often, *in the interests of the writer and not of the paper*, does not like absolutely to refuse a contribution, because one has a vague (often quite impossible) hope that one may some day find room for an article, and one would like to give it a chance.

But of course not all editors were, or are, as honest as Strachey; and they commonly took deliberate advantage of the ordinary author's diffidence in this situation.

Parting with copyright in an article, surreptitiously by cheque endorsement, still occurs though relatively rarely. It can also be lost, deliberately or inadvertently, where there is a chance of syndication. Strictly under copyright, and in the absence of any written agreement to the contrary, the author of an article sells first British serial rights only. In fact, the law runs counter to 'the custom and practice' of Fleet Street, where the big newspaper and magazine groups operate a two-tier system:

> 1. If a story or article is initiated by the editor, then the contributor becomes, in effect, a staffer . . . and is paid once for the piece, the payment to include syndication rights.
>
> 2. If a story is initiated by the contributor, then the editor is buying first British rights only.

In practice, unless he is so well-known as to be able to command his own terms, or has other good reasons for reserving syndication rights, an author usually falls in with the first category—providing he is paid enough—on the grounds that, with a worldwide clientèle, the publisher is far better placed to arrange reprints. Alternatively the author can hand the whole business over to a syndication service, with which he will split the proceeds. In either event it is the automatic and undeclared assumption of copyright ownership by the publisher that creates bad blood and is wrong in principle—no less now than in 1920.[2]

Rates of payment have at all times varied widely within the market, from hundreds of pounds per article paid to a star name (political, literary, or otherwise), down to tens of pounds handed out to the rank and file, or lower still to the zero level common among numerous professional or 'little' magazines of different persuasions. The *pattern* of payment however, as distinct from the rates, has not markedly changed over the past half-century or so. Thus it is only of archaeological interest to know that in the 1920s seven guineas[3] was paid for a short story in a shilling magazine, or that a serial earned one guinea to thirty shillings per thousand words, or that the average rate paid by an established periodical for an article or a book review was two to five guineas per thousand words. American magazines paid, as always, far better; but few British writers leapt that barricade, and most of those who did were able to command their own price. What *has* markedly changed in a notably ephemeral world is neither the pattern of payment, nor even the quantity of publications, but the identity of the periodicals themselves.

R. H. Langridge, writing in *Smith's Trade News* of 11 October 1958, listed some striking fatalities among the weeklies and monthlies—those which died just before or at the beginning of the Second World War, and those which vanished within ten years of the end.

GENERAL	LITERARY
Pre-War	Pre-War
Bystander, Family Journal, Grand, Happy, Man and Woman, Nash's, Pearson's, Red, Violet, Windsor	*T.P. and Cassell's Weekly, Athenaeum, Criterion, London Mercury, Life and Letters, Nation, New Verse, Night and Day, Saturday Review, G.K's Weekly*

Answers, Band Waggon,
To-day, Picture Post, Leader,
London Opinion, Strand,
Parade, World Review,
Illustrated

John o'London's, Public
Opinion, Chamber's Journal,
Truth, Books and Art,
Literary Guide, Adelphi

These lists are indicative, not comprehensive. They omit certain revivals and, for example, the war-time literary phenomenon of *Horizon*, edited by Cyril Connolly, and *Penguin New Writing* (and his earlier ventures) edited by John Lehmann.

Since 1958 there have been further notable casualties, especially among the politicals and literaries, of which surviving readers are well aware: *Time and Tide, Books and Bookmen* (subsequently revived), *Twentieth Century, Blackwood's Magazine, Cornhill, The New Review*, and a host of 'littles'; also the temporary interment of *The Times* group including *The Times Literary Supplement*, which stimulated the publication of a clutch of new titles, some of them clinging to life for only a few numbers—but there is no end to listing. Reasons for demise include competition from television and the inability of a limited circulation to cope with a regular rise in the cost of production. What *has* remained relatively stable, despite intermittent crises, is a core of weeklies and 'less frequents' dependent either upon special interests (from fashion to finance) or upon strictly professional or trade support, often a captive readership deriving from membership of a profession (e.g. medicine) or academic discipline (e.g. chemistry). In contrast and alongside, there is a constant flow of arrivals and departures among journals of every type, but this, as indicated, has always been a characteristic of journalism. A glance through *The Writers' and Artists' Year Book* or any press guide reveals an astonishing quantity and variety of publications (national and provincial) in business at any one time, and still nominally open to the freelance, be it for a short story, a statistical review, or an investigative feature in a Sunday supplement. However a closer look at the market taken in the summer of 1967[4] was less optimistic, and in essence is still valid today (1982).

This stated bluntly that the freelance as he used to be, i.e. 'the brave loner outside the big battalions' was fast becoming obsolete.

> Today the traditional dreams of freedom through journalism come true for few book writers; just how few was made clear . . . in the Society of Authors' survey, which demonstrated that a quarter earned *nothing at all* from what the poll lumped together as 'other literary earnings' and that the next quarter earned no more than £70 a year.

Several reasons were advanced for this 'contraction of opportunity'.

1. The ownership of magazines had radically changed. Hundreds of editors worked on the payroll of only two employers—the International Publishing Corporation with over 80 women's and general magazines and over 130 trade and technical magazines; and the Thomson organisation with 127 British newspapers and periodicals. The inference was that few independent magazines were left 'that could *pay*'.

2. Newspapers, already reduced in numbers, had themselves become more like magazines, some publishing their own magazine supplements. The contents were increasingly the business of staff writers: a policy vigorously pursued by the National Union of Journalists which was working towards a closed shop in journalism and making it difficult even for freelances to join the NUJ.

3. The rates of pay for freelance work, always too low, had not kept pace with the cost of living or with comparable rises in staff salaries and the cost of producing a publication.

In this connection Julian Symons, prominent book writer and journalist, compared reviewing rates per thousand words over a period of 15 years:

	1952	1967
The Listener	7 guineas	12 guineas
London Magazine	—	10 ,,
New Statesman	10 ,,	18 ,,
Spectator	10 ,,	16 ,,
TLS	7 ,,	10 ,,
Tribune	2 ,,	2 ,,

He added that *Punch* paid 6 guineas for a 150-word review, 10 guineas for 250 words, and 16–18 guineas for the lead review of 700 words. *Encounter* paid £9 per 1,000 words, *Stand* 25 shillings, and *Twentieth Century* 5 guineas. Rates were not always linked to circulation.

> ... it is strange that *The Listener* and the *TLS* both pay less than the *Spectator*, although they have larger circulations. How can such a situation exist? It does so because reviewers are unorganised and easily replaceable. Any reviewer who gives up writing for a paper in protest against its rate of pay has simply lost a job. The embarrassment to the paper will be minimal; his own financial problem may be acute.

By 1982 the rates for both book reviewing and features had all moved up sharply. In general national dailies and Sunday papers paid a basic £100 per thousand words plus or minus, according to circumstances and the standing of the contributor; prominent weeklies £50–£70; literary magazines £25 upwards (dependent in several instances on a subsidy from the Arts Council). But the fact that the purchasing power of £1 sterling in 1970 was the equivalent of £5 in 1982 brings these rates into line with those quoted earlier; thus, as before, only a handful of regular contributors could hope to live off their freelance earnings in journalism or supplement their other sources of income to any marked degree.

Despite these discouraging facts and figures, writers have never stopped trying to break into journalism, and it is this ceaseless pressure that has given established editors and owners the whip hand. More significantly it explains the extraordinary proliferation of little magazines since the last war, some of which have provided future talents with their first appearance in print—as have their predecessors throughout the history of literature. Few of these publications have been commercial ventures in the ordinary sense, and very few have paid their contributors; rather they should be regarded as a symptom of the creative urge to find a means of expression at whatever cost—hence the fact that the majority have been devoted to fiction, belles lettres, and poetry.

In his 1972 report to the Arts Council of Great Britain, *Little*

Magazines in England, Jim Burns categorised magazines of this type in four groups; and I quote:

1. Relatively well-established publications enjoying a reputation for their regularity of appearance, and their insistence on good literary standards: e.g. *London Magazine, Stand, Ambit.*

2. Experimental or avant-garde magazines, designed to feature the new and often representing the work of a group or 'school' of poets: e.g. *Grossteste Review, The Park, New Departures.*

3. Magazines which tend to concentrate on poets writing in what might be termed a modern, though not particularly experimental style: e.g. *Phoenix, Priapus, Outposts.*

4. The sporadic, often badly produced publications . . . the editorial impetus appears to derive more from a desire to be an 'editor' rather than from any interest in searching out promising work or making a contribution to literature: e.g. *Scrip, Headland, Viewpoints.*

Burns concluded his comments by quoting Cyril Connolly:

Little magazines are of two kinds, dynamic and eclectic. Some flourish on what they put in, others by whom they keep out. Dynamic magazines have a shorter life, and it is around them that glamour and nostalgia crystallises. If they go on too long they will become eclectic although the reverse process is very unusual. Eclectic magazines are also of their time, but they cannot ignore the past nor resist good writing from opposing camps. The dynamic editor runs his magazine like a commando course where picked men are trained to assault the enemy position: the eclectic is like an hotel proprietor whose rooms fill up every month with a different clique.

If freelance outlets and opportunities have seriously diminished, not so the prospects offered to aspiring writers by commercial schools and tutors of writing. While, for example, the London School of Journalism—founded by Max Pemberton at the suggestion of Lord Northcliffe after the First World War—has sustained a reliable reputation, others have at best merely added to the surplus of supply over demand, or at worst teetered on the edge of false pretences within territory occupied too often by bogus colleges and adventurers. Some of the latter have however been attractive rogues.

One, Hargreaves, alias Frank White (or vice versa), spent more than one stint 'inside'. After emerging on one occasion he turned his attention to the cider industry and offered a very special brew in the back pages of *The Farmer's Weekly*, privately informing enquirers that unfortunately (sic) his article had 'aphrodisiac' properties. Sales burgeoned and I bought a flagon myself. Alas, it was just ordinary rough cider and so Frank White tumbled again—but it was a stunning idea, if only for its simplicity.

In America teaching writing is big business, but no less suspect. Jessica Mitford investigated the Famous Writers School in the July 1970 issue of *The Atlantic* magazine.[5] She found that, in practice the school was organised in two parts—the Guiding Faculty, and the instructors and salesmen. The former was illuminated by some 16 famous names, headed by Bennett Cerf, Chairman of the board of Random House, columnist and television personality. From him she discovered that neither he nor his famous colleagues had any idea of how the school worked, they did no practical teaching, and performed no serious duties beyond allowing their names to stand on the writing paper and prospectus. The hard graft was done by the instructors

> ... former freelance writers and people with editorial background [operating from] cheerful little cubicles equipped with machines into which they dictate the 'two-page letter of criticism and advice' promised in the advertising.

The most important element was the 800 salesmen, who outnumbered the instructors by 14 to 1 and were deployed throughout the country working on commission. From them, and them only, was it possible for an aspirant to discover what the course cost: namely $785 cash down, or about $900 in instalments—'roughly twenty times the cost of extension and correspondence courses offered by universities'. Joining necessitated an 'aptitude test', not a serious bar, it seemed, to 'enrolment for professional training'. At the time of the enquiry the school had enrolled 65,000 students.

Each student is supposed to send in twenty-four assignments over a three-year period, an average of eight a year. With 65,000 enrolled, this would amount to more than half-a-million lessons a year, and the fifty-five instructors would have to race along correcting these at a clip of one every few minutes. But in fact (the instructors assured me), they spend an hour or more on each lesson, and grade a total of only about 50,000 a year. What happens to the other 470,000 lessons? 'That's baffling,' said Mr Carroll [the director]. 'I guess you can take a horse to the water, but you can't make him drink.'

Miss Mitford estimated that the drop-out rate was close to 90 per cent. A similar answer was given to me by the tutor of a British writing school, currently advertising in the Sunday supplements, which offered to refund tuition fees if not covered by writing income earned—a seemingly impossible offer to honour if all or most of the students managed to stay the course. Significantly a separate survey of the US twenty-six top magazines had elicited the fact that

> . . . of 79,812 unsolicited article manuscripts, fewer than a thousand were accepted. Unsolicited fiction manuscripts fared far worse. Of 182,505 submitted, only 560 were accepted. Furthermore, a study based on the earnings of established writers, members of the Authors League with published books to their credit, shows that the average freelance earns just over $3,000 a year, an income which . . . very nearly qualifies him for emergency welfare assistance.

So the US experience did not differ much from that revealed in the surveys conducted by the Society of Authors.

CHAPTER EIGHT

Patronage

Patronage of literature. Civil List pensions. 'Desert and Distress'. The Royal Literary Fund. The state and the arts. Honours. Literary Prizes. Support of literature by the Arts Council. Writers' Grants 1964–81. The McGuigan Report. Need for patronage if contemporary writing is to survive.

If journalism cannot fill the gap for the great majority of those who write for print, what is the alternative? This is not a rhetorical question, for there is a clear and positive answer with an established role in the history of art—*patronage*.

In the 16th and early 17th centuries patronage was not primarily concerned with the giving and receiving of money, but formed part of the social system. Writing was not yet regarded as a profession to which you devoted your life, hoping that it would yield you a livelihood. Rather, it was a form of civilised communication that, among educated people, was quickly replacing the oral traditions of the past . . . What the writer received by way of reward, apart from acclaim, was security: a job as a secretary, tutor, chaplain, actor, librarian, or political agent . . .

In time the social stigma of print evaporated, partly through the popularity of the theatre which knew no class distinctions and made good money, and partly because certain kinds of work were never so stigmatised. For example, street ballads, broadsides, and pamphlets—the forerunners of modern journalism—found a ready market . . . Again, books of instruction and improvement were well received.[1]

As the 17th century advanced, the Puritans exerted a growing influence on literature, to the detriment of the humanities; and although, after the Restoration in 1660, royal patronage recovered its primacy for a time—notably in science and the theatre—thanks to the liberal interest of Charles II, the monarch no longer had a free hand. Military matters became the prerogative of Parliament which assumed increasing responsibility for the cost of all public services and of the royal household, in exchange for the surrender of hereditary Crown revenues.

Besides this, royal patronage declined for other reasons under the first three Georges—wasn't it George II who said, 'I don't like Boetry and I don't like Bainting'?—although it revived sumptuously under George IV who, as heir to the throne and sovereign (1820–30), gave solid support to institutions such as the Royal Literary Fund and the Royal Society of Literature, and made no bones about extravagances like the Brighton Pavilion; but he was the last of his kind. For over a century—and particularly after the passage of the Copyright Act, 1709, which gave them limited security as copyright owners—authors had been moving into the commercial market. Instead of relying solely on the favours of the Court and the aristocracy, they had turned more and more for support to members of the public to *buy* their books and *subscribe* to their magazines, with such success that some leading *literati*—Alexander Pope among them—made small fortunes. However the need for patronage did not disappear, as we know from the history of Grub Street, the sad suicide of Thomas Chatterton, and the records of the Royal Literary Fund. Nor did the sovereign's personal interest vanish, although royal patronage gave way to the public purse, so that, under the Civil List Act, 1837, the first Lord of the Treasury (usually the Prime Minister in person) became responsible for pensioning needy and deserving authors. But, as Nigel Cross has explained:[2] 'The 1837 Act provided for an annual sum of £1,200 to be spent on new pensions, including those for scientists, artists and public servants as well as authors.'

By the end of the century, however, most of the public servants had been taken care of by contributory and other schemes, although the impression long remained that, as far as authors were concerned, the Civil List was being mismanaged. In 1889 the Society of Authors issued a pamphlet, *Literature and the Civil*

List, the work of William Morris Colles, who gave himself the gargantuan task of listing all the pensions granted between 1838 and 1888, the names of beneficiaries and amounts paid, and of trying to make sense of the result. He asked by what criterion choice was made? Wordsworth had deserved his pension of £300 in 1842, but what about Eliza Cook, recipient of £100 in 1863, in recognition of such works as *Lays of a Wild Harp*, or *The Old Arm Chair* contributed to the *Weekly Dispatch* in 1837? Nigel Cross states:

> To qualify for a pension an author had to demonstrate both 'Desert and Distress'. Explaining why the Government pensioned so many second-rate authors, F. S. Parry, the civil servant in charge of the list under Balfour,[3] commented: 'First rate merit is far more generally recognised and rewarded by the public, and it is, as a rule, only second-rate Desert that is sufficiently unremunerated to pass the Distress test.'
>
> Failure to receive a pension did not necessarily mean that the supplicant author came away empty-handed ... the Prime Minister was also responsible for the distributions of the Royal Bounty fund, [which] covered payments to 'females in distress', 'alms', 'privy purse' and 'special services' ... The criteria ... were much the same as for pensions, except that the standard of literary merit was lower or the applicant was younger.
>
> In some cases it is quite clear that the Prime Minister took a personal interest in the Pension list.
>
> In Balfour's ten years as First Lord of the Treasury, he gave pensions to Henry Bradley, Mrs Trollope, Margaret Oliphant, W. H. Hudson, W. E. Henley and Sir James Frazer. He also pensioned Gissing's sons in their minority ... Perhaps Balfour's most laudable act of literary patronage was the Royal Bounty grant he made to Conrad in 1905 of £500.

Asquith[4] supplemented this grant with a pension of £100, which Conrad, in happier circumstances, was later able to return, the first author to do so. Another was W. H. Hudson; but these were rare exceptions.

Asquith conferred pensions on Yeats, Arthur Symons, W. H. Davies, Edith Nesbit, Constance Garnett and Walter de la Mare, though the latter was only 42 at the time. For this he was severely criticised by Edward Thomas and Ezra Pound, who wrote abrasive letters in support of James Joyce, then only 34, whose works were still widely regarded as a bad joke. Nonetheless, on the recommendation of Edward Marsh, editor of *Georgian Poetry* and generous patron of the arts, he received a Royal Bounty grant of £100.

Today Civil List pensions and Royal Bounty grants continue to be awarded on the recommendation of literary and other organisations, subject to the approval of the Prime Minister, but their level is very low.

In 1880 the average value of a Civil List Pension was £125 or £120 after 3 per cent income tax. In current values that £120 represents £2,400. In 1980 the average value of a literary pension is £600, which if tax is paid at 30 per cent is further reduced to £430. This tiny sum may well be a vital addition to a perilous literary income, but as a reward for 'distinguished literary services' it is hardly complimentary.

Cross's comment is reinforced by further, no less striking statistics. In 1981–2 the total value of Civil List pensions awarded for services to literature was £29,360. In the same financial year the Royal Literary Fund expended (in short-term grants and long-term pensions) £81,285, or nearly three times the Civil List figure.

This strange, typically English, institution, which I had the good fortune to serve as Secretary for nearly 16 years (1966–82), was described by John Lehmann, President from 1966 to 1976:

The Fund was the brain child of a remarkable enthusiast, by the name of David Williams, would-be religious reformer, lover of literature and philosophy, an educationalist far in advance of his time, and friend of many eminent men including Benjamin Franklin and Josiah Wedgwood. He was born in 1738, ordained as a Dissenting Minister at the age of 20, but had virtually abandoned the ministry by 1780.

The idea of founding a society for the relief of distress among authors had long been in his mind: the moment of crystallisation arrived in 1787, when public opinion was shocked by the death in prison of an aged man of letters, Floyer Sydenham, who had been confined there for a trifling debt. By the end of 1790 the Literary Fund had been established on a sound basis by the efforts of Williams and his friends in the learned world, and from the subscriptions received had relieved its first case of distress with a gift of 10 guineas.

The Prince Regent became an early and keen patron of the Fund. He subscribed 200 guineas a year towards the rent of its first headquarters in Gerrard Street, Soho. Through his efforts, the Society was granted a Charter of Incorporation in 1818. By the time of his death (as George IV) his constantly renewed donations had amounted to a total of £5,455.

Later the Fund was permitted by Queen Victoria to call itself 'Royal' and, under a zealous and upright Secretary, Octavian Blewitt, who placed the hitherto somewhat haphazard administration upon a sound basis, established itself as the principal literary charity, graced by a Council of distinguished persons and, by 1850 at least, widely regarded as a 'national institution'. In fact it remains today, as in the past, a *private* organisation—registered with the Charity Commissioners but not subsidised by the state—its affairs conducted by a General Committee of 27 members: authors, publishers, booksellers, literary agents, critics, and others concerned with literature, who dispense grants and pensions entirely at their own discretion according to criteria similar to those of the Civil List, viz., 'Desert and Distress', but, as noted, on a far more generous scale though backed by smaller resources. The Fund's income derives from legacies, investments accumulated since the foundation, royalties on certain literary estates, and subscriptions. Although no longer the sole source of charitable aid for authors,[5] the Fund's praiseworthy record over a period approaching 200 years reflects the national attitude towards artists in general, at any rate until relatively recently, in that, while support by private benevolence is respectable, public expenditure is suspect, to be extended only in the last resort to the old and ailing, when creativity is at an end.

The concept of state support for the arts, in terms other than charity, is comparatively new. It was only a combination of chance, private munificence, and the efforts of a few enlightened men that forced past Governments to found and maintain (often parsimoniously) such national institutions as the British Museum, the National Gallery, the Victoria and Albert Museum, the National Portrait Gallery and the Tate Gallery. As late as 1938–9 Government expenditure on the arts amounted to less than £1 million p.a., most of the money going towards museums and galleries containing 'dead men's treasures'. Nothing was provided by the Treasury for the performing and creative arts. This attitude is traceable partly to deep-seated Puritanism, still alive today, that tends to equate art with immorality, and partly to the influence of *laissez-faire*, the economic theory propounded by Adam Smith in his *The Wealth of Nations* (1776), 'which held that the State should exercise the least possible control in trade and industrial affairs', and which inevitably extended to other spheres, as when Lord Melbourne, Liberal Prime Minister in the 1830s, said, 'God help the Government that meddles with art.' A hundred years later, John Maynard Keynes, the economist, described this view as

> . . . the utilitarian—one might almost say financial—ideal, as the sole, respectable purpose of the community as a whole; the most dreadful heresy, perhaps, which has ever gained the ear of civilized people.[6]

Of Keynes's part in rectifying this view, more in a moment. Suffice it to say at this point that, by comparison with other culturally advanced countries, e.g. France, where state patronage and recognition of the arts has always been generous and fruitful, Britain's record—taken as a whole—is miserable. This judgement can be tested in several ways: by honours conferred for service and achievement, by prizes as rewards for specific works, and by grants and bursaries to stimulate fresh activity.

Honours arouse conflicting feelings. By comparison with members of other professions, the civil and defence services, industry or the trade unions, which all receive a substantial share of the Birthday and New Year Honours, writers so recognised can be counted in ones and twos; often they do not figure in these lists at all. It is true that some British writers have been honoured abroad through, for example, the Nobel prize for literature, the most prestigious of all international awards and coupled with a considerable sum of money. Some too have received the Order of

Merit, the highest British honour, which is in the gift of the sovereign and limited to 24 recipients (exclusive of foreign honorary members); but these are in their nature exceptional for members of any profession. It is among the life peers, knights, CBEs and OBEs, i.e. the general categories of public honours, that authors find themselves in a very small minority: so much so that a strong feeling has grown up in literary circles against receiving or even being recommended for them. None has any financial advantage, except ironically the nominal sum allotted to the Poet Laureate, a post now widely regarded as an eccentric and ludicrous anomaly, which requires the unfortunate incumbent to hammer out celebratory verses to order; indeed no one—with the possible exception of Tennyson—seems to have performed this invidious task with any success since the 17th century. Outside the state, the only source of honours for literature as such is the Royal Society of Literature, whose gold and silver medals are respected and valued, but not widely known outside the immediate circle of that Society.

As for literary prizes, these are almost entirely the product of private initiative in the broad sense, be the donor or administrator an individual, club, society, foundation, university, etc., or a commercial enterprise. Between the wars the number of such prizes was small. Two that survive from that era are the James Tait Black, founded in 1918 in memory of a partner in the publishing house of A. & C. Black, and consists of two prizes, one for the best biography, the other for the best novel published in the previous year. The second is the Hawthornden, founded by Alice Warrender in 1919, and awarded annually for the best work of imaginative literature by a British author under 41 years of age. Apart from these and a limited number administered, for example, by the Poetry Society and the Royal Society of Literature, there was little else, outside the universities, beside occasional competitions sponsored by publishing houses, some of them qualified by objectionable conditions, such as equating the prize money with the advance on royalties and a lien on future work.

Since the last war however prizes have proliferated—Britain can no longer be criticised on that score, although the state is not a prize giver. Well over a hundred are listed (1982) in the *Writers' and Artists' Yearbook*, and in the *Guide to Literary Prizes, Grants and Awards*, published jointly by the National Book League and the Society of Authors, in which the author, Margaret Drabble (then chairman, NBL) remarked:

> Prizes can and do stimulate interest in books, and benefit more than the winning author alone, as readers, publishers and booksellers acknowledge.

This has not always been the case. While prize money is naturally useful to the winner, especially when supplemented as it sometimes is by the Arts Council, and otherwise a source of gratification, its effect on sales has usually in the past been negligible. This is no longer true, at any rate in the case of rich prizes, such as the Booker, Whitbread, and W. H. Smith, which carry plenty of publicity and reflect success not only in ordinary volume sales, but in subsidiary rights and fresh engagements and commissions as well. Whether this development will spread to many other prizes and invigorate prize-winning as such remains to be seen. But there is this to be said. However strict the rules and however conscientious the judges, the process of selection is intrinsically a lottery, and cannot benefit more than a tiny proportion of those engaged in serious literature, whatever the *genre*.

The greatest need for patronage lies not in honours and prizes, but in generous financial aid to writers engaged in or preparing worthwhile work, and in sponsoring the production of such work if it is not commercially viable: in short a grant or bursary of possibly an academic appointment in order to 'buy time' for the writer to do the job without having to earn a living by other means while so engaged; and, where necessary, a subsidy to the publisher as well. This applies particularly to books of less than 100,000 words in length and expected to sell less than 5,000 copies: in other words large numbers of well-written novels and general non-fiction which, in the present economic climate, do not secure sufficient sales or which publishers dare not publish at all.

Aiding a writer in this way does not replace the need for a fair contract, but it does find money additional to the advance where this is insufficient for the writer's support, even if it represents the total royalty income on the initial print-run. Subsidising the publisher so that, for example, he can price a book at £5 instead of

£10 means that he, and others like him, can continue to issue books of quality but which, owing to limited sales *have* to be priced high—the price itself contributing to that limitation. As it is publishers, following an American trend, are concentrating more and more of their resources upon potential bestsellers—some deserving of popularity, others manufactured according to a formula (e.g. violence, soft porn, etc.) and often team-written—at the expense of the kind of books referred to, which until recently composed the corpus of publishers' lists. Not only are fewer of these books appearing, but those already in print are vanishing from back lists before their time, owing to the high cost of warehousing and because 'old' stock no longer sells fast enough to justify its retention as an asset. As is well known, remainder bookshops have become a growth industry.

If these publishing trends continue, as they will if left solely to the vagaries of the free market, then they will deplete and may ultimately extinguish the rich sources of native talent which, over the centuries, have given our literature and language its prime place in the world.

Who are the patrons of literature?

Clearly the principal patron since the Second World War has been the Arts Council of Great Britain, founded in 1946. Its predecessor, the Council for the Encouragement of Music and Art (CEMA) had been set up by the Pilgrim Trust in 1939 to sustain the cultural life of the country during war-time, primarily in music, drama and art; and, nurtured by a handful of visionary administrators, it had been immensely successful. Happily John Maynard Keynes was adviser to the Chancellor of the Exchequer when acting as Chairman of CEMA 1942–5 and was Chairman-elect of the Arts Council, though unhappily he died at Easter 1946 before he could assume office. By then however he had ensured that

> The Arts Council was placed directly under the Treasury, which permitted it to administer its funds with greater freedom and flexibility than if it had been made a government department.

In 1964 the Council became the Parliamentary responsibility of the Department of Education and Science,[7] but without apparent detriment to its independence, and at about the time when the appointment of Jennie Lee as Minister for the Arts and of Lord Goodman as Chairman of the Council ensured, together with the publication of the Government White Paper, *A Policy for the Arts* (February 1965), a great increase in support for the arts, especially for the living artist. Oddly the Council's objectives, as defined in the original charter, had seemed—by their insistence on 'fine arts'—to exclude literature. However a poetry panel was instituted in 1950 which thereafter promoted the *genre* by various means: e.g. grants to poetry societies and festivals, subsidising poetry magazines and, in 1954, forming the Poetry Book Society that has since operated as a book club distributing selected volumes of new poetry to subscribers. The panel also formed a poetry library and, in co-operation with the British Library, has created a national collection of manuscripts and associated material by contemporary poets. This is a fine record, remarkable for the fact in the early years it was financed on a shoestring. Only £9,443 was spent in 1965–6, some sixteen years after the panel was founded.

In 1964 the first move was made to add prose to poetry and, after a brief brush between A. P. Herbert and Reginald Maudling, then Chancellor of the Exchequer, as to whether or not literature was a 'fine art', the poetry panel was replaced by, and its functions incorporated in, the literature panel, with effect from January 1966. The first Chairman was Cecil Day-Lewis, who had been the last Chairman of the poetry panel, and had long played a leading part in promoting poetry and poets.

I do not propose to dwell on the details of the work of the literature panel since 1966, for these can be studied in the annual reports of the Arts Council and elsewhere. In principle it pursued a course similar to that of the poetry panel, though of course on a much larger scale, by subventing organisations such as the National Book League, Poetry Society and PEN, subsidising literary magazines and other publications of cultural value, supplementing literary prizes (e.g. the Hawthornden), grant-aiding festivals, financing writers' tours, visits to schools and academic appointments, supporting residential courses in creative writing of the type offered by the Arvon Foundation, funding for seven years (1974–81) the New Fiction Society, and much else designed to enlarge opportunities and create new openings for writers. Instead, I propose to refer to two of the panel's activities that stand out as essential acts of aid, and of which I have first-hand knowledge.[8]

One is the part played by the panel and the Arts Council itself in the campaign for Public Lending Right, which is described in Chapter Four. The other is the Writers' Grants scheme which evolved out of a handful of bursaries awarded to poets in 1964–5. In my view this scheme fulfilled in large measure the very purposes suggested as the prime function of patronage: namely to 'buy time' (however that might be interpreted in practice by the recipient) for the writer. In his history of the Arts Council Eric Walter White, who served as the Council's first literature director from 1966 to 1971, wrote:

> The competitive element was felt to be invidious: and by 1969/70 a simplified scheme was in operation, which seemed to avoid most of the defects of earlier schemes. Under the new dispensation, applications on behalf of professional writers who were actively engaged in writing and had published at least one book in the particular category of their work in progress were invited from publishers, literary editors, or other responsible members of the literary profession.[9]

White added that this method gave the 'examining committee' a chance to get an outside view of the writer's needs, and that the grant (if approved) would rank as an *ex gratia* award, not subject to income tax—an assertion that was contested by the Inland Revenue in 1978. But the essential point was the first one. However imperfect the methods of the 'examining committee' proved to be, the scheme—by comparison with prize judging—reduced the element of lottery to a minimum. Far more writers who deserved aid and got it at the essential early stages of their tasks benefited under this scheme than was ever possible in a prize competition.

The Writers' Grants scheme ran for seventeen years, from 1964 to 1981, at an average output of 40 grants a year. At one time it absorbed approximately half the literature budget. On this and other grounds it had always attracted controversy: for example, that its criteria were too narrow, excluding as they did numbers of non-fiction titles because they were not 'creative', or because as works of scholarship their authors should look to academic foundations for support; that some writers benefited too often from the scheme or that they possessed sufficient means to do without assistance; that there were not enough writers of quality to justify grant aid on this scale—a view pursued by the polemicists of *The Times Literary Supplement*.

However when the scheme was abandoned in 1981, there was a howl of protest. It was widely assumed that the decision had been dictated by a report commissioned by the Arts Council, *Writers and the Arts Council*, by Jim McGuigan, completed in 1979 but not published until 1981. This was an intelligent and interesting report providing much information about and constructive criticism of the scheme. For example it found that, up to 1978, most of the beneficiaries had been well-educated people of professional and middle-class backgrounds, living in the south of England, and thus did not represent a fair cross-section of the writing population. On the other hand an impressive body of work had been produced, though much of it might have been written without grant-aid. But McGuigan's main complaint was levelled at the structure of selection—the fact that grants were decided by a small executive committee independent of the literature panel itself. This meant that the ultimate decision was left to the subjective judgement of a handful of people, conscientious and well briefed no doubt, but as human beings possessed of private prejudices and tastes, and therefore fallible.

How could it be otherwise?

While human fallibility can never be eliminated, organisation can always be improved, and that was what McGuigan recommended in his report. He did not advise abolition. Instead he discussed changes in methods of application and sponsorship, the definition of 'buying time', the need to be explicit about refusals, emphasis on help to the young writer, reporting back on the use of grants, and the eternal difficulty of striking a balance between literary merit and financial need.

In the event the report was used as an excuse to end the Writers' Grants scheme altogether, summed up by Charles Osborne, the literature director, when he said: 'It is not part of our job to shield authors against the harsh realities of life.'

That remark misconceived with a half-truth the essence of artistic patronage: not to featherbed artists so that they become a burden upon society but, by enabling some to survive, to help sustain and enrich a culture that, in the case of literature, has been a national glory since the days of Chaucer.

Moreover patronage is cost effective and will stand up to the closest scrutiny in terms of pounds and pence, should that be regarded as the ultimate criterion. In 1980–1 the Writers' Grants scheme cost £74,150 or less than 11 per cent of the literature department's annual expenditure of £680,421, itself barely 1.2 per cent of £54,699,613 which was the total cost of the Arts Council to the nation in that financial year. And that figure—to draw a comparison nearer my home—was the equivalent of only 71 per cent of Somerset County Council's bill for education in 1980–1. And Somerset is one of the least generous of local authorities.

Patronage must be for merit, but the discovery of merit can never be an exact exercise. Assessors have to spread their net wide, be prepared to make mistakes, and help many more authors than ultimately their works seem to justify. What does it signify if, out of a hundred authors helped, only five make good? The answer is that only by helping a hundred can you expect to find five, who may include a future Keats or a Conrad or a Joyce.

The literature department replaced the Writers' Grants scheme with the award 'only in exceptional circumstances to a few writers of proven achievement (up to five bursaries of not more than £7,500) for work on a specific project': in other words, 'to him that hath . . .', thus a return to competition, an experiment already tested and rejected after two years with the National Book Awards 1980–1. Any prospect of assisting young and 'unproven' writers, for whom patronage is a lifeline, was extinguished. It could certainly not be made good, as regards scale and the immediate needs of writers, by the aim 'to increase the audience for literature', i.e. by 'devoting increased funds to the distribution of books' via community (non-profit-distributing) bookshops, sales points in libraries, and so forth—admirable as these ideas might be in their own right; nor by double talk about the aims of

Creative Writing Fellowships . . . no longer to be regarded primarily as a means of support for writers; the priority will be to use them to stimulate the students' interest in and appreciation of literature.[10]

It might be argued that the loss of support by the Arts Council in London would, in time, be made good in other parts of the country. The records of the Scottish and Welsh Arts Councils, each with a defined territory and each coping with more than one language, read well. In 1981–2 the Scots spent over 5 per cent of the total arts outlay on literature, the Welsh 8 per cent, compared with 1.2 per cent by the Arts Council of Great Britain. The regional arts associations, partially financed by the Arts Council but all chronically short of cash, have necessarily accomplished less, despite notable exceptions. But all arts associations suffer from a lack of cultural identity by comparison with Scotland and Wales; and that in turn is a reflection of the centralisation of our national life, which is mainly dictated by geography and economics. London remains the power house of the arts; regional culture in England is still a mirage.

There remains one other potentially fruitful source of patronage—industry. Whereas industrial sponsorship of sport, and of performance in the arts, notably music and drama, has grown greatly in the past decade, literature has hardly benefited at all. This is surprising, for performance is essentially ephemeral. While a sponsor's name in an opera programme lasts one evening or perhaps a week, its imprint beside the author and publisher on the title page of a book stays as long as the book is read, or for that matter as long as the paper and ink survive.

What are the prospects of writing for print, seventy years after the passing of the Copyright Act, 1911?

Clearly making a living, however modest, by writing books, backed by freelance journalism of whatever sort, remains the preserve of the few. Ten per cent of *bona fide* writers who fall into this bracket—and that includes the handful of immensely successful—is the maximum figure revealed by the most recent surveys, the real one is almost certainly less. Secondly it can no longer be assumed that literature will continue to be fuelled by all those part-time writers who have the talent and persistence to go on turning out books and articles and broadcasts, while relying on other kinds of jobs for their bread and butter. Commerce unaided will inevitably pinch that source into extinction; neither will Public Lending Right, tax reliefs, or other necessary and rightful measures make good the deficit in the foreseeable future. If literature is to survive as it has done for the last six hundred years,

PART TWO

WRITING FOR PERFORMANCE

when Bernard Shaw began to treat social problems as theatrical entertainment; when J. T. Grein of the Independent Theatre pioneered the production of plays with 'a literary and artistic rather than a commercial value', notably those of Ibsen; when William Archer and Bernard Shaw set new standards in dramatic criticism; and when actor-managers such as Irving and Bancroft were giving acting a new professional respectability, crowned by Irving's knighthood in 1895 (the first actor to receive such an honour) and Bancroft's in 1897.

These pioneering efforts gathered momentum in the decade before 1914 with, for example, the work of Harley Granville Barker (in collaboration with the manager John E. Vedrenne) 1904–7 at the Royal Court in London, where some of Shaw's and other outstanding plays were presented for the first time; with the enterprise of the American impresario, Charles Frohman, at the Duke of York's, where the production of John Galsworthy's *Strife* in 1909 and *Justice* in 1910 roused the theatre-going public to an emotional awareness of social injustice; with the launching of serious repertory by Annie Horniman and Ben Iden Payne at Manchester, Alfred Wareing at Glasgow, Basil Dean at Liverpool, and Barry Jackson at Birmingham; and with the growth of the Stage Society[1] and other theatre clubs that put on experimental pieces in special matinées and on Sunday evenings.

Among men of the theatre, however, Shaw perhaps did most to raise the standards of drama, thanks to the character and scope of his own plays and to his critiques of other contemporary work whether by British or foreign authors. Nor was this all; for out of the renaissance of the theatre and out of efforts by Shaw and other playwrights came fresh impetus to organise collective action through the Society of Authors to improve terms and conditions for playwriting. The campaign did not start from zero. Gone were the days when a playwright commonly sold his work for £100 outright, or was tied to a theatre for a pittance. While Charles Reade had fought hard for dramatic rights, waging war in particular against piracy and plagiarism, it was Dion Boucicault who, in the 1860s, traded upon his popularity as an actor to insist upon receiving, as an author, royalties on box office receipts. And when in 1874 Bancroft raised the price of seats (stalls at 10s each) at the Prince of Wales's Theatre (later the Scala) in order to pay for improved comforts and attract a moneyed and middle-class audience of both sexes, he was able financially to benefit actors and authors alike. Even so, although by the early 1900s 'a successful dramatist could make more from one play than any of his predecessors had earned in a lifetime', it was still the manager who called the tune, and that is still true of the commercial stage.[2]

As Richard Findlater relates in his book, *The Unholy Trade*, it was possible in the 1880s to rent a West End theatre of moderate capacity for £50 a week. There was no Entertainments Duty or surtax, while income tax stood at 8d in the £. Overheads and production costs were relatively low, and publicity quite a minor item. The period of prosperity for this kind of régime lasted at least until the First World War, and although costs inevitably rose, it was still possible for Vedrenne and Granville Barker to regard takings of £600 a week at the Royal Court as a 'guarantee of success'. Theatre business was exceptionally profitable in those halcyon days of free enterprise, and several actor managers (e.g. Bancroft and Wyndham) died worth a fortune.

So far as the authors were concerned, it is possible to make a critical distinction—then as now—between playwrights and dramatists. The former might be defined as skilled pragmatists, like Alfred Sutro, who, by pleasing the public, found ready outlets in the commercial theatre. The latter, as innovators, had a far harder task, having often to rely on the 'other theatre'[3] (experimental ventures, theatre clubs, even amateurs) to gain a hearing. Shaw was remarkable in that he started in the latter category and moved by sheer genius and persistence into the former one, and he used his experiences to fight for his fellows. However the distinction cannot rigorously be sustained in the present attempt at an economic assessment of playwriting. Obviously not all 'commercial' plays have been devoid of art or experiment, nor 'other' plays of commercial intentions.

In 1897 the Society of Authors had formed a small drama sub-committee under the chairmanship of Henry Arthur Jones, to whom Shaw wrote on 12 October of that year:

> . . . it seems to me that we ought to try to work up some sort of an organisation with a view to getting a *minimum* price established for plays, and putting a stop to the ridiculous jobbing of 'rights' that goes on at present through the silliness and ignorance of the authors . . . The difficulty is, of course, to

find time for Trade Union work; but one feels that it ought to be done. It is all very well for you or me to pit our individual strength against Irving or Wyndham and the rest; but the small fry are bound to crumple up without an organisation behind them.[4]

The sub-committee lay low until 1899 when it was stiffened by the addition of Sydney Grundy and Arthur Wing Pinero, at a time when a number of other well-known playwrights were being recruited into the Society, among them R. C. Carton, Haddon Chambers, W. S. Gilbert, W. Somerset Maugham, Clement Scott, Louis N. Parker, and H. V. Esmond. These men were soon followed by a fresh intake which included Alfred Sutro, J. M. Barrie, John Galsworthy, John Masefield, and Harley Granville Barker. Within a few years, most leading playwrights had joined the Society, and the total of members who had written plays, or who regarded themselves as connected with the theatre, was stated to be in excess of 300.

Shaw served on the sub-committee from 1906 to 1915, attended practically every meeting and galvanised its activities by his own inimitable character and force of personality, despite displays of envy and apathy among some of his colleagues. He conducted, for example, the campaign against stage censorship in 1909. Although it did not achieve its aim, it was a personal *tour de force* and helped liberalise the attitude of the Lord Chamberlain. He ensured that dramatic rights were properly protected by the Copyright Act, 1911, so that the law vested in the author the sole right to dramatise his novel or to novelise his play, abolishing the need for 'copyright performance'.[5] But Shaw's most arduous campaign was to try to secure a minimum terms agreement (then known as the 'managerial treaty') with the Society of West End Managers. The negotiations lasted until 1915 when the managers rejected three conditions upon which the authors insisted:

1. The author's right to a voice in the selection of the cast.

2. The author's right to coach individual members of the cast.

3. The author's right to cancel the contract in case of bankruptcy of the manager.

At a meeting held in November 1915, it was decided to break off negotiations. It was felt by then that the Society was strong enough to deal effectively with individual managers, treaty or no treaty. Shaw retired at this point, not so much because he felt he had done his stint, but to avoid dissension within the Society owing to the unpopularity of his opinions about the war.

By this time theatre business was contending with fresh problems. One was the ironical fact that, despite Zeppelin raids and the imposition in 1916 of Entertainments Duty (a 'temporary' war-time measure), West End theatres were experiencing a boom that threatened to destroy serious drama in London. Men and women back from France were demanding entertainment at any price, with the result that speculators moved in to buy or lease theatres and put on productions regardless of quality, but which made a lot of money. Some shows had such long runs that they took certain theatres out of circulation for years at a time. At His Majesty's, for example, *Chu Chin Chow* ran for five years and earned Oscar Asche, who wrote the dialogue and the lyrics, and produced and acted in it as well, over £200,000 in royalties. At the Criterion *A Little Bit of Fluff* lasted for three years.[6]

Success of this kind was harmful. Not only did it reduce the number of theatres available, but it aggravated risks by inflating the amount of investment required to finance a play. As Findlater explains—a characteristic of the process, which continued in the West End between the wars, was the influx of middlemen between the landlord and the manager whose job it was to mount a production.

> Mr X. buys a lease at £50 a week, and sub-lets it to Mr B. at £70 a week; Mr B. sub-lets it at £100 a week; and so the process went on. It is in this way that the level of London theatre rents was forced up without any relation to the level of prices or costs, for these were irrelevant to the 'bricks and mortar' magnates.[7]

A new trend emerged in London in the late 1930s: namely the increasing involvement of the landlord/lessee in play production business, to the extent that the two sides became more closely committed to each other—the former investing in management, and sometimes the manager buying an interest in the theatre. Either

way a vertical structure evolved and resulted '. . . in a concentration of capital, the close association of production and distribution, and the consolidation of monopolist power'.[8]

With the disappearance in the 1920s of most of the
old-established theatre managements, whose methods of business
were relatively straightforward, the Society found that a
disproportionate amount of time had to be devoted to its
dramatist members—collecting royalties, coping with bankrupt
enterprises, and litigating over infringement of copyright and
contingent matters. Nor was this all, for similar obligations were
being generated by the new medium of the cinema, which had
greatly benefited from the war and was making serious inroads
into theatre business. Film making was already a near-monopoly
of American companies, which were inclined to make free use of
plays and plots and were difficult to bring to court. In its turn the
competition excited theatre managers, who not only insisted on a
share of film rights as a *sine quà non* of play contracts, but an
excessive share at that.

Such was the background to opinion among the Society's
dramatists after the First World War that a more formal and
effective body than their existing group should be set up, either on
the lines of the French Société des Auteurs et Compositeurs
(SACD), which had long secured a tight hold over theatre
managements all over France and acted virtually as an agent for
its members; or as a trade union on the model of the Actors'
Association (forerunner of British Actors' Equity).[9] The French
proposition had been investigated in 1907 by Shaw and Henry
Arthur Jones who, in their report, had declared it inapplicable to
the United Kingdom. For one thing it was far too late—the French
Société had been founded in 1829 and had long consolidated its
position. For another, any similar move in this country was likely
to be successfully opposed by the managers and might even induce
anti-monopoly legislation. Nonetheless Shaw and Jones recommended what amounted to 'free collective bargaining', which
duly led up to the campaign for the managerial treaty; but this had
petered out as explained and because, in the last resort, the
dramatists—by no means united—had been unable to apply
sanctions as a body. Even so, thanks to persistent pressure upon
individual managements, the issuing of leaflets and other
publications setting out terms for a variety of agreements (*West

End, Repertory, Collaboration, Agents, etc.), and ultimately to the foundation of the League of British Dramatists in 1931 (which acted both as an agency and a pressure group in its own right), the Society went far towards establishing a new and powerful dramatists' lobby.

Meanwhile the process of creating such a lobby developed slowly. As early as 1919, due to the energy of R. C. Carton, Harold Brighouse, Justin Huntly McCarthy, Ernest Denny and others, ideas were advanced for the formation of a 'Playwrights' Union'. A constitution was hammered out by Herbert Thring, Secretary of the Society; but when it came to signing the 'bond of covenant' which required members to accede to, and stand by, the basic conditions, the response was lamentable. Even Shaw was unable to convince his colleagues of the need for practical unity, and appeared to share their hesitation over solidarity. At a meeting on 28 October 1921 he said that the young author should resist the temptation to get a first play produced on whatever terms he could obtain, and would be in a better position to say 'No' if he could state that he was abiding by 'standard terms'. But Shaw did not press for the definition and acceptance of such terms beyond adopting the purely negative stance of rejecting the worst sorts of exploitation, e.g. the sale of copyright, profit sharing (a familiar mirage), or an abysmally low rate of royalties with the manager reserving a substantial cut of the 'extra' rights.

The fact was that in the 1920s most authors with plays in the West End—the undisputed centre of commercial theatre production—were getting the terms they wanted (a royalty of 5 per cent—10 per cent on the box office returns preceded by a substantial option) without the aid of a union, that is by individual negotiation with or without the Society's help or through an agent. *The Author* regularly published lists of London productions by dramatist members as, for example, in October 1928:

ADELPHI. *Clowns in Clover* by Ronald Jeans.
ALDWYCH. *Plunder* by Ben Travers.
APOLLO. *The Squeaker* by Edgar Wallace.
DALY'S. *Blue Eyes* by Jerome Kern, Guy Bolton and Graham John.

HAYMARKET. *Alibi* by Michael Morton (from the story by Agatha Christie).
LITTLE. *The New Sin* by Basil Macdonald Hastings.
LONDON PAVILION. *This Year of Grace* by Noël Coward.
LYCEUM. *The Flying Squad* by Edgar Wallace.
NEW. *A Damsel in Distress* by Ian Hay and P. G. Wodehouse.
QUEEN'S. *The Trial of Mary Dugan* by Bayard Veiller.
ROYAL COURT. *Yellow Sands* by Eden and Adelaide Phillpotts.
ROYALTY. *Bird in Hand* by John Drinkwater.
ST. JAMES'S. *The Return Journey* by Arnold Bennett.
WINTER GARDEN. *So This is Love* by Stanley Lupino.
WYNDHAM'S. *Loyalties* by John Galsworthy.

The list is remarkable for its light weight and for the fact that it omits two plays that made 1928 a memorable year for the theatre: *Young Woodley* by John Van Druten and *Journey's End* by R. C. Sherriff; nor of course does it include performances in other months of works by established dramatists such as Shaw, Barrie, St. John Ervine, Somerset Maugham, Frederick Lonsdale, A. A. Milne, and Sean O'Casey and his predecessors in the Irish school.

In sum the West End, where survival depended on making good money, was not the likeliest place for enforcing collective agreements or for reforming the theatre for whatever purpose. Indeed making money was and is today only exceptionally an effective armament for fighting moral battles. It meant, for example, that innovators and others writing plays of minority interest were kept out of the inner ring of stages patronised by the London public. And so, of necessity, the author's case owed much to the growth of the 'other' theatre—fringe in character and location—both professional and amateur—that attracted support by its contribution to drama as a dynamic art, by presenting experimental and/or banned plays or—no less speculatively—by staging try-outs with an off-chance of commercial transfer.

In a number of cases experiment was synonymous with banning because the themes automatically aroused controversy, e.g. sex, religion or politics. Despite the 1909 assault on the censor, the Lord Chamberlain was fighting a rearguard action between the wars and exercised his powers over a number of plays that have long passed into the repertoire. *Young Woodley* for example was held up for over a year because it dealt with the calf love of a schoolboy for the wife of his housemaster. Marie

Stopes's *Vectia* was vetoed for its concern with male impotence. Laurence Housman ran into trouble over the 'adultery' of Queen Caroline. Marc Connelly's *Green Pastures* was banned because Jehovah was represented on the stage and as a negro at that; while in the period of political appeasement several plays had to be amended or dropped altogether owing to irreverent remarks about Hitler and Mussolini. On the other hand nudity on the stage was permitted provided the naked female did not *move*, but serious treatment of sexual deviation had to wait until after the Second World War,[10] and stage censorship was not abolished until 1968.

In these circumstances the part played by a handful of 'other' theatres in London and elsewhere was of paramount importance. Examples include two theatres in Hampstead—the Everyman where, between 1920 and 1926 Norman MacDermott introduced some of the works of O'Neill, Pirandello and other foreign dramatists, besides staging first performances of Sutton Vane's *Outward Bound* and Noël Coward's *The Vortex* which went on to become West End successes; also the Embassy which launched a number of successful try-outs between its opening in 1928 and final closure after the war. The Gate was a club theatre that opened under Peter Godfrey in 1925 in Covent Garden and moved to Villiers Street, Charing Cross, two years later. Under Norman Marshall it gained a considerable reputation in the 1930s for good theatre in various *genres*, including a series of witty revues. The Lyric, a Victorian theatre in Hammersmith, was given a new lease of life when Nigel Playfair took charge in 1918. Over the next fifteen years he made it as popular as any theatre in central London with new plays, such as Drinkwater's *Abraham Lincoln*, with a notable revival of *The Beggars' Opera* and several Restoration pieces, and with *Riverside Nights* and other revues by A. P. Herbert and Thomas Dunhill. The Mercury, Notting Hill Gate, was opened in 1933 by Ashley Dukes and his wife, Marie Rambert, the ballerina. Dukes adapted and presented a number of European plays and—ballet apart—gained the Mercury a high reputation for verse drama: outstandingly for T. S. Eliot's *Murder in the Cathedral*, which received its first London performance there. Perhaps the most important of the club theatres was the Arts, opened in 1927 near Leicester Square, where *Young Woodley* was first played, and succeeded soon after by Reginald

Berkeley's *The Lady with the Lamp*, Gordon Daviot's *Richard of Bordeaux*, and other arresting plays that have since secured a strong hold in repertory. After 1942 the Arts enjoyed a decade of great prestige under Alec Clunes who, in 1948, put on and acted in Christopher Fry's *The Lady's Not For Burning*. Outside London an 'other' play might be given its chance at a drama festival, or at one of the bolder repertory houses, e.g. by J. B. Fagan at the Playhouse, Oxford,[11] or by Terence Gray at the Festival Theatre, Cambridge.[12]

Another alternative resided in the growth of the amateur theatre, which at its best was rapidly divesting itself of the taint of 'theatricals' and raising standards of performance among hundreds of play-producing societies all over the country. The movement received powerful impetus from the formation of the British Drama League in 1919 and from the vision and energy of its first director, Geoffrey Whitworth. Although the League aimed to arouse interest in *all* aspects of theatrical life and work, its initial concern was for the amateurs who benefited immeasurably by a centre in London, equipped with a library and play-lending service, publishing a journal, supplying information and advice, and representing the interests of its members at all levels.[13] One of the best amateur theatres was the Maddermarket, Norwich, which Nugent Monck converted into an Elizabethan playhouse seating 220 in 1921. Thereafter he was responsible for a programme that compared favourably with that of any professional enterprise: classical Greek and Japanese Noh plays, Shakespeare, Molière, Alfieri, G. E. Lessing, Ibsen, Chekhov, and works by contemporary British and European dramatists.[14]

No working playwright, however, could rely on the 'other' theatre for a livelihood. Often he was expected, virtually if not actually, to make a present of his creation in exchange for a first performance. Before the age of subsidies, the overriding problem for the experimental theatre was of course that of survival, but economics degenerated into exploitation when art was offered as a substitute for cash. It was on these grounds that St. John Ervine criticised the contract offered him by the 'Q' Theatre, Kew Bridge, managed by Jack and Beatrice de Leon.

The managers demand from the author the sum of £150 as 'a contribution towards the expense of production and running of' his play . . . My wonder is increased when I read Clause 7 in which the managers stipulate that the author shall supply them 'with four copies of the play, and one copy of each part' . . . why should they not make the author pay for sweeping the stage after each performance? The wages of the programme girls and the money paid to the bill-stickers might also be charged to the author.

The author's share of the weekly box office receipts were: nil up to £200; 25 per cent between £200 and £300; 33⅓ per cent £300 to £400; 50 per cent over £400. Ervine calculated that if the total receipts for a week's performance amounted to £400, the managers took £341 13s. 4d, and the author £58 6s. 8d—'pretty good for the managers'. After taking into account options on outside productions of the play in the UK and abroad, plus a 50 per cent share of the film rights, Ervine concluded: 'I can only imagine that the managers of the "Q" Theatre consider that money is very bad for authors.'[15]

As to the author's income from amateur productions, this was the subject of a lengthy discussion in the 1920s between the Society of Authors and the British Drama League, the latter arguing for a royalty rather than a standard fee.

. . . It is neither reasonable nor fair that a small dramatic group in a village of 500 inhabitants should be asked to pay the same fee for the performance of a play as is asked from the dramatic society attached to a large bank or insurance office in the centre of London.[16]

The proposal was steadily opposed by the majority of playwrights on the grounds that, however apparent the equity of the principle, they nearly always lost money by it. Nor did they alter their view when the League suggested a sliding scale. Inevitably Shaw joined in the discussion.

The fees I charge to amateurs are the old fees of the 19th century: five guineas for a performance of a full-length play, and two or three guineas for shorter ones. And my fees to professionals are what they were when I began thirty-four years ago: that is, a sliding scale of percentages, ranging from 5 to 15 per cent of the gross receipts according to their magnitude, and applying alike to a first-class metropolitan production and to a performance on a village green. Cheques for £300 and stamps to the value of eighteen pence arrive on the same morning and are acknowledged with equal courtesy.

The difference, he continued, between his practice and that of some others arose from the method of defining 'amateur' and 'professional'.

When a party of ladies and gentlemen get up a play to amuse themselves, and, to excuse that sin, promise to give the profits to charity . . . then they are amateurs. They pay five guineas; take their licence; and are never heard of by the author again. But any person or persons striving to establish a permanent theatrical organisation and to make a profession of acting, or managing, keeping all the profits in the concern except what they need for their bread and butter, are entitled to business terms whether they are novices or veterans, whether they act well or ill, whether they are paid or have to contribute to the expenses out of their own pockets, whether they play in the village school or in the Metropolitan Opera House. If anyone can propose any better basis of classification, let him speak or be for ever silent.[17]

Ian Hay refused to accept Shaw's ostensible common sense.

How does he [Shaw] prevent a goat from coming to him and posing as a sheep? In other words, how does he deal with a society of well-to-do fun-seekers who are posing as poor but deserving servants of art in the hope of evading a five-guinea fee? Some amateurs do these things . . . Amateur finance is a mysterious and unfathomable thing. To render a return of gross takings is comparatively simple, but there are frequently certain indirect assets, in the form of club subscriptions and private donations, which ought rightly to be included, but seldom are . . . Many dramatists are already bound by contract to such firms as Samuel French, on terms which make it impossible for them to reduce their fee below a flat five guineas

... His [Shaw's] scheme seems to involve almost insuperable complications of accountancy.[18]

And so amateur fees remained in force.

This excursion into the 'other' theatre, professional and amateur, is not meant to imply that interesting and sometimes adventurous work was not staged in the West End between the wars. As at most other times, the period was characterised by its variety—by the fading of old hands such as Barrie; by the sustained activity of familiar practitioners such as Shaw, Maugham, Frederick Lonsdale, A. A. Milne, Ben Travers, St. John Ervine, *et al.*; by the transient success of occasional or one-off works by, say, Clemence Dane, Ronald Mackenzie, Walter Greenwood, Charles Morgan, Dodie Smith, and many more; and by the intrusion of new names and fashions. As J. C. Trewin, the drama critic, points out in his history, *The Theatre since 1900*,[19] not many plays from the 1930s stand out today. Among those that do and were written by authors whose output was substantial, continuing into the 1940s, we find the names of Noël Coward, Emlyn Williams, James Bridie and J. B. Priestley. Nowadays Coward's 'musicals' do not bear repetition, but his brittle comedies, such as *Private Lives*, and some of his one-act plays survive by their wit and truth to the superficiality of the age. Williams's work has all the poetry and exuberance of the Welsh temperament, combined with the expertise of the professional actor; but, taken, as a whole, his plays are not likely to be staged outside the occasional revival. Bridie (O. H. Mavor), a Glasgow doctor, was prolific and discursive, taking his themes from sources as disparate as medical history (*The Anatomist*) and the Apocrypha (*Tobias and the Angel*). In almost all his work he travelled in and out of fantasy with varying success, but there is no doubt that he was an original artist who broke out of a purely Scottish enclave into a world of far wider appeal. Like Bridie, Priestley was concerned with plays of ideas, but he was a profounder dramatist and a more important figure in the history of the theatre. Both prolific and versatile, he was able, at one end of the scale, to write a broad Yorkshire comedy (*When We Are Married*) and, at the other, to compose imaginative plays on the subject of time in its reactive aspects of memory and premonition (*I Have Been Here Before*) and (*Time and the Conways*). He was also remarkable for his ventures into management, and for forcefully arguing the author's case inside and outside the theatre.

This essay however is not intended as a critique of dramatic values, so much as an attempt to assess the rewards and conditions of playwriting. One of the most illuminating examples is that of Terence Rattigan, whose career as a highly successful dramatist from the 1930s to the 1960s is described (with helpful notes on his income) in *Terence Rattigan: the Man and his Work* by Michael Darlow and Gillian Hodson.[20] Rattigan's first play, *First Episode*, was a success of a kind. Written with a friend, it was put on at the 'Q' Theatre in 1933, with the help of £200 out of Rattigan's own pocket. It then ran for three months at the Comedy Theatre, but the young authors had failed to read the contract with sufficient care, for it reserved too high a minimum 'take' at the box office to allow them any royalties. Nonetheless the experience confirmed Rattigan in his determination to write plays and he stuck to his last for the next two years, despite every discouragement. During that time he earned £50 from Bronson Albery for an adaptation of *A Tale of Two Cities* and landed a job as a scriptwriter at £15 a week with Warner Brothers at Teddington, where he offered the head of the studio a play of his own for £200 outright. The offer was refused and his work disparaged—but then his chance came. The '£200 script' started a new life on straight terms as *French Without Tears* and was slipped as a stop-gap into Albery's production programme at the Criterion. The rest is theatrical history. The play was a fairy tale success and ran for over a thousand performances, from 1936 to 1939. Shades of Shaw's advice to a young playwright, quoted on p. 173!

By now Rattigan was beginning to earn money at the rate of £100 a week and spending much of it on high living and playing the Stock Exchange. But his luck held more or less despite a near-flop, *After the Dance*, the outbreak of war, and the failure of a farce against Fascism, staged far too late, in January 1940. What kept him going was working with Anthony Asquith on the film version of *French Without Tears*, and the fact that the play had earned him over £20,000 from film rights and stage productions in London, the provinces, Paris and New York, where he broke with Warner Brothers and managed to escape abduction to Hollywood as a tame scriptwriter. What sobered him up and dissipated what had become a writer's block was service as an air gunner in the RAF which he joined in 1940, flying in Sunderlands in Coastal Command. He liked the RAF and the RAF liked him, eventually seconding him when he needed to return to writing. In this way he got back into his stride with *Flare Path* which opened at the Apollo in August 1942 and ran for 670 performances, and with *While the Sun Shines* which ran for 1,154 performances at the Globe from December 1943, earning him over £21,000 from the London run, plus £30,000 from the sale of film rights, plus further income from provincial and foreign productions.

By the end of the war, at the age of 34, Rattigan was reported to be receiving over £600 a week from royalties, the highest earning playwright in Britain. He had reached these heights by his gift for comic invention, by his sure and sensitive grasp of human situations, and by his ability to react to the public mood of the moment—all conveyed in taut and naturalistic dialogue, though without the wit and glitter that characterised, say, Coward's plays.

I do not propose to proceed with a catalogue of Rattigan's career. Suffice it to say that his run of stage success continued with plays such as *The Winslow Boy* (1946), *The Browning Version* (1948), *The Deep Blue Sea* (1952), *Separate Tables* (1954), and *Ross* (1961); and that his work for stage and screen (some 30 film and TV scripts) meant that his writing income regularly exceeded £30,000 a year. His natural extravagance was restrained by the accountant whom he had the good sense to employ, so that his wealth enabled him to survive, without difficulty, the critical reaction against his work that followed the publication of the prefaces he wrote to the first two volumes of his *Collected Plays* in 1953.[21] In these he argued against the idea that the enormous popularity of his plays implied that they were critically second-rate. He wrote, he said, for 'Aunt Edna', who lived in a West Kensington hotel and who knew what she liked. Her likes and dislikes (Kafka, Picasso, William Walton) were a reliable guide to theatrical success and no playwright could afford to disregard them, although he himself aimed slightly above her level without losing touch with her ability to appreciate the best.

[181]

Intended partly if not wholly as banter, these remarks landed Rattigan in trouble with the critics, such as Kenneth Tynan, who heralded the new wave of playwriting associated notably with the English Stage Company at the Royal Court and specifically with the production in 1956 of John Osborne's *Look Back in Anger*. Of that and more—shortly. The 1950s were a watershed for the British theatre, and so Rattigan's place in the history of drama must await assessment.

So far as making a living from the theatre was concerned, Rattigan—like most other popular playwrights—was able to stand on his own feet. His experiences therefore did not bear on the collective efforts needed to secure fair terms and conditions for all playwrights—to which I now return.

The inability of British authors to form a 'Playwrights' Union' in 1921 compared unfavourably with the action taken in 1925–6 by their counterparts in the USA. There the Dramatists' Guild of the Authors' League of America, apprehensive of the way that theatre managers were forcing disadvantageous contracts upon authors, banded themselves together to make a stand. In January 1926 leading members of the Guild, under the guidance of Arthur Richman and George Middleton, set about drafting a set of terms and conditions which, when agreed, would bind every member of the Guild and compel the observance of the majority of managers. In a remarkably short time a Minimum Basic Agreement was drawn up and presented for negotiation to a representative committee of the opposing party. After hard bargaining both sides ratified the final text on 14 April 1926. As was made clear, this was a *basic* agreement which allowed anyone to obtain better terms if he could, but which—thanks to the 'dramatists' shop'—ensured that members would only do business with managers who agreed to deal with them on the *basis* of the terms set out in the document. Penalties were imposed on both sides for breach or 'unethical behaviour', and a small weekly levy placed on every member of the Guild with a play in production in order to pay for the composition and maintenance of the Agreement which, inevitably, had to be monitored. Success was immediate. By January 1927 at least 150 managers were observing the terms, while the Guild increased its membership from 185 to nearly 700, including a number of British authors such as Galsworthy, Maugham, Coward, Michael Arlen, Ian Hay, Ashley Dukes and Dion Titheradge.

The American Agreement was published in full as a supplement to the July 1926 issue of *The Author* and raised a good deal of controversy. It seemed to some that, while protecting themselves against exploitation (especially in regard to ancillary rights), the Americans were trying to corner foreign markets and impose unacceptable conditions upon foreign, notably British, playwrights. Herbert Thring asked the Guild:[22]

> 1. Is the British author, having contracted with a British manager for the production of his play, and having leased the British and Colonial rights, and having sold his kinema rights, and having dealt with the other rights mentioned in the Minimum Basic Agreement, with the exception of the United States and Canadian performance rights, still empowered to enter into an agreement with a United States manager under the terms of the Minimum Basic Agreement?

> 2. And is the manager empowered to enter into such a contract without contravening the Minimum Basic Agreement while keeping a good standing with the Dramatists' Guild? It would appear that an interest in the British rights of every play has been implicitly promised to the manager under the agreement, and this of course would conflict with the interests of original British authors.

On 12 April 1927 the Guild replied 'Yes' to both questions, and in *The Author* Ian Hay defended the Guild's position, reiterating that the terms were minimum not maximum, and only applied in their entirety to a play first produced in the USA. While the doubts were not dispelled in all the correspondence that followed, the lesson was clear: that it was open to British playwrights to 'go and do likewise' and effect a similar agreement with British theatre managers—in other words to revive the battle begun by Shaw and others before 1914. Such were the preliminaries to the formation of the League of British Dramatists in 1931.

The man who brought matters to a head on this occasion was Benn Levy, who chaired a general meeting at the Hotel Victoria in Northumberland Avenue, London, on 15 June 1931. The immediate reason for the meeting sprang from an earlier conversation at the Dramatists' Club, at which John Drinkwater and St. John Ervine had complained that they were paying 'hundreds of pounds' to the Dramatists' Guild (in addition to their annual subscription) by way of the weekly levy on plays of theirs running in New York. What were they getting in return? The Guild did not place their work, nor did it collect royalties for them, nor would it fight their legal battles (indeed it was forbidden by US law to do so). It only provided the Minimum Basic Agreement which stated terms far inferior to those they customarily secured through agents and, worse still, it permitted theatre managers a share in ancillary rights which, in their opinion, was entirely unjustified. Ervine also referred to the iniquitous Canadian Copyright Act, 1931, which, *inter alia*, deprived a dramatist of the right to object to mutilation of the script; which laid down limits to royalties; and which even permitted charitable bodies to perform copyright works free of charge. These and other developments made it essential to set up an organisation within the Society of Authors which, from a position of strength, would negotiate with managers, bargain with the Dramatists' Guild, and make reciprocal agreements with similar societies in Europe (where, in France, for instance, a minimum 10 per cent royalty was mandatory).

None of these things could be achieved by individual effort except occasionally by 'heavyweights' such as Shaw, who happened to be present on 15 June and spoke with his usual force. He too poured scorn on the American Agreement and backed the proposal to set up a new organisation. But he reminded his hearers how he himself had worked hard on the Society's dramatists' sub-committee for ten years for the same or similar objects. Although they had made a good deal of progress, what had defeated them in the end was not the recalcitrance of the managers but

... the burden of hatred I had to endure from fellow-members. They thought that I was an interfering, pushing fellow with a commercial mind, and what business had I to interfere in their affairs, and all the rest of it.

He added:

For years we [The Society of Authors] have been collecting royalties and things of that kind for English authors for 5 per cent, but the English author says: 'No, I am not going to do that, I will go to an agent and pay him 20 per cent.' If you ask them why they do it, they say: 'I have been for a long time paying this sort of thing, and so-and-so is a very nice fellow and I do not care to change.' You know the kind of thing—absolute weak-mindedness—this curious feeling that you always find in England that you must not do anything unamiable. The result is that you fall a helpless prey to a large number of business gentlemen who put business first and amiability afterwards, and who naturally say: 'Here is a flock of sheep, let us shear them.'

   You have to form a very powerful trade union . . . unless you combine and unless you are prepared to pay our Society of Authors as handsomely as you seem to be prepared to pay the American Society, we shall not make real progress . . . but you must have a real sense of what can be done by combination . . . I just recall Sydney Grundy telling me: 'You are wasting your time, my boy. I have been all my life at it trying to get British authors to combine, and they never will; it is no use; you may just as well save yourself all the trouble you are proposing to take . . .' I am now prepared on the whole to say to the young author of today exactly what Sydney Grundy said to me long ago. But I suggest it is up to you to falsify my prediction.[23]

In all that followed—with speeches by Harley Granville Barker, Lionel Britton, Ashley Dukes, J. B. Fagan, Mrs Belloc Lowndes, C. K. Munro, Conal O'Riordan, and Benn Levy himself— discussion revolved round the central problem of 'combination'. Was it possible to launch and maintain an organisation, a trade union without 100 per cent membership and—what was more important—100 per cent loyalty to the union's actions and decisions? If 'no', then what advantage had the new body over the existing dramatists' section of the Society of Authors which in fact had done a great deal for members by vetting contracts, supplying information and advice, issuing warnings about bad business practices and bad managements, fighting legal battles and collecting royalties? Benn Levy, who took a stand against any kind of standard or basic agreement, felt that expanding the agency work and making reciprocal arrangements with the American and European societies would be the most effective method of conducting any new organisation, however small the beginnings. It would, for example, be of most use to young dramatists who were of small interest to agents, on which point Shaw had this to say:

I have had young men come to me and say, 'You get your 10 and 15 per cent, but how can I ask as much as you?' I always tell them, 'My young friend, you imagine you are in competition with me; you are not in competition with me for a moment. If you imagine there is any Manager in his senses who will produce a play by you, an unknown man, as long as he can get a play by Noël Coward, or Sir James Barrie, or possibly by me, you are very much mistaken; he never will. He will not produce your play until he finds that neither Coward nor Shaw nor Barrie, or the rest of them, have got a play for him.' He has to keep the thing going at all hazards and therefore if he can get plays from any of the established authors the beginner has no chance at all, but if he cannot get them from established authors the beginner has as good a chance as the big man, because the Manager has to keep his theatre going. I remember saying to the Manager of one of the biggest London theatres who wanted to produce a play of mine, 'This will not do for you. I know what your running expenses are and if you revive this play it will only draw £800 a week. Your expenses are £1,600 a week, so do not think of it.' He said, '. . . If I have to shut my theatre it will cost me more than £800 a week to do it . . . it is worth my while to produce your play at a loss of £800 a week because that would be less than my loss if I closed.' So that managers are in a much weaker position than you imagine. They are always in desperate need of plays, and in fact most of us know that all authors have got into the theatre first as stop gaps.[24]

A second meeting took place on 15 October with Sir James Barrie in the chair, but with Benn Levy again in charge. By this time detailed resolutions had been prepared, principally that a League be set up, under the auspices of the Society, and that it should offer to draft contracts and collect royalties at low rates of commission (2½/5 per cent), thereby attracting a strong and loyal membership. Further, as several authors argued, agents stood to gain by accepting indifferent terms in order to keep managers sweet, while the League would have no such axe to grind. However, if a member did retain an agent, then he should follow the American example and pay a weekly levy on any play currently in production (10s on a West End run, 4s for a provincial or colonial tour). The main doubt was that, if the League was to operate as a placing agent, then it would be flooded with scripts, many of them bad, and be forced to set up a large and expensive organisation that would be unable to offer the low rates of commission proposed. By arguing both ways, Shaw made it difficult for the meeting to reach a decision, but in the end all the resolutions were passed in principle, the details to be referred back 'for amplification'.

During the next twelve months a constitution was hammered out, and the League of British Dramatists ('British' was soon dropped) launched with wide-ranging powers. It was not and never became a closed shop but, through concentration of effort and a small increase in resources, it was able to offer more effectively all the services that had generally been available from the Society before, with the addition of registration of plays and scenarios, assistance in protecting members' interests in foreign countries, and a department for leasing amateur and repertory performances for which it prepared a catalogue of plays. All this for an annual subscription of £2.10s and a modest scale of commission charges starting at 4 per cent.

In the event the League became an important and influential body with an initial membership approaching 200, representing almost every facet of the living theatre, year by year.[25] Inevitably most of the practical work fell on the shoulders of the Secretary (successively Aubrey Blackburn, Harold Rubinstein, Elizabeth Barber, Julia Jones). It was they who dealt with the day-to-day business of advice, negotiation, and income collection; who kept in touch with agents and managements, served on representative committees, and drafted letters to the press. Such work rarely becomes apparent except to those intimately affected, but it constituted the main sub-surface business of the League, whose public face was occasionally revealed in other ways. For example, the League did much to restore cultural relations with former enemy countries (British plays had always been popular in Germany); to secure the spread-back of dramatists' earnings in the Finance Act, 1953; to achieve the abolition of Entertainments Duty in 1957 and of stage censorship in 1968. It harried the BBC for improved rates for the use of dramatic material. It was represented on the Theatres Advisory Council and on the drama panel of the Arts Council, and it gave strong support to the cause of the National Theatre.

The League also made public the needs of dramatists and the state of drama at open meetings, usually held in a theatre or in a hotel, attended—according to the occasion—by actors, agents, and managers, as well as by League members. It was at one of these discussions held at the Royal Court Theatre in 1959 that Ted Willis[26] said:

> The first fact is that for 95 per cent in this country, theatre does not exist. Serious playgoers are in a tiny minority . . . The second fact is that audiences are drawn mainly from the middle class . . . Managers must put on plays to make money. So they select plays which appeal to the theatre-going audience, mainly a middle class one . . . Now the music hall is dead. The working class no longer goes to it, but is drawn to the box in the living room . . . The next fact . . . is that we have got to do some really serious re-thinking about the position of the theatre in order to wipe away this snobbish approach . . . There is far too much snobbery about television. *Look Back in Anger* reached an audience in this theatre as a result of an appearance on television. My own play, *Hot Summer Night*, failed to find an audience in London last year . . . It went out on television. And I have never had such appreciation as I had from that production . . . I believe this snobbish contempt for television is holding back the theatre. Why don't our playwrights write for this medium?

Willis's remarks, pertinent enough in 1959, when television

was fast capturing the public at the expense of the cinema and the theatre, read oddly now. For one thing the snobbery has long vanished and most dramatists write for any medium they can. For another, the theatre had weathered this kind of situation before, having—after initial shocks—recovered to co-exist successfully with both films and radio. Television on the other hand appeared the more menacing, in that it combined both sight and sound, and was extremely cheap to the consumer on whom it imposed no inconvenience other than the small size of the screen. In short, as Willis said, it provided 'total' entertainment in the home. No expensive tickets, no cramped seats, no need to go outside the front door; alternatively nothing 'onerous' like having to use your imagination to supplement the hints and implications of a radio play.

However, as we now know, adjustments have indeed taken place, at any rate as between television and the theatre; indeed—thanks to subsidies—the living stage has regained some important territory, notwithstanding the advent of Channel Four and the prospect of a multitude of television programmes via cable and satellite.

During the 1950s and 1960s television's threat to the theatre had coincided with a new alignment of writers, already referred to in Part One and to be further discussed in the chapter on 'Writing for the Screen', namely the action by a number of film and TV scriptwriters to form a new organisation that had begun life in 1937 as the Screenwriters' Association within the Society of Authors; but which, by stages and after various changes of title, had broken away to become the Writers' Guild of Great Britain in 1965. Willis had played a leading part in the evolution of the new body and later became its President, though without personally leaving the League of Dramatists. At a public meeting on 4 June 1964 he had this to say:

> Every benefit that we have has been achieved by the League . . .
> If it had not been for the League, we should be paying about 60
> per cent of our film royalties away and giving away our
> repertory and amateur and international rights. When the
> managers began to ask for more than 40 per cent of the film
> rights, the League protected the dramatists and brought the
> figure down again.

He then added:

> Has the League a function any more? Is there a need for it, or
> has time overtaken us? Is it any longer possible to speak of a
> 'theatre dramatist' as such—is it true that a dramatist is one
> who writes for the screen as well as for the stage? How many
> people earn their living just by writing for the theatre?[27]

The question was not simply rhetorical. Its implications were
accepted by the Society of Authors itself when it formally
dissolved the League in 1975, and re-integrated responsibility for
drama into the services provided for all its members, including
those who wrote plays in whatever medium; and, as a 1977
survey showed, there was a large number of them. In short, stage
dramatists as such had, as Willis suggested, indeed become a
rarity; and it was perhaps significant that John Mortimer, the last
chairman of the League, had started his dramatic career by
writing scripts for the Crown Film Unit and then radio plays.[28] On
the other hand, a decade later, yet another organisation appeared,
the Theatre Writers' Union,[29] dedicated—as the name implied—
to the cause of stage writing, and initially to negotiating terms
with the subsidised theatre.

When the League of Dramatists was founded in 1931, the theatre
was losing ground to the cinema as the main medium of public
entertainment in the suburbs and provincial towns, while the
world slump was adding to the problems of survival. In spite of
this the attitude of *laissez-faire*—of doing without support from
central or local authority—prevailed in the theatre,[30] as generally
in the creative arts, at least until the Second World War. But the
war was the rubicon.

In the autumn of 1939 the official fear of blitz bombing and the
dislocation caused by evacuation put a temporary stop to all live
performance; and although the situation was eased by the 'phoney'
war over the winter of 1939–40 and by the ordinary processes of
human adjustment to emergency, it was clear to those who
thought ahead that—apart from the BBC's lifeline of communication—some public body would have to revive and help
sustain the means of entertainment, if the arts were not to starve

to death from neglect and the population die of boredom. While ENSA and ABCA[31] were formed to serve the troops, nothing similar existed for civilians—hence the origin of CEMA[32] in January 1940. Briefly stated, the objects of the latter were to preserve the highest standards in the arts, and to make it possible for people to enjoy them, partly by their own efforts, and partly by giving employment to professionals who would otherwise suffer seriously from lack of work. Hardly had CEMA got into its stride when Hitler assaulted and conquered most of Western Europe and followed this with the night bombing of London and other large towns during the winter of 1940. None of this fatally hindered the progress of CEMA which was being flooded by a tidal wave of demand for the arts all over the country. Aid to drama consisted in the main of subsidies or guarantees against loss to a handful of touring companies and festivals; but, most important of all, CEMA persuaded the Old Vic to take to the road, playing Shakespeare and other works in Wales and Northern England, followed by opera by Sadlers Wells and a further Old Vic tour in 1941. By the end of that year it was calculated that live plays had been seen by $1\frac{1}{2}$ million people, many of whom had never seen a professional performance of serious drama before.

CEMA's success was given great impetus by the appointment in April 1942 of Lord Keynes as chairman. This was important, not only for his foundation in 1936 of the Arts Theatre, Cambridge, and for his other enlightened services to the arts, but also for the fact that his had long been the principal voice in promoting the idea that the state *should* subsidise the arts. Thanks to him, CEMA's work was consolidated and expanded, and—significantly—support given to the campaign against the crippling handicap of entertainments duty which, as already mentioned, had been first imposed as a 'temporary' tax in 1916, but had nonetheless remained in force ever since. In the 1930s however exemption had been granted by HM Customs and Excise to charitable trusts and certain companies 'not established for profit', including the Old Vic and Sadlers Wells. In 1942 exemption was extended to all companies conforming to constitutional requirements and where the entertainment could be shown to be at least 'partly educational'. Difficulties over definition led to further extension of the rule under the Finance

Act, 1946. In this way a large number of enterprises, both amateur and professional, were relieved of the burden of this tax.

Among the professionals which benefited and used the concession to great cultural advantage was the theatre management of H. M. Tennent Ltd. which, under the dynamic direction of Hugh ('Binkie') Beaumont, set up a subsidiary non-profit-distributing company for the purpose, Tennent Plays Ltd. This unit not only gained exemption but was permitted to plough back its profits into mounting ambitious Shakespeare and other revivals, and to promoting new and often experimental plays by J. B. Priestley, Christopher Fry, and other native and foreign dramatists—all with star actors, designers and producers. Beaumont's success however aroused several storms. His production of Tennessee Williams's *A Streetcar Named Desire* exacerbated the familiar problem of 'educational' entertainment, while his practice of deducting royalties and other percentages from box office takings *before* calculating entertainments duty was challenged and had to be reversed. Thereafter the duty became the first charge upon the gross. Then in 1946 Inland Revenue decided, on a constitutional point, that Tennent Plays Ltd. was liable for income tax. As a result a heavy sum had to be found to meet the demand, while the company was wound up and replaced by a new one, Tennent Productions Ltd., which met the requirements of the Commissioners. Beaumont survived all these troubles and remained the most powerful manager in the business, to the extent that he was feared and attacked for running a near-monopoly. In the autumn of 1949, for instance, Tennents had seven plays in production in the West End, but all their presentations, then and later, were characterised by high standards and big names. In this and their choice of works, a number of which lost money, they did much to enhance the prestige of the British stage.[33]

It is an irony of history that it takes a war to introduce fundamental changes in society which would have taken decades to achieve, if ever, in the ordinary course of events. That happened in the First World War and, more strikingly, in the Second, which generated a revolution, no less in the arts than in other aspects of national life. As regards the theatre, what was begun in the 1940s became a reality beyond the wildest guesses in succeeding decades—a movement springing in essence from three sources. First, the work of CEMA and its successor, the Arts Council of Great Britain founded in 1946. Secondly, the passage of legislation such as the Local Government Act, 1948, which permitted local authorities to spend money on the arts, and the National Theatre Act, 1949. Thirdly, the creation of a new public for the theatre, especially outside London, which contributed to the new wave of playwriting that surged up in the 1950s and was itself an expression of social change.

This is not the place to describe in any detail the post-war revival of the theatre, beyond a brief reference to the construction of new theatre buildings (e.g. the Belgrade at Coventry, opened in 1958, the first ever at the entire expense of a municipal authority) or the renewal of old ones; to the reorganisation and financing of repertory with resident companies playing to new audiences within a wide radius or on circuit; to the replacement of weekly by fortnightly or three-weekly productions in many companies; or to the various schemes developed for taking theatre into different strata of society. This is a very large and diffuse subject ably described in other publications.[34] The important fact here is that such moves enabled the live theatre to revive, survive, and even flourish, and thus to provide not only a medium for the presentation of classics and other reputable plays by past authors, but a market for contemporary dramatists. Without such a base, little fresh work of quality could expect to find a hearing in the highly speculative conditions of the ordinary commercial theatre—most of it in London—where escalating costs forced many managements to rely on the familiar fare of farces, musicals, thrillers, and drawing-room comedies, some of which were so successful that they took certain theatres out of circulation for years on end. Of this, more in a moment; but the point of significance for writers was that the war gave birth to the age of the subsidised theatre.

However the base was not and could never be the whole edifice. Subsidies had to do more than help maintain buildings and bolster the general finances of theatre companies, although obviously without such indirect aid few plays could be performed. Additional money was needed to make it possible for authors to write new plays and ensure that companies staged them, if the *living* theatre was to justify itself in the fullest sense. That is where the Arts Council, and the Scottish and Welsh Arts Councils, have played such a vital role over the past thirty years, described by one critic as helping to 'change the face of the regional theatre, and to influence the attitude of actors, directors and (most important) audiences to the work of living British writers'.[35]

Direct aid to dramatists began in 1952 with the award of a small number of bursaries, worth initially £500 each, to enable the recipient to concentrate for a limited period of time on writing a new play. This scheme, in expanded form, is still in operation (1982); but the whole policy of direct aid has since been enlarged by three more schemes. One is the Resident Dramatists' Attachment Awards 'designed to enable a playwright to work with and for a theatre company for a period of 6–12 months'. This scheme has been applied at a number of centres such as Newcastle, Sheffield and Stoke, where plays of a documentary kind have been written and produced, reflecting local life and idiom.[36] Another scheme is the Contract Writers' Awards 'available to theatre companies to assist them to commission or employ playwrights on new play projects'. The company is expected to find at least half the cost of commissioning or otherwise employing the author, e.g. on a salary basis. Yet another scheme is the Royalty Supplement Guarantee 'designed to ensure that playwrights receive a reasonable reward from the first production of their plays'. This has proved an essential counterpart to the other schemes in that, as the name implies, it makes up to a fair figure the actual royalty income received and calculated usually at $7\frac{1}{2}$ per cent of the box office gross. Audience attendances apart, in many subsidised theatres the box office accounts for only a small part of the total income. The Octagon Theatre, Bolton, for instance, has some 374 seats selling at a top price of £3 per seat to the public, but the subsidy per seat works out at over twice that figure; yet the author's royalty is calculated on the seats sold.[37]

It is significant that direct aid to playwriting did not begin to show real results until the mid-1970s when the commissioning and royalty guarantee schemes were linked, and more recently when responsibility for administering the schemes (except the busaries and the residencies) is being transferred to the companies themselves—86 of them at present (1982). In all, money for theatre writing has risen by 34 per cent per year over the past decade, from £86,000 in 1971 to £312,000 in 1981, although still slight when related to the total sums spent on subsidising theatre. Here are the figures (exclusive of housing and aid to the national companies) for 1981–2.

Arts Council: £10,296,964 (about ⅛ of total annual expenditure) including £7,771,586 to 55 building-based companies, £1,716,070 to 30 touring companies, and £708,143 on theatre projects.

Scottish Arts Council: £1,797,545 (about 1/9 of total annual expenditure)

Welsh Arts Council: £1,513,355 (about 1/5 of total annual expenditure)

Distinct from these figures is the money allotted by the Arts Council to the two national companies—£5,770,000 to the National Theatre and £2,880,000 to the Royal Shakespeare Company. I mention this without attempting to enlarge on the role played by these great enterprises in the artistic life of the country or, for that matter, in the world at large, but simply to comment on their function as patrons of contemporary drama; likewise the English Stage Company at the Royal Court Theatre, Sloane Square, which, though listed in the Arts Council report as *one* of the building-based companies in London, received the largest single subsidy of £430,425—alone indicative of its importance—but also because it is generally regarded as a *de facto* national company with a special place in the history of post-war contemporary drama.

As regards new plays and playwrights the record of the English Stage Company outdistances by far that of the National Theatre and the Royal Shakespeare Company. Indeed the English Stage Company was launched in 1956 specifically to 'encourage new writers and to combat the decline of the vital theatre clubs'.[38] Between 1956 and 1973 it presented 273 productions, of which 221 were by contemporary writers, 178 of these being British. Between 1978 and 1981 it presented over 50 new plays compared to 21 by the National Theatre and 26 by the Royal Shakespeare Company. As regards rewards, none of these three companies (collectively known as the Theatres National Committee or TNC) differed in principle from other subsidised companies before the conclusion of the Minimum Terms Agreement with the Writers' Guild and the Theatre Writers' Union in 1979.[39] This was based on the view that the author's remuneration should represent six months' work, taking into account all the rehearsals and other preparations—although in many cases, of course, it would take far longer to conceive a play and put it down on paper. The agreement therefore provided for a commissioning fee of £2,000 (more if an uncommissioned play was accepted), to be treated as an advance against royalties if the play was performed in one of the larger auditoria, but as an addition to royalties if performed in one of the smaller ones (e.g. the Cottesloe at the National Theatre). Secondly the royalty rate would start at 10 per cent and vary thereafter according to receipts. Thirdly the author would have the right to attend rehearsals and be paid for doing so. Lastly, the extent of 'participation' or share by the management in the future income of the play would, in view of the subsidised status of the company, be strictly limited.[40]

With a few exceptions no dramatist makes much money out of a subsidised production, even when mounted by a Theatres National Committee company. The real value lies in prestige and the play's potential: by transfer to the West End; to Broadway and on tour in the USA; to similar realisations in other English-speaking countries; to performance in translation in Europe and Latin America; in film rights, broadcasting, and publication in volume form. What otherwise have playwriting subsidies, direct and indirect, achieved so far? Not certainly a regular and reliable living for playwrights. On the other hand they have created a positive climate of interest in new plays, by increasing the size of the theatre-going public, especially outside London, and by propagating the idea that new drama is the lifeblood of the theatre, which cannot thrive on a diet consisting solely of classics and other revivals.

This contention is supported by the extraordinary flowering of new drama over the past 25 years, and with its radical approach to most of the themes central to our society, from political protest to love, liberation and violence. In the 1940s and early 1950s serious new work had principally been expressed in the poetic dramas of Christopher Fry, Ronald Duncan, and T. S. Eliot; in innovative plays imported from abroad by, for example, Anouilh, Brecht, Sartre, and Tennessee Williams; in a handful of plays by established British and Irish writers, such as Rodney Ackland, Samuel Beckett, James Bridie, Noël Coward, Charles Morgan, J. B. Priestley, Terence Rattigan, R. C. Sherriff, and Sean O'Casey; followed—to take a random sample—by well-written but otherwise unadventurous pieces by Wynyard Browne, Denis Cannan, William Douglas Home, N. C. Hunter, and Peter Ustinov. Much promise had also been discerned in two plays by John Whiting in 1951[41] and one by Graham Greene in 1953.[42] Nonetheless,

> The image which most readily springs to mind when one tries to recall the British theatre before 1956 is that of the curtain parting to reveal a maid dusting a white telephone in a well-furnished drawing-room. The maid—inevitably, being working-class, was comic; the French windows in the carefully constructed set suggested the presence of a spacious garden, with which mostly middle-class patrons could comfortably identify.
>
> Such an approach to the 1950's theatre is not altogether fair . . . but for the most part the plays that were nightly performed in the West End theatre were not distinguished by their ability to portray much other than a picture of a settled, untroubled society.[43]

1956. That was the year when the English Stage Company put on, as its third production, John Osborne's *Look Back in Anger*[44] which 'caught the imagination of a whole generation both inside and outside the theatre, and turned the Royal Court into a centre for plays, not of protest in the "agit-prop" sense, but of general indignation at the state of civilization'.[45] This then was the play that, in the opinion of most theatre historians, catapulted the new age of native drama into life.

Taking 1956 as the starting point, it is possible—as already indicated—to compile a list of several hundred serious new plays that followed in the wake of *Look Back in Anger*, many of them 'barrier-breakers' in their various themes and treatments. Most, but not all, were first produced in subsidised theatres in and out of London. Some received single performances or otherwise suffered short shrift; but overall the quantity and quality of work by new writers, together with the achievements of actors, directors and designers, have contributed to an astonishing transformation of the British theatre, and this in turn has mainly been made possible by the policy of state support.

Among the playwrights launched since 1956, who have already made their mark in the annals of the theatre, are John Arden, Alan Ayckbourn, Robert Bolt, Edward Bond, Howard Brenton, Michael Frayn, Christopher Hampton, David Hare, Ann Jellicoe, Henry Livings, David Mercer, John Mortimer, Peter Nichols, Joe Orton, John Osborne, Harold Pinter, James Saunders, Peter Shaffer, N. F. Simpson, Tom Stoppard, David Storey, Peter Terson and Charles Wood.

Of necessity this is an arbitrary selection, and so I would refer the reader for details and discussion of the merits of these and many other post-war dramatists to the works listed in the Notes.[46] Not every experimental play or playwright has owed success to the subsidy system. Despite high risks, the commercial theatre has also played an important part, notably in running plays transferred from subsidised houses. In 1973, J. W. Lambert wrote:

> There are in London 34 commercial theatres. In the last ten years they have housed some 350 productions. Of these 134 have been what may be called straight plays, just over 100 light comedies and farces, all these have first been produced in a subsidized theatre . . . Some were mounted by the subsidized theatres in direct association with a commercial management. Some, after initial success, were taken over by a commercial company, with or without changes of cast designed to enhance the play's appeal to the general public . . .
>
> Of the notable new plays to reach the commercial theatre by these channels, those of John Osborne, David Storey and Christopher Hampton came from the Royal Court; Frank Marcus's *The Killing of Sister George* from Bristol; Peter Nichols's *A Day in the Death of Joe Egg* from Glasgow and his *Forget-me-not-Lane* from Greenwich; Ronald Millar's *Abelard and Heloise* from Exeter; Alan Ayckbourn's comedies from Scarborough; John Mortimer's *A Voyage Round my Father* from Greenwich; Peter Barnes's adaptation of Wedekind's, *Lulu,* and his *The Ruling Class,* from Nottingham . . .[47]

Lambert went on to say that the gradual dissolving of barriers between different kinds of theatre was one of the most encouraging cultural signs of the times, although—as he observed later—the process was by no means inevitable; nonetheless that 'what is dismissively called the theatre of entertainment' had also made its contribution as the vehicle for works by such 'eminently respectable writers' as William Douglas Home, Hugh and Margaret Williams, Terence Frisby, Hugh Leonard, Alan Bennett and Muriel Spark.

I propose now to insert an interlude, not concerned explicitly with the economics of playwriting, although plenty of money is involved. It is devoted to Alan Ayckbourn, stage playwright *par excellence*, who has regarded the theatre as his prime medium from the outset of his career.

In his book, *Conversations with Ayckbourn* (Macdonald Futura, 1981), Ian Watson describes how Ayckbourn began life as an actor; his association with Stephen Joseph at the Victoria Theatre, Stoke-on-Trent, and at the Theatre-in-the-Round, Scarborough; the proliferation of his plays; and his ideas about acting, writing, directing, and running a provincial theatre. I need therefore only recall, by reference to this book and to a talk I had with Ayckbourn himself, that his first two comedies were produced in 1959, followed by a play a year until 1963 when *Mr Whatnot* was performed under his own direction and with considerable success at Stoke. Next year—the last incidentally in which he appeared as an actor—*Mr Whatnot* was transferred with a fresh cast and a different director to the West End, where it failed. That failure so depressed him that he promptly got himself a job as a radio drama producer at BBC Leeds, where he stayed for six years and earned far more money than he ever received before as an actor-writer-director. Although he never wanted to write a radio or television play, the Leeds experience was probably beneficial, but it might well have signalled the end of his career as a playwright. In fact 1964 was the end of his apprentice period—the end of the beginning—because working at Leeds did not stop him writing stage plays, and it was Stephen Joseph who commissioned him to write *Meet My Father* and produced it the very next year at

Scarborough. Re-titled *Relatively Speaking*, it became a runaway success in the West End. He had almost arrived.

By 1970 Ayckbourn had written five more plays, including *How the Other Half Loves* (Scarborough 1968, London 1970 with Robert Morley in the lead, and the first of his plays to be put on in the States); and he was beginning to be recognised as a possible successor in *genre* to Noël Coward. That possibility was translated into reality over the next decade, thanks to his extraordinary fertility and facility; to writing one new play each year (sometimes more than one); to directing and launching it himself at Scarborough, thereby starting the process of a London, American, and/or European production, inclusion in repertory, translation (into 24 languages), adaptation for television, publication, and a harvest of awards. His success was phenomenal, *vide Absurd Person Singular* (1972), *The Norman Conquests*—three plays (1973), *Bedroom Farce* (1975), *Just Between Ourselves* (1976), *Joking Apart* (1978), *Suburban Strains*—with music by Paul Todd (1980). Here in more detail is a breakdown of the performances of *Bedroom Farce*, 1975–82.

Scarborough 33. National Theatre 184. British tour prior to National Theatre 27. Prince of Wales Theatre, London 373. Broadway, New York, 104 plus 160 on tour in the USA. Canada 32. UK repertory, 51 productions of 2–4 weeks each. UK amateur productions, uncounted but numerous. Performed in every country in Europe and in many further afield, e.g. Argentina, Chile, Japan, Uruguay, Venezuela. It was also broadcast on television in 1980, and issued in book form by three publishers, Samuel French, Chatto, and Penguin, yielding substantial sales.

Ayckbourn's exceptional success has made him a rich man, and when success comes on this scale it multiplies money on a geometric scale. I sense however that, for him, playwriting is not an end in itself. His overruling passion is the theatre and, before all others, the theatre at Scarborough, of which he took charge in 1970, three years after Stephen Joseph's death. At that time it was still a fit-up installation on the first floor of the public library which Joseph had originally leased for a limited summer season of six to eight weeks. In 1976 a move was made into permanent quarters in a converted school, now called the Stephen Joseph Theatre-in-the-Round. Equipped with 305 seats, it is in use 48 weeks out of the 52, provides full-time employment for a company of eight actors and supporting staff, offers facilities to local schools and amateur groups and attracts a solid audience. It also operates a bar theatre, with about a hundred seats, as a means of enticing hesitant males, afraid that drama might sap their virility or tempt them down the path of decadence. The theatre is supported by the Arts Council, Scarborough, and the County Council, and is an interesting example of the way in which a subsidised theatre—by putting on about a dozen new plays a year—fulfils a multiple purpose. It gives new writing a chance, it takes risks which few commercial producers would dare take, yet it offers them the opportunity of profiting from a promising try-out. Ayckbourn's own success as a playwright and play director, and as the man in charge of the whole enterprise, is an essential component of it all.

The fact is that in order to make a fair living out of writing for the stage—leaving aside for the moment income from ancillary or subsidiary rights—an author has still to depend on commercial production, the costs and risks of which have increased enormously since the war.

In 1952 it was said that a manager had to close down if he was not doing 60 per cent capacity business by the second week of the run.

In 1967 it was calculated that to produce a one-set play, with eight characters and four weeks' rehearsal, cost (pre-first night) £6,050, and a weekly outlay of £2,590. With an average box office return of £3,000 a week, thus a profit margin of £410, it would take 15 weeks to recoup the initial cost. Ten years later these respective totals would have more than doubled, and the ticket prices and takings have moved up accordingly.

By 1982 the statistics had rocketed. According to an article by Jon Catty in the winter 1982 issue of *Drama*,[48] the table of costs for a 'typical' production (subject of course to many variations) might look like this:

	Production	Weekly Running
MUSICAL	£460,000	£50,000
PLAY	£95,000	£15,000

Within the weekly figure, provision would have to be made for the rent and overheads and a cut of 15 to 20 per cent for the theatre owner, two to four per cent for the director, a half to one per cent for the designer, one to two per cent for the producer, ten per cent to the star actor, and five to ten per cent for the author.

In one show I handled the two stars each got 10 per cent, the director 4 per cent, the author 10 per cent, the designer one per cent, and the theatre 20 per cent—leaving a mere 45 per cent of the takings to pay for all the basic costs of running the show.

Even this figure of 45 per cent did not represent the final figure, as all box office returns are subject to VAT (successor to Entertainments Duty) currently at 15 per cent (1982).

Catty continued:

If we look at the example of the straight play which costs £15,000 to break even, it does extremely well to take £25,000 in a week. Yet even with this level of business it will only make a weekly profit of £7,000–£8,000 and will therefore need about three months to recover its initial production costs. For the musical, if the takings are £80,000, the costs £50,000 and percentages 30 per cent, the weekly profit is just over £20,000, which will take nearly six months at that level of business to recover its costs.

These figures are based on the show playing to 80 per cent capacity or more. Unfortunately, the majority of shows play to much less than this.

If a show falters for any reason, climatic possibly, it is usual for the royalty earners (the author included) to reduce or forgo altogether their participation, in the hope of recovery; but this is just one aspect of the speculative nature of an immense speculation.

Catty concluded:

My estimate is that of every ten shows produced, half lose more or less all their money, two others lose some of their investment, one breaks even approximately, one makes a modest profit and one makes, by any standards, a handsome profit.[49]

To return to the playwright. Apart from the original option paid by the producing management, which will be set against royalties, he will be entitled—as explained—to say five per cent until production costs have been recouped, rising to seven and a half percent and ten per cent, or perhaps a straight ten per cent at the second stage. What this means in terms of money depends on the capacity of the theatre, the volume of business, the length of the run, and the time it takes to recoup. If the play flops he will get his option money (say £500) and very little more. If it is a smash hit, he stands to earn a very large sum at the rate of say £1,500–£2,000 per week. It is a case of 'to him that hath', because success on the stage is likely to bring in important sums deriving, as already mentioned, from UK repertory and touring; from American, other overseas and foreign presentations; from amateur fees (at £10–£15 or more per performance); from broadcasting (both radio and TV), film rights and volume publication. The latter can be considerable in the light of demand from drama departments at universities (another source of promising dramatists) and from local education authorities interested in reading texts for schools and, generally, in using the theatre as a medium for teaching. Bolt's *A Man for All Seasons* is reputed to have sold at least half-a-million copies.

It is obvious that no clear answer can be given to the question, 'What does a playwright earn?'—other than that he can range from nil to £100,000 or more in a year (if he has a 'hit'), or any sum in between.[50] However there is this to be said. First, that almost every playwright with sticking power and faith in his future needs an agent who will have the ear of producing managements and who will be alive to all the possibilities of exploiting the property of his author. A good agent will earn his commission of ten per cent ten times over and, not least, offer a shoulder to sob on. Bernard Shaw handled his own theatre business and a few other writers do to this day, but they are exceptional. Secondly, that although the potential is enormous, the number of writers who approach or achieve it is very small, despite the undoubted renaissance of the theatre since the 1950s. Even the wider opportunities offered for performance by subsidised theatres have not meant that more than a handful of contemporary playwrights, household names notwithstanding, can live off their plays after the first flush of success.

A recent survey (1982) issued by the Theatre Writers Union, based on a very small sample, states that only about 25 playwrights succeed in earning the average national wage of £8,000 p.a. from the live theatre alone.[51] Among many facts and suggestions arising out of the report, one proposal stands out as possible and practicable, that of a 'Dead Writers Levy'. Applied to the theatre it would mean that productions of out-of-copyright plays would yield royalties as a means of financing new plays by contemporary, in-copyright, authors. The Theatre Writers' Union would restrict the scheme to subsidised theatres, with the proviso that if the money so yielded were not spent on new plays, then any subsidy devoted to the performance of an out-of-copyright play should be withdrawn.

This proviso would be regarded by some people as blackmail, and in any event might be difficult to monitor. Moreover what does a company do if it cannot find sufficient new plays of quality during a season? But the principle of calling on the past to promote the present is sound and was, for example, one of the proposals advanced during the course of the Public Lending Right campaign, although it had to be discarded in the face of opposition by publishers. Almost certainly managements would oppose it in the theatre and, as a first step, it would necessitate a change in the law of copyright; but that is no reason to dismiss it. The idea is far from dead.

To conclude. With very few exceptions, writing for the theatre remains—like freelance authorship in general—a part-time job and a part-time source of income. Even well-known and seemingly established playwrights usually have more failures than successes and have to look elsewhere for means of making or supplementing their living. Most playwrights make ends meet from alternative roles as scriptwriters for screen and radio, actors, directors, critics, novelists, journalists, lecturers, teachers—or in occupations outside letters altogether. It is an experience that runs true to form throughout the entire writing profession.

CHAPTER TEN

Radio

Origins of the BBC. Broadcasting fees in 1923. Copyright protection. A. A. Milne's criticisms in 1926. Collective agreement for minimum terms. American radio fees in 1930. Playwriting for the BBC. Role of Performing Right Society. Popular broadcasters in 1930s. Early television transmissions. Growing dissatisfaction of authors writing for radio during Second World War. Confrontation between Society of Authors and BBC in 1947. Radiowriters' Association founded in 1947. Some personal experiences of radiowriting and broadcasting in the 1950s. Competition of television. Pilkington Report, 1962. 'Broadcasting in the Seventies'. Commercial radio and local radio. Annan Report, 1977. Fees for radiowriting in 1980–1.

Public transmission of programmes of speech and music by radio telephony, or 'wireless' as it was familiarly called, began in USA in November 1920 and in UK in November 1922.[1] The British Broadcasting Company, the organisation responsible, was a private monopoly operating under Government licence and controlled by the manufacturers of receiving sets. Its headquarters were at Savoy Hill on the Victoria Embankment in London; and its general manager, later managing director, was Major J. C. W. Reith. By 1925 over one million licences had been issued by the Post Office to owners of receiving sets; but the obvious popularity of the new medium, and its potential influence on public opinion, militated against the continuance of a private monopoly. Equally strong was the dislike of any idea that broadcasting should become the business of a department of government. A Broadcasting Committee was therefore appointed to review the future of the enterprise. Its report, issued in 1926, recommended the formation of a semi-independent public corporation to run the service in the national interest, without political, commercial or other interference. This led, in January 1927, to the constitution of the British Broadcasting Corporation under a 10-year royal charter. Technical supervision rested with the Post Office, which found the necessary finance by the issue of 10-shilling annual licences for receiving sets, already in excess of two million by this date. Reith became Director-General, responsible to a board of governors. Thanks to these preliminaries and to Reith's strong, didactic personality, which he exercised over eleven years of office,[2] the BBC achieved a high reputation—acknowledged world-wide—for the breadth, performance, and integrity of its programmes, which, in particular, were to stand the country in good stead during the Second World War.

These high standards depended not only on the planners, producers, and artists employed by the BBC, but also of course on the material provided by authors and composers of music.[3] And it was in this area that, in the first flush of enthusiasm, the value of the 'primary producer' was often overlooked—a not unfamiliar phenomenon. As early as 1922 the Society of Authors was warning its members about copyright infringements on the air, and asked everyone who 'listened in' to report such cases to the Society's office. Meanwhile it was left entirely to the individual to make his own arrangements with the BBC as to payment (if any); but at the Society's AGM held in June 1923 the following resolution was passed unanimously:

> That this meeting recommends members ... not to give permission for their works to be broadcasted without payment of a fee, and that in cases where they give permission for payment of a fee members should notify the Secretary of the Society of the terms on which they are dealing with the British Broadcasting Company ...

A rider was added that, while it was impossible at that time to standardise fees, it was essential that *some* fee be paid; further, that any author requested to broadcast his own work was entitled to claim a fee as a performer, in addition to that to which he was entitled as an author.

Shortly afterwards Herbert Thring, the Society's Secretary, began an intensive correspondence with the BBC on the whole subject of authors' remuneration, to such effect that before the end of 1923, while still leaving it open to any author or composer to fix his own terms, a table of minimum fees for published work had been agreed between the two sides—a document of interest historically and for its occasional odd phraseology, summarised here:

1. £2.2s per Act or Canto, or division, for a single performance, providing that it exceeds 200 lines in length.

2. £1.1s for a single performance of shorter poems, excerpts, monologues, etc., not exceeding 200 lines in length.

3. In the case of short stories, excerpts from a book in prose or serial matter, £1 1s for the first 1,000 words and pro rata for every succeeding 1,000 words, for a single performance.

4. No abridgement or alteration without the author's sanction.

Thring also offered to submit a list of works available for broadcasting on the automatic payment of a fee by the BBC to the Society who would pass it to the authors concerned. This offer was not approved by everyone, as it soon became clear that the BBC never paid more than the minimum unless the author or his agent bargained for better terms. Among those however who fell in with the idea were Laurence Housman, Jerome K. Jerome, Harold Monro (of the Poetry Bookshop), and John Drinkwater, who seemed quite content with three guineas for the broadcast of his play, *Oliver Cromwell*, and a similar sum for *Robert E. Lee*. Among those who objected were A. E. Housman (who flatly refused to have his work broadcast at all), Gilbert Frankau, W. W. Jacobs ('no cuts'), John Galsworthy, and Bernard Shaw.

Shaw objected on specific and characteristic grounds: namely quality not quantity.

The reasonableness of a quotation from a stage work cannot be measured by its length.

Now take the case of Antony's oration from *Julius Caesar*, which Benson[4] has been broadcasting lately. Quantitively it is a negligible fraction of the play. But the fact that it is broadcast as a recitation, and has often been made a separate item in an entertainment by professional elocutionists proves that it is a work of art by itself, with a value independent of the context. Shakespear [sic] could, if alive, claim performing right accordingly.

When the BBC suggested that I should give a reading viva-voce in my own person . . . I believe I asked a hundred guineas. When it was proposed to broadcast a performance of *The Dark Lady* with four performers, of whom three were doing leading business, I told the manager to ask £50, with the result that the project fell through . . .

The money doesn't matter if we can nail them to the principle.[5]

In a later letter,[6] Shaw wrote:

But I have never given a *personal* performance of any kind for money, though I have been offered prodigious sums by the Americans. When it came to the point I could not overcome my repugnance to breaking this record; and I told the BBC that I would do it for fun as an experiment, which naturally relieved them enormously, as they were expecting me to open my mouth very wide indeed. Fortunately for us the experiment was a very great success. The testimonies are overwhelming as to the superiority of a good reading to a performance by invisible actors; and now is the time for those of our members who can read effectively to make hay while the sun shines. Far from intending to create a precedent of broadcasting for nothing, I wanted to test the market; and any member who is confronted with 'Shaw did it for nothing' can reply 'Then there is all the more left for me. Shaw is not a professional reader, and I *am*'.

Bargaining about money paled into insignificance compared with the bogey raised in 1925. In a statement published in *The Times* on 22 June, the BBC was quoted as holding the view that:

There is no legal criterion for copyright in broadcasting, but we have been careful not to take advantage of this fact. Our policy is to consider all copyright claims on their merits and to compensate owners on a basis of moral justice.

Reference was slyly made to the value of advertisement in the broadcast of a work.

Thring challenged this statement in *The Times* at once, and shortly afterwards Reith attended a meeting of the Society's dramatists at which the point was discussed, without conclusion. Next year Thring, accompanied by J. B. McEwen, Principal of the Royal Academy of Music, gave evidence to the Broadcasting Commitee, at which they asserted, without compromise, that broadcasting was a performing right under the 1911 Copyright Act. This had some effect because, in its subsequent report, the Committee recommended that the services of those who provided the raw material for broadcasting 'should be adequately rewarded'. In fact the BBC did not sustain its negative attitude, and the principle regarding payment for the use of copyright material on the air was never seriously questioned again.

Apart from Shaw, who could always be relied upon not only to speak out for authors' rights but to make the public listen to him, it fell to another successful author, A. A. Milne, to fly the literary flag in *The Evening News*,[7] in which a correspondent had criticised the BBC's literary programmes.

Authors have never been taken very seriously by their fellow-men. 'A singer is a singer,' the attitude seems to be, 'a painter is a painter, and a sculptor sculpts; but, dash it all, a writer only writes, which is a thing we all do every day of our lives, and the only difference between ourselves and Thomas Hardy is that Hardy doesn't do anything else, whereas we are busy men with a job of real work to do.' And since writing is, in a sense, the hobby, or at least the spare-time occupation of the whole world, it has become natural for the layman to regard the professional author as also engaged merely upon a hobby, the results of which, in accordance with the well-known vanity of the hobbyist, are free for the inspection of anyone kindly enough to take an interest in them.

For instance, you who read this would not think of asking a wine merchant, whose nephew had been at the same school as your son, for a free dozen of champagne on the strength of that slight connection; but you would not hesitate to ask an author, similarly connected, for a free article for some ephemeral publication in which you were interested, or for permission to perform his play without the usual payment of royalty. Indeed, you would feel that you would be paying him the same sort of compliment that I should be paying you if, dining at your house, I asked to see the fret-work soap-dish in your bathroom. 'Oh, are you really interested?' you would say. 'Fancy your having heard about it! How awfully nice of you!' But this is not what the author says.

Now the BBC exploits to its highest power this attitude of kindly condescension to the author. To the BBC all authors are the same author. There is a 'regular fee' for the author, whoever he is; the fee is what advertisers call 'nominal'; and with any luck the BBC can avoid paying even this ridiculous amount by an ingenious scheme of its own. It says to the author, 'If we pay you a fee, we won't mention your name or your works or your publishers or anything about you, but if you will let us do it for nothing we will announce to our thousand million book-buying listeners where your work is to be bought. And if you don't like it, you can leave it, because there are plenty of other authors about; and, if it came to the worst, we could write the things ourselves quite easily.'

Now imagine if other concerns behaved like this. Suppose, for instance, that Mr John Galsworthy wrote an article in *The Evening News*. Would *The Evening News* (with certainly as many readers as, on any one night, the BBC has listeners) say to Mr Galsworthy: 'Well, if we give your name and tell our readers who you are, of course you can't expect to be paid?' Would the Editor ask Thomas Hardy for a free poem on the ground that it was a good advertisement for him? Does a Theatre Manager tell a young dramatist that he mustn't expect a royalty on his first play, as it will undoubtedly help to sell his second? Of course not.

But the BBC is obsessed by the thought of advertisement. Publicity might never have been heard of until the BBC was born. After all, if the BBC says to the author, 'I shan't pay you, because I'm helping your books to sell,' why on earth shouldn't the publisher also say to the author, 'and *I* shan't pay you, because I'm helping you to get taken up by the BBC'? Why should the Broadcasting Company be the one, and the only one, not to pay?

I suggest, then, that the reason why the literary standard of the BBC is low is simply that the Company has made no effort to attract authors, and is entirely out of touch and sympathy with authors. Let me give an example or two from my own experience.

1. I was offered two guineas to read one act of one of my own plays. Whether this was an attractive proposition for listeners-in is not for me to say, but how could anyone think that it was an attractive proposition for the author? Let anybody consider what, in the way of preparation and performance, the author would have to go through, and ask himself if the offer was likely to be accepted.

2. On a very special 'Gala Night' I was asked to read something of my own during the Children's Hour. I was offered five guineas, and it was explained to me apologetically that the Children's Hour had to be run cheaply. (As if that was any reason why I should help the BBC to run it cheaply!) I replied that I didn't want to read my work aloud. An Editor, a Manager, a Publisher, would then automatically have said, 'Would you do it for *ten* guineas?' or 'What *would* you do it for?'—or something of that sort. The BBC voice at the other end of the telephone said in heart-rending accents, 'Not even for the sake of the Little Ones?'

In any collective agreement, there is always a tendency for the employer—epitomised in this case by the BBC—to convert minima into maxima, so that the onus rests upon the contributor, i.e. the author or his agent, to bargain for better rates if he can get them. Once it becomes clear that a number of popular or established authors are regularly paid above the minimum, then it enables the collective organisation to use this fact as a strong—though not the only—argument for raising the basic level when the current agreement has run out. In later years the BBC adapted this pattern to its own purposes, offering two rates, one for beginners, the other for established writers—a reasonable proposition at first sight, though much depended on its interpretation; but it also made it harder for any individual author, unless exceptionally popular, to sell his work above one or other of these rates. In practice it also meant that in each new collective agreement two categories of minima had to be considered instead of one, but it did not of course remove the need for re-negotiation at regular intervals to keep abreast both of the market and of the cost of living. In short, the very existence of minima collectively agreed (however low the rates may seem to us all these inflated years later) served two essential purposes: one to prevent exploitation by underpayment, the other to provide a basis for bargaining upwards. It was in this sense that, soon after the first agreement was signed in 1923, Thring wrote to the leading literary agents—A. P. Watt, Curtis Brown, A. M. Heath, *et al.*—and gained their support; and one assumes that A. A. Milne soon benefited from the intervention of *his* agent in subsequent dealings with Children's Hour and other sections of the BBC.

While fresh agreements were signed by the Society of Authors and the BBC at intervals of approximately three years,[8] minimum rates were not the only points at issue. One, for example, was the principle blandly assumed that contributors to school and children's programmes should be paid less (generally at two-thirds of the full rate), and broadcasters to the Empire even less than that. Another was the objection that the term 'broadcasting rights' which appeared in every BBC contract gave far too much away. It should be replaced by 'one British broadcasting use', and so leave the way open for repeat fees and sales abroad.

In this connection Ivan Firth, an executive of the National Broadcasting Company of America, gave some useful information in 1930 about the use of radio material in his country.[9] After describing the pattern of commercial broadcasting, how programmes were shaped by the necessity for advertising breaks, how the problem of time-changes over a vast continent were countered by the use of recording so that a popular programme in, say, New York could be slotted in at the appropriate hour in San Francisco, he continued:

> There is no hard and fast rule with regard to the price paid. The material has to be sold, just as a story to a magazine, but as much as £100 for a half hour sketch may be obtained on a commercial programme. Sustaining programmes, on the other hand, will rarely carry more than £10.

Detective stories are always popular, stories of adventure on land and sea, love stories, in fact, any sort of series in which there can be both human interest and suspense.

The market, although not very lucrative at the present time [1930], brings writers into the world of business. George Bernard Shaw may consider it 'an offence to the Holy Ghost' to use his genius in writing an advertisement for Harrods, but in America, where advertising is definitely linked to entertainment, through the medium of radio, both dramatists and writers would do well to consider entering the field.

Whatever the prospects for British writers on American radio, and while there was no question of advertising on the BBC, the potential of the medium—according to an editorial in the winter 1930 issue of *The Author*—had as yet hardly been explored.

It is time for authors and composers to realise that broadcasting is no longer to be regarded merely as a by-product of publication and performance. It is beginning to be a distinct and important market not only for work which has already been exploited in other directions, but also, as a distinct and definite technique is being developed, for new work of every kind.

The point was underlined by Val Gielgud, head of productions at the BBC where, by 1931, as many as 40 play scripts a week were already being received. Because a radio play had an entity of its own, it followed that it required a technique of its own. First and foremost, everything had to be conceived for and received by the ear. Unlike sight which produced an instantaneous reaction, hearing was a relatively slow sense in terms of response, demanding more time, closer attention, and a positive application of intelligence on the part of the listening audience.

In the very first play ever specially written for the microphone, Mr Richard Hughes, with a very typical ingenuity, solved the problem by placing his characters in a coal-mine disaster. His characters were in the dark, their eyes were useless to them. It was, therefore, easy enough for the audience to listen and react without feeling all the time that they were missing something by not being able to see. But for all its ingenuity this was only a makeshift.[10]

However, while the disadvantages of the medium were obvious enough, the strengths were no less impressive—complete freedom to tell a story without ordinary limitations of dramatic time and space, or the need for scenery, but reinforced by a wide range of sound effects, particularly music, always a powerful means of inducing the right mood, and which must 'form an integral part of the complete dramatic structure'.

Gielgud regarded Tyrone Guthrie and L. du Garde Peach[11] as 'up to the present, the most successful practitioners of this new craft', and referred to their respective plays, *Squirrel's Cage* and *Ingredient X*, as examples of how to write drama effectively for the ear, 'entirely independent of visuality' with 'sound construction as definite and as satisfying as a musical symphony'. In the end there was no substitute for good writing.

> No amount of mechanical ingenuity, no knowledge or comprehension of sound pattern—not even a good situation— can compensate for poor writing, and in the case of a radio play a high standard of writing is the more necessary because it cannot be balanced by luxurious appointments in the shape of scenery or dresses, and because the radio audience, split up as it is into individual units by their firesides, each one of whom is completely isolated, is far more immediately critical than the massed units of the audience of the theatre or the cinema, subject to every kind of emotional mob-reaction.

Music was important, not only for its emotional stimulus in the presentation of radio drama and other programmes, but because—as an art in its own right—radio opened up vast new vistas for performance, which in turn meant important prospects of employment for players and composers. Music moreover entered into the dialogue between the Society of Authors and the BBC for historical reasons. The following quotation from Volume One (p. 213 *et seq*) of my *Authors by Profession*[12] explains the background.

Unlike authors, composers had done virtually nothing to assert their rights by corporate action, notwithstanding repeated invitations by Walter Besant [founder, the Society of Authors] 'to combine with the authors and band themselves together to protect their own property'. A few prominent composers did join the Society and form a sub-committee as early as 1899 but, with the exception of Charles Villiers Stanford, they failed to pursue 'a virile and energetic policy'; so this initial effort petered out and had to be replaced by a more vigorous body after 1911. Publishers dominated the music world. Although the royalty system was belatedly finding its way into music contracts, it was still customary for composers to dispose of their copyrights (both publication and performance rights) to their publishers, who made most of their money from the sale of sheet music: for which purpose they promoted public concerts and subsidised artistes to perform new works.

The situation however radically changed in the first decade of the 20th century.

For one thing public concerts, even the 'pops', were losing money, and so music publishers gave up promoting them. Another factor was the escalation of pirate music publishing and sale by street hawkers, especially of songs . . . A third factor was the rapid growth of the pianola and gramophone industries and doubts as to whether 'mechanical music' . . . constituted an infringement of copyright. These events induced a change of attitude towards the enforcement of performing right as a source of income, and ensured its inclusion— together with mechanical right—in the Copyright Act, 1911.

All this contributed to the formation in 1914 of the Performing Right Society Ltd. (PRS), a collecting organisation to which composers, lyric writers and publishers assigned their performing rights and agreed to share in the resulting income. The foundation of the PRS did not however dispense with composers' representation at the Society of Authors, where several heavy-weight musicians took exception to the fact that the PRS was publisher inspired, and who *faute de mieux* used the SoA—one has the impression—as an instrument of protest.[13]
One of the most vociferous was Rutland Boughton who wrote

the music for the immensely popular music drama, *The Immortal Hour*, and who had been the driving force behind the Glastonbury festivals before and after the First World War. Boughton was a natural protestant and had enlivened not only Glastonbury, but the music establishment generally, with polemical, political and marital bombshells—the story is well told by Michael Hurd in his book, *Immortal Hour* (Routledge, 1962). Although his star was falling fast by the 1930s, Boughton's was still a name to reckon with; and so his comments on the plight of the composer were of some interest.[14]

> Radio has made an end of the greater commercial value in printed music.
>
> The total fees paid to me by the PRS for the year just ended (to June 8, 1933) have amounted to £56 2s 4d of which £38 0s 6d was for broadcasting. Nor is my case one of the worst, as I get occasional fees for performances of operas not controlled by the PRS. But at one time, my royalties from the sale of published music amounted to two or three hundred pounds a year; now they have dwindled to a mere pittance, while performing fees, which should have taken the place of the old main source of income, do not provide the barest livelihood.

Boughton's hopes of a substantial income from broadcasting were premature, as indeed were those of many other musicians and authors. Three years later, Thomas F. Dunhill, a respected academic composer and a member of the Society, reiterated Boughton's sentiments even more cogently.[15]

> Broadcasting, and broadcasting alone, is responsible for the reduced sale of music in printed form, and that, in bringing the artist's work to a wide audience, the BBC is, first and foremost, providing itself with the material it needs to carry on at all. The composer's former public, in plain words, has been wrested from him by the BBC to its own advantage . . . the sale of sheet music, taking into account all classes of musical composition, has fallen to about one-fifth of what it was in 1925.

Dunhill, on the other hand, thought well of the PRS—its

administration and service to members—but that in dealing with the BBC much remained to be done both by the PRS and by the Society.[16]

In his history of broadcasting Asa Briggs describes the rapid growth of radio in the 1930s, evident in the extension of listening time, the addition of alternative programmes (national and regional), and the broadening of subject matter broadcast— whether light entertainment (variety, musical comedy, dance music, sport, etc.), drama, features, talks, or the special transmissions for schools, children, and overseas listeners. These programmes made household names of a number of writers— new or already established in other *genres*—who wrote and broadcast their own scripts, such as Harold Nicolson, Vernon Bartlett, Ernest Newman, Stephen King-Hall, James Agate, Alistair Cooke (who began his radio career as a film critic in 1934). They also brought to the microphone unexpected *literati* such as E. M. Forster and Roger Fry; popularised the classics (not only Shakespeare, Milton, Restoration dramatists, 18th century poets, *et. al.*, but by serialising some of the novels of 19th century giants—Scott, Dickens, Thackeray, Trollope); expanded audiences for a mixed company of contemporary writers (alphabetically, at random—T. S. Eliot, Ian Hay, John Masefield, J. B. Priestley, Dorothy Sayers, Bernard Shaw, H. G. Wells); and provided a twice-weekly preaching platform for the immensely popular incumbent of St. Martin-in-the-Fields, the Reverend Dick Sheppard. By 1938 98 per cent of the population could listen in, and there were 73 licences for every 100 households in the country. By then too the BBC had firmly established three weekly publications, *Radio Times, World Radio*, and *The Listener*.

This remarkable development was not without its critics. In 1935 Ian Hay, giving evidence for the Society before the Government Commission appointed to consider the revision of the BBC's charter, praised the Corporation for its efficiency and high standards, but deplored the low scale of fees deriving from the days of the BBC's 'impoverished infancy' and no longer justified on that account. He also asserted that authors should be compensated for the 'various inroads made by the listening habit upon their previous sources of income'. This latter point (the same, in principle, as Boughton's and Dunhill's) seemed real enough at the time, especially to dramatists, of whom Hay was one.

> Today there are just about enough regular theatregoers left in London to fill—to profit point, that is—half a dozen West End theatres. Certainly not more . . . What do we see? Half the theatres in London struggling to keep afloat, with two-tickets-for-the-price-of-one in front of the curtain and half-salaries behind it, and the rustle of paper audible from floor to ceiling.

In the same (autumn 1935) issue of *The Author*, W. J. Turner, the critic, hoped that the BBC, having saved music (at any rate for the performers), would do the same for the theatre—by means of television, already on the scene in experimental form. Trial transmissions had started in 1930, a daily half-hour in 1932, and by 1936 a regular service was in progress from Alexandra Palace, mainly of outside events. Shortly afterwards Ashley Dukes[17] attended an indoor production, which he found exciting and artistically challenging, but he wondered how the service could be funded out of the annual 10s wireless licences, and prophesied the beginning of the end of the film industry 'as we know it'. In February 1937 the BBC adopted the Marconi system (in preference to that of Baird, the pioneer of television in the UK) and steadily expanded the coverage. Outside broadcasts included the Boat Race, Test Match and Cup Final, while J. B. Priestley's *When We Are Married* was the first play televised direct from a theatre. Opera, ballet, the circus, comedy shows, and much else appeared on the TV screen; and it seemed clear that television was beginning seriously to challenge the dominance of radio, until the contest was abruptly terminated by the outbreak of war in September 1939, when all TV transmissions ceased until the return of peace.

Meanwhile the remuneration of writing, whether for radio or TV, remained unsatisfactory and unsatisfied. Television was regarded as still too raw and poverty stricken to justify high-pressure tactics for improved payments, although the League of Dramatists had a small success in doubling fees for the transmission of one-act plays.[18] Although the minimum terms agreement for the use of published material on radio remained in force, an argument developed with the publishers, represented by Geoffrey Faber, who claimed a 50 per cent share in the broadcasting rights of a book. The Society stated flatly that any claim to an interest in an author's broadcasting rights, merely because the claimant happened to be the publisher of the work in book form, was both ethically and logically unjustifiable. A compromise was eventually reached, without concession of principle, so that in September 1942 a fresh agreement was drawn up between all the interested parties.[19] But the authors' basic complaint about BBC rates remained.

Ernest Raymond, author of *Tell England*, *We The Accused*, and many other popular novels, expressed his dissatisfaction in the spring 1942 issue of *The Author*.

Let us now consider the BBC. That may seem an unoriginal and oppressive opening, since the pastime of criticising the BBC has been indulged in by the Press *ad nauseam*, but really, if a patient persists in remaining sick, there is nothing to do but go on considering him. A further reason for disliking to consider, with disapproving and even despairing comments, this remarkable corporation is that everyone connected with it is so extraordinarily nice . . . It is only when you consult the clauses of your contract that you perceive that Broadcasting House is a place where every person pleases and only your prospects are vile.

I am going to ask you to examine with me the clauses of the standard contract for talks . . . The more I study these clauses, with their impudent disregard of the limitations to which other business houses and publishing or producing concerns have learned that they must submit—do you remember Mr Duff Cooper's, 'To be asked to speak for the BBC is a *privilege*'? Soon they may be suggesting that we pay for the privilege—the more I feel that in the socialised state which will come upon us after the war, and which I desire to see come, there'll have to be two of every socialised service, whether it is the post office, broadcasting system, railway system or army, so that we may keep the advantages of competition, and no single monopoly may get too mightily above itself.

He then drew attention to the fact that the contract was 'subject to the Corporation's acceptance of your final manuscript'.

I cannot imagine that any established author can accept the position that commissioned work upon which he has spent valuable time is subject to summary and uncompensated rejection by his publisher or producer. No author can regard such an arrangement as a contract at all. It is merely and precisely an invitation to offer a manuscript for acceptance or rejection.

A second objection was that the Corporation claimed the manuscript as its own property. A third that the author was expected to attend as many rehearsals as the Corporation thought necessary.

But clause 6 is the real villain. The rights it pinches are quite astounding . . . all wireless and wire broadcasting rights in the English language; the right to translate and broadcast in all other languages; the right to make a mechanical record . . . for subsequent reproduction without restriction throughout the world; for 28 days from date of broadcast all rights of publication in all languages in Great Britain and Northern Ireland; for six months . . . all rights of publication elsewhere throughout the world.
The impudence of it! The anachronism that it is!

The final insult was that the Corporation reserved the right to cancel the talk, subject only to payment of the fee *'assessed by the Corporation for work already carried out* . . . or to the offer of an alternative engagement *as the Corporation alone shall decide'* (Raymond's italics).
This blast by an author, too popular and respected to be dropped by the B B C, assisted the Society—after further sustained pressure—to secure a few of the improvements sought by Raymond: e.g. no unilateral rejection of commissioned work, the payment of a small additional fee for publication, the author to retain his own manuscript, and payment on acceptance (not merely when broadcast) of specially written short stories and

plays, though nothing would induce the BBC to upgrade Children's Hour and overseas rates, which continued to be paid at two-thirds or less of the full fee. However, as noted, a fresh agreement for the use of published material was signed in September, and a Standing Committee was set up by the two sides to deal with current complaints, which was welcome so far as it went. At best this was patchwork negotiation, partly dictated by wartime conditions and by a tendency to regard confrontation as unpatriotic. It did nothing to dispel widespread resentment of the arrogance inherent in the BBC's monopoly, liable at any time to bare its teeth.

One such incident occurred in December 1944, when the BBC broadcast a performance of R. L. Stevenson's *Treasure Island*, reported in the *Radio Times* as 'one of many programmes to commemorate the fiftieth anniversary of RLS's death'. Now the Stevenson estate was managed by the Society, which had not been notified. Legally the BBC appeared to be acting within its rights, on the grounds that works published or performed after fifty years had elapsed since the author's death were no longer protected by copyright; and Stevenson had died on 3 December 1894. As it happened the Society was able to prove that most of the scripts in question had been prepared during the period of protection, and in consequence secured the payment of a 'sum which the Corporation would have been required to pay had permission been applied for at the outset'. But the implications went far deeper than a matter of dates. If, the Society commented, the BBC insisted on sticking to the letter of the law in every case without regard to moral liability, and made it a practice to honour an author's name by broadcasting commemorative programmes directly his works ran out of copyright, then the renewal of the Corporation's Charter would have to be called in question.

Monopoly will have a hollow sound as distances diminish and America, North and South, become in the ether as near neighbours to Britain as Radio Luxemburg. Government subsidy is unlikely ever to equal funds derived from advertiser-subsidised programmes . . . The BBC will have to look to its only stock-in-trade for outbidding its more opulent competitors: a civilised regard for the author himself and a sensitive respect for his artistic interests.[20]

This incident turned out to be the first shot in a grand campaign waged by the Society from 1945 to 1947. Letters from members appeared in almost every issue of *The Author*. Adrian Conan Doyle, who managed his father's estate, reported that a Sherlock Holmes story earned £200 on American networks but only 25 guineas on the BBC. Hilary St George Saunders wrote:

> The fees ... offered by the BBC are in the best tradition of Grub Street, and they are only too often accompanied by a Pecksniffian observation to the effect that they are paid out of public funds and therefore should be as low as possible.

Two letters proved a mine of information about most types of broadcasting in the mid-1940s. One from 'Sinbad' (Captain A. E. Dingle, RN):

> Fifteen guineas for fifteen minutes in my first broadcast, a talk; for various talks covering many subjects, and each taking fifteen minutes, fees ranging from ten guineas down to six guineas. Bits in programmes such as *Men Talking* (unscripted), *The World Goes By*, *Ack-Ack-Beer-Beer*, *ABC of the BBC*, etc., five and six guineas; Children's Hour, Schools, eight and ten guineas. For *Desert Island Discs* (unscripted) and *Essays in Adventure* (with script), the same fee, six guineas. For the *Brains Trust* I received a cheque for fifteen guineas ...

Another letter from L. A. G. Strong, popular fiction writer and a regular broadcaster since 1928, was less censorious. He agreed that talks were notoriously the worst paid branch of radio work, though they compared reasonably with the fees offered to the rank and file of drama competition adjudicators, lecturers, and the like.

> I can't generalise on the fees I get for talks, but they work out at roughly twelve guineas for a quarter of an hour, and a guinea a minute for shorter talks, up to five minutes in length.
>
> I have sold more than seventy short stories to the BBC. The usual length is two thousand words, or a little over, which takes a quarter of an hour to read. The basic rate is a guinea a minute. I get twenty-five guineas for the fifteen minutes, plus

four guineas for reading the story. I have never been a fashionable short story writer . . . Nine out of ten writers . . . would regard it as a good price. I have only once been paid a higher price by a British periodical for a story of that length. What is more . . . after twenty-eight days from the date of the first broadcast all rights revert to the author, and he can sell first serial rights to a magazine.

Radio plays are paid for at the same rate. Dramatists of reputation get very much more: I get a little more. For a programme on the life of John McCormack, which was played twice, I received a hundred and ten guineas, plus twenty for taking part in the broadcast. The programme lasted for three quarters of an hour; the ordinary fee would have been ninety guineas.

I have had several tussles with the BBC copyright department on prices, particularly in the matter of adaptations for which in my opinion they pay less than they should . . . informing me that when I adapt I work on a lower plane than when I do what they are pleased to call 'original' work. (The fact, of course, is that they have to pay a fee to the victim of the adaptation, and so try to save it at the expense of the adapter.) My retort that there is only one plane, the writing of good radio . . . has so far failed to move them.

It is clear from a study of the Society's records that a large number of authors were thoroughly disenchanted with the BBC; and so, in the autumn of 1946—after the Government had refused to appoint an independent Committee of Inquiry prior to the renewal of the Corporation's Charter—the Society intensified the attack. It maintained that, as a result of wartime expansion, too many top jobs in the BBC had gone to veterans and pioneers of broadcasting, who had become stale after the strain of war; nor was long service necessarily a sound qualification for a high appointment. Such men were responsible for the niggardly attitude towards those who provided the raw material for broadcasting, and had entrenched themselves behind the parapets of public service. Here is another comment from the autumn 1946 issue of *The Author*:

Negotiation with a monopoly is almost inevitably a one-sided affair unless the other party to the negotiations is also a monopoly. In this respect composers have been better placed than authors for battling with the BBC, since the Performing Right Society has a more or less monopoly-control of musical performance in this country, and can impose its own conditions on the BBC, so long as it does not run into stormy weather at Westminster. On the other hand the composer almost invariably has to share with his music publisher the fees paid for radio performances of his work. The author, in the majority of cases, gets the whole of the fees paid for literary material, but they are relatively much smaller fees; and although the Society of Authors and its affiliated League of Dramatists have applied constant pressure to improve the rates for literary and dramatic work, these two organisations have been handicapped by lack of sanctions and by the absence of any united front or agreed broadcasting policy among literary agents.

Moreover it transpired that the minimum terms agreements, signed since the early days with the BBC, especially those for different categories of specially written material, had—for reasons already explained—been allowed to run too long. The war was a ready-made and specious excuse for resisting change. That had to be faced and, in view of the BBC's continued intransigence, the Society 'took to the streets', called a press conference (conducted by Osbert Sitwell, then chairman of the Committee of Management) on 29 May 1947, and issued a manifesto listing and analysing the principal grounds of complaint, backed by personal statements from John Masefield, the Society's President; from St. John Ervine, President, and James Bridie, Chairman of the League of Dramatists; and from ten or more other prominent members including Michael Foot, J. L. Hodson, Margaret Storm Jameson, H. J. Massingham, Charles Morgan, J. B. Priestley, V. S. Pritchett, Herbert Read, and H. M. Tomlinson.

The complaints were specified under three main heads, with random examples:

Poverty of Fees
  1. Author A: 5 guineas for world broadcasting rights in a

specially written 2,000-word story. No additional fee, other than £1 12s 9d expenses allowance, for rehearsing and delivering it, and a further one guinea if the BBC exercised its option to publish.

2. Author B (Bernard Shaw): an offer of £70 for permission to record *The Devil's Disciple* in English and foreign language versions with the right to broadcast it three times from every broadcasting station in the world outside the UK for a period of three years from the date (unspecified) of recording.

3. Author C: had received 25 guineas from the *Strand* magazine for a 500-word article. The BBC expected him to write and deliver a talk of four times that length on the same subject for about half the *Strand* payment, plus free option to publish it in *The Listener* for 2½–3 guineas.

Further examples of 'penny-splitting' were quoted:

1. Author D (a leading short-story writer): the BBC took a 6,000-word story, cut it to 4,500 and declined to pay more for it than 3s 6d above the minimum for a story of 4,500 words.

2. Author E (Norman Douglas): on being told that, for substantial quotations from his works, a fee of one guinea more than the fee offered was required, the BBC cancelled the broadcast.

3. Author F (H. J. Massingham): commissioned talk of about 2,000 words, offered 10 guineas after delivery of script, raised to 12 after much argument, and finally to 18 after hint of legal action by the Society.

4. Author G (a distinguished woman dramatist): the BBC offered 10 guineas for a 2,000-word talk, then suggested 12. After further haggling, the author told BBC to send the cheque to a hospital.

Unreasonably Wide Rights

Under its standard form the BBC—for a single fee, ranging usually between 8 and 15 guineas—took all broadcasting rights in English and foreign languages without restriction throughout the world, together with a free option to publish in *The Listener* and its other journals for payment of a fee equivalent to one-fifth of the sum paid for the broadcasting rights.

After protracted negotiations with the Society, the BBC agreed that under the talks contract repeat fees should be paid for repeat broadcasts, but at cut rates. But it appropriated the right to record the talk in the Transcription Service—3 broadcasts from every transmitting station in the world for three years from date of recording—all in return for a single fee of about 3 guineas.

High-Handedness in Negotiations with Authors

Any attempt by an author to negotiate over terms tended to be treated by the BBC's contract and fee-paying departments (not the producers) as a presumption. Although persistence sometimes extracted a better fee, the author had to be prepared to fight inch by inch for every penny and risk the arbitrary cancellation of the programme and rejection of his future work.

The Society then stated its terms:

Fair fees, in return for a properly limited licence in conformity with established editorial and publishing practice, no free option to publish in the BBC's journals other than at rates comparable to those paid by reputable publications, free negotiation over terms without threat or dictation, and any offer of fee and contract to reach the author well *before* the date of the broadcast.

The Society concluded:

Preparations have already been made for a wide boycott should the BBC persist in its refusal to recognise the existence of a state of affairs which has repeatedly been brought to its attention and has now been made fully public. If such a boycott is imposed, authors will be notified of the date on and after

which they should decline to have further dealings with the
BBC.

In short this was a real threat to disrupt BBC programmes by
the withdrawal of material and labour; but what differentiated
the move from similar 'strike' notices was not only that it came
from writers (itself an exceptional event outside journalism), but
that it was subscribed to by leading authors and broadcasting
personalities of the day, i.e. those at the top, thus reversing the
normal pattern of revolt by the rank and file. Moreover the
inclusion of men like J. B. Priestley, whose wartime broadcasts
had helped to herald the post-war welfare state, and the
Parliamentary activities of the popular dramatist, Edward Percy
(E. P. Smith, MP) added significantly to the protest.

The Society's action was successful. Following a high-level
meeting[21] on 29 July, the BBC came forward with the following
offer;

1. A 20 per cent increase in fees paid for specially written work
in the shape of plays, adaptations, dramatisations, features,
variety scripts, dramatico-musical works, and dramatised
schools scripts.

2. A further increase of 25 per cent in the repeat fee for talks,
bringing the repeat rate to 75 per cent for domestic services and
50 per cent for overseas—the original talks fee having already
been improved.

3. An increase from 20 per cent to 50 per cent of the original
talks fee for reproduction in *The Listener*.

4. Permission for the producer to quote an approximate fee in
his initial approach to an author.

5. The 'standard' scale of fees in force for the use of published
work on the air to be regarded as negotiable.

The Society accepted these terms at a special meeting of
members on 29 October and called off further militant action,
although negotiation in matters of detail continued—and was
protracted. Moreover the formation of the Radiowriters' Association (RWA) in December 1947—with L. du Garde Peach as

Chairman and Ted Kavanagh as his deputy—as an affiliated group within the membership of the Society, analogous to the League of Dramatists, ensured that the interests of those who wrote for radio would be continuously monitored and advanced.

The revival of BBC television after the war and the introduction of independent television in 1954–5 is described later: likewise the conflict between the Radiowriters' Association and the Screenwriters' Association over the right to represent those who wrote for television. These developments were however incidental to radiowriting, even though they came at a time when the very survival of radio as a medium began to be questioned. Yet, just as the 1820s–30s were the heyday of stagecoaching before the era of railways, so the 1950s–60s provided a wealth of opportunity for radio producers and writers, especially in the regions. I had personal experience of this.

I began my broadcasting career on 8 November 1946, all due to a fluke. I had been demobilised from the Army early in the year and was farming in a small way at Inkpen in Berkshire, working in London mid-week. Sitting in a bus one Tuesday or Wednesday morning, I spotted a BBC producer whom I had known as a fellow undergraduate at Cambridge before the war. We chatted, and I told him I had submitted a talk to the BBC but supposed it had vanished without trace, if only because of the insignificance of the subject. What was it about? I replied: 'Inkpen Parish Council, of which I was elected chairman last March, what its powers and limitations are, and what we are doing despite our lowly estate.' He promised to look into the matter, and that—I thought—was the end of that. Not at all. Within a week I had a telephone call. The script had been found and approved, subject to normal editing at rehearsal, and I was booked to broadcast it live on the Home Service at the plum time of 9.15 pm, immediately after the News, on the following Friday. I was both elated and petrified. I barely slept the next two nights, learned the whole thing by heart, gargled repeatedly against 'frogs' in the throat, and rang up all my friends and relatives about the forthcoming event. By the grace of God the talk went off splendidly, thanks to the expert tutelage of the producer, Donald Boyd, and to the fact that I am blessed with a resonant voice that comes over well on the air. This—after an interval of two years when I moved westward into full-scale farming near Dulverton in Somerset—was the beginning of a dozen or more years of regular freelancing on BBC radio at Bristol and in London, much of it in collaboration with Robert Waller, himself a talented author and one of an imaginative band of producers[22] who helped make the West of England an outstanding regional service.

I was never in the front rank of freelances, not like A. G. Street, Ralph Wightman, Ralph Whitlock or John Cherrington, who belonged to the West Country by birth or long residence, and became household names on the air; but I find, on looking back at old scripts and accounts, that I broadcast frequently enough to earn over £500 p.a. from radio alone in most years; and that was not only a considerable sum of money in those days, but an invaluable supplement to scratching a living on a 130-acre hillside farm on the edge of Exmoor. Of course at the outset, like all beginners, I was delighted to be paid anything at all; but once in the saddle, and once I had begun to earn money from other media as well, such as books and journalism, I became wiser, joined the Radiowriters' Association, and pressed my producer for the best terms I could get or that he could get for me. Even so, until the late 1950s, except for occasional additional payments for research, my rate of remuneration rarely moved above the basic 21s to 25s a minute air time, plus the current terms for repeats and publication in BBC journals.

At first I concentrated on one subject—the village—its history, institutions, recreation, sources of income (farming, forestry, small industries, retail trade, etc.), its people, and its future. It was—and indeed still is—a rich subject that appealed to a very wide audience, not only nostalgically (always a factor in a highly urbanised country like ours), but practically too: for this was a period when post-war Governments passed a succession of important laws relating to rural planning, land use, farm support, National Parks, and other related subjects, in an effort to re-invigorate the economy of the countryside and conserve the diminishing stock of valuable agricultural land and fine land-scape. I wrote, edited or chaired four or five series on village and country life, each of about six programmes, for the West of England Home Service, Forces Educational Broadcasting, and the

East European Service at Bush House. I had a regular slot on Woman's Hour for a number of years and, besides this, poured out a variety of talks on subjects ranging from milk recording to haymaking, church interiors, eccentric parsons, dialect, forgotten rural writers, a water mill, waymarking, a tramp over Exmoor, all kinds of customs and festivals, and soil evaluation. Book reviewing was a regular commitment, as was participation in debates, discussions, quizzes and, in 1955–6 a panel game about local lore called 'County Count', for which I chaired over 30 programmes, all recorded at the Playhouse Theatre, Charing Cross, where my most exacting task was to warm up the audience beforehand. I hated having to do that!

Once typecast as an expert on village life, it was very hard to break into new territory; but thanks largely to Robert Waller I was given a change of diet now and then. Waller ran a lively series called 'Apollo in the West', devoted to contemporary arts activities and the artistic heritage of the region. I took part in several programmes and met some interesting contributors, some of them well known or who have made their mark since: among them the critics, Colin MacInnes and D. S. Savage; the poet, Charles Causley; the dramatists, R. H. Ward and Ronald Ducan; the naturalist and novelist, Henry Williamson; the historian, E. W. Martin; and an ex-farm worker, who wrote about country life and work with all the force and articulate expression of experience, Norman Goodland. One of the most effective programmes was called The Glastonbury Romance, which I devised and broadcast with Geoffrey Sale, then headmaster of King's School, Bruton. It lasted the best part of an hour, made up of a central theme narrating the history and legends, illustrated with short dramatised scenes spoken by actors, and punctuated with excerpts from Wagner's Parsifal, Gregorian chants, and Parry's Jerusalem. It had all the ingredients of a rich plum cake and we really let ourselves go. The mystique of Glastonbury is so strong that you can't really miss, and the listeners loved it. The programme got a very high rating!

Glastonbury was the link to another 'Apollo' programme, devoted to the work of Rutland Boughton, already mentioned as the composer of The Immortal Hour, who had inspired the Glastonbury Festival of music from 1914 to 1925. My collaborator was Reginald Nettel, the music critic, and together we visited the old composer, long living in retirement near Newent in Gloucestershire. We found him, as expected, to be at heart a William Morris-type Socialist, with rather a pathetic belief in the heavenly prospects of Communism: but, in character, a man of strength, with a crusading gleam in his eye when he spoke of past experiences. He broadcast well and we imported the actor, Denis McCarthy, to take the part of Bernard Shaw who had been one of Boughton's strongest supporters. I also interviewed Roger Clark, head of the shoe-making family at Street, who had acted as treasurer to the Festival and stood loyally by Boughton during all the rows that had characterised the Glastonbury enterprise. Musically it was a feast and a considerable undertaking for the West of England but, with the help of four soloists, the West of England Singers and Light Orchestra, conducted by Reginald Redman, we performed two oboe pieces and parts of *The Immortal Hour, Alkestis, Bethlehem* and *Galahad*, the latter a hitherto unperformed music drama in the cycle of five that Boughton had written around the Arthurian legends.

To conclude this digression. By the late 1950s I was beginning to lose touch with Bristol. Waller and certain other producers, such as Gilbert Phelps, with whom I had worked happily, had all left. In 1959 I sold my farm near Dulverton and migrated to London to work part-time for the Society of Authors, and continue broadcasting—mostly for Bush House. I was also deep in a 15-year assignment with Dartington Hall, where the Trustees had commissioned me to write the whole history of the enterprise—a complex collection of commercial, educational, and amenity undertakings, loosely linked by the social and personal ideals of the founders, Leonard and Dorothy Elmhirst—and set up a records office at the same time. That is altogether another story,[23] but it had started back in 1951 when the BBC had given me the job of writing a 50-minute programme about the place, with Robert Waller and Alan Gibson as co-producers. It was eventually transmitted on the West of England Home service. There was no repeat that I can recollect, except a shortened version for the Third Programme. The fees totalled less than £100 plus expenses; but it gave me the chance later, as mentioned, to write the full story, and salve the essential documents, of the boldest and most comprehensive private enterprise in rural reconstruction that has ever been attempted in Britain.

Although, throughout the whole history of broadcasting, writers have had to make extraordinary efforts to achieve even the most minimal improvements in fees and conditions, there was no doubt about the importance of the confrontation in 1947 between the Society of Authors and the BBC, and the formation of the Radiowriters' Association as a constituent body of the Society, devoted to the interests of scriptwriters and broadcasters. The Radiowriters' Association made an immediate impact, with a membership rapidly approaching 400, a lively and distinguished executive committee,[24] and an efficient secretary in the person of Helen Lehmann.[25] Day-to-day problems and complaints by members were regularly taken up by a permanent panel[26] while, however difficult the going, the Association never ceased to prosecute its two main aims: to improve fees and conditions; and forcefully to present its views in any major discussion about the structure and policy of the BBC and the behaviour of its departments.

One such opportunity arose in 1949, when the Government appointed Lord Beveridge to chair a committee on the future of broadcasting and invited comments from interested parties. The Radiowriters' Association promptly canvassed the opinions of its members, the majority of whom had no doubt that the virtues of public service broadcasting were heavily outweighed by the defects. It was Lord Acton's aphorism, in adaptation, all over again. Not that 'power tends to corrupt . . .' but that monopoly tends to generate complacency and arrogance. Such was the conclusion of many experienced broadcasters based on the plain fact that the radiowriter had no alternative to the BBC.

> His material is seldom of use in another medium. And, if, for any number of reasons, his material is unacceptable at the fount of broadcasting, his stock there not unnaturally falls and any scripts he offers may suffer from that handicap. In short, there is what is called a permanent buyer's market in radio scripts. . .[27]

This raised the whole question of competitive broadcasting. The Radiowriters' Association did not advocate sponsored programmes to the exclusion of the BBC, but suggested that the whole subject be re-examined in the light of technical advances, which would make possible the provision of alternative stations, be they independent and commercial, or truly autonomous under the aegis of the BBC. Another point—never settled—related to the gap between staff producers and payers.

> It often happens that work is commissioned, written, and even broadcast before the author hears anything from the Copyright Department, or knows what he is to be paid; and if he delayed in order to learn the full terms of his contract, the script, especially of a talk or topical feature, would often be out of date . . . If the producer, who is given an over-all financial allocation for each feature, were authorised to discuss fees, the author would not be left in the dark.[28]

The Beveridge Report, published in 1951, did *not* however recommend competitive broadcasting, but expressed the opposite view that the BBC should remain a monopoly, although it did hint at the possibility of local broadcasting under BBC licence. The Radiowriters' Association had therefore to be content with the *status quo*; but, within that limitation, and stimulated no doubt by all the public interest generated by the enquiry, the BBC did a great deal to improve the cultural and technical quality of radio during the 1950s. It devoted the Third Programme to serious music, prose, poetry and drama, and fully justified its minority appeal by the standards set and by the opening offered to the then obscure talents of writers such as Dylan Thomas, Louis MacNeice, Giles Cooper, Harold Pinter and many others. In short the Third contributed significantly to the cultural life of the country. Again the increasing use of magnetic tape (replacing the cumbrous cutting of discs) gave writers and producers far greater flexibility in mounting programmes; while the introduction in 1955 of very high frequency (VHF) transmissions made it possible to listen free of interference.

These advances came however at a time when television was rapidly gaining ground. By 1958 the total of combined radio/TV licences had forged ahead of those issued for radio alone by about a million a year,[29] and the ultimate survival of radio as a medium was continually being questioned. Even so, although by then television had captured the bulk of the evening public, radio still ruled the daytime and, for the time being, listening figures remained remarkably stable. In 1958, for instance, some 20 million people were listening to radio every day, while 22 million viewed TV. The BBC sustained an annual output of over 300 radio plays, while *Saturday Night Theatre* continued to attract an audience of 10 million. Add to that the perennial popularity of radio news bulletins, quizzes, magazine-type programmes, prose readings, and much else—quite apart from music, radio's strongest card—and it will be seen that sound was in many respects still holding its own. It was also of course far cheaper to operate than television.

On the other hand the anticipated decline of radio was not all due to the rival attractions of television. As Helen Lehmann pointed out in 1960, when she retired after twelve years as Secretary of the Radiowriters' Association, the BBC had only itself to blame owing to its continuing refusal to pay writers properly and to recognise in hard cash the value of their work as the prime source of broadcasting material.[30] During her icumbency—despite constant pressure—the minimum rate for talks had only risen from 1 guinea to $1\frac{1}{2}$ guineas per minute, while that for drama had barely moved at all. It was true that experienced writers (in radio or any other medium) were usually able to secure better terms, so that in practice the minimum rate applied only to newcomers. This forced the BBC to make some concessions to reality and institute the two-tier system of payment—for Beginners and Established. Even so it compared very unfavourably not only with television rates but, for example, with national freelance rates in journalism, and failed therefore to attract the quality of writing that the *genre* deserved. For that reason the standard argument advanced by BBC negotiators—when facing writers' representatives—that the Corporation could only pay 'what the market would bear' was self-defeating.

I do not propose to describe the events of the following 21 years (1960–81, when this chapter ends) in any detail, but rather to try to discern some pattern in what happened and in what became of radiowriting during that time.

First, as to policy. In 1960 the Government appointed a committee, chaired by Sir Harry Pilkington—more or less on the lines of Beveridge a decade earlier—to investigate the state of broadcasting and make recommendations, a number of which were duly implemented. This new report, published in 1962, concentrated in the main on television—a second channel for the BBC, colour, 625-line definition, etc.—but what it said about radio was no less important, for it saved sound broadcasting, at any rate for the time being. While declaring that there was no need to add to the national network, it re-stated the principle that broadcasting should be *comprehensive* in character and thus ensure a place for minority as well as for majority tastes.[31] This was reassuring, and the declaration stood the BBC in good stead when the Corporation ran short of money a few years later and had to make economies, though not seriously at the expense of sound. By 1969 the financial crisis had arrived, due partly to rising inflation, but more importantly to the failure of the Government to increase licence fees sufficiently or in time. The situation was reflected in a policy document issued by the BBC, entitled *Broadcasting in the Seventies* which, in proposing a re-organisation of sound programmes, appeared at first to confirm the radiowriters' worst fears. In fact sound came out of it very well, although no notice was taken of Pilkington's sensible criticism of the segregation of programmes into Home, Light and Third, as if all listeners were strictly separated into middle, low and high brows, without inter-connection. In the end the new pattern was, in essence, a repetition of the old—with, broadly, Radio One and Radio Two taking care of pop and sweet music, chat and quizzes and a few other popular programmes, Radio Three dedicated to serious music (classical and jazz) and some ten hours of speech (talks, plays, poetry) per week, and Radio Four devoted to news, current affairs, plays, some music, and a variety of speech programmes. It was the year's vintage in old bottles but carrying new labels.

Pilkington had also recommended that a trial be given—by the BBC only—to local sound broadcasting, i.e. to set up radio stations in selected provincial towns, transmitting programmes of purely local interest for a few hours a day. The idea was approved by the Government in 1967, prompted partly by the inroads of pirate radio ships in the North Sea. The BBC started work at once and planned to cover most of the country with about 40 stations; but, after the Conservatives were returned to power in 1970, commercial radio was introduced. The Independent Television

Authority (ITA) became the Independent Broadcasting Authority (IBA), and the local radio market was allotted to both organisations. At the start local radio offered very little indeed to freelance writers, other than a handful of journalists and disc jockeys, in terms of cash or opportunities. Programmes were stiflingly parochial: the kind of news and chat already provided— and better provided—by the local press. Gradually the situation improved. Negotiations for minimum terms and conditions began—at any rate with the BBC, for the Association of Independent Radio Contractors (AIRC) dug defences at once. It was however a good sign that a handful of local programmes won places in the annual awards scheme organised by the Society of Authors and Pye Ltd., and this gave encouragement to companies like Capital Radio to develop an output of drama, both adaptations and original scripts.[32] Indeed it seemed that until local radio (BBC or otherwise) made perceptible advances in terms of quality, it had little chance of establishing a recognisable identity, and thus of commanding support. Such advances depended upon an increase in resources of staff and programme finance, without which most stations were unable to do much more than duplicate network transmissions and rely on second-rate talent for their own restricted output.

Perhaps this was the conclusion contained in the proposal to set up a Local Broadcasting Authority, advanced by the Annan Report in March 1977, whereby the new Authority would take responsibility for all local radio stations with the object of supplying the whole population with at least one local radio service. The idea was not adopted and maybe, unlike its predecessors, Beveridge and Pilkington, Lord Annan's Committee[33] wanted to invent too many Authorities. Whereas it proposed leaving the BBC alone (minus its local radio), it would have downgraded the IBA into a Regional Television Authority, and set up not only a Local Broadcasting Authority but an Open Broadcasting Authority as well to run the Fourth Television Channel. This proposal, along with many other of its 500 or so recommendations, was negatived or ignored; but, as explained later, it was to be the creation of the Fourth Channel, plus the prospects for satellite TV and cable transmission that engaged public attention after 1981.

The principal conclusion from this brief review of policy from

1960 to 1981 is that, so far as radio was concerned, the BBC retained its traditional position, virtually intact, as the main source of radio and thus as the chief patron of radiowriting. Without question it stood in a class by itself by comparison with commercial radio in the UK and with foreign radio services, in terms of quantity, quality and variety of listening, transmitted by its four national channels, 30 local stations, and its phalanx of external services. Furthermore, despite criticism from within and without, despite neglect of its very existence in the periodical press, and despite the attractions of television which threatened at times to overwhelm 'steam radio', it had not only kept radio in being but gone far towards confirming, for instance, radio drama as a *genre* with a future as well as a past.[34] At the same time it did not eradicate the fear that, when money was short, radio would always be treated as the poor relation of television and be the first to suffer.[35]

One area in which radio has offered frequent and continuing opportunities to the freelance is that of education, interpreted in its broadest sense, either as direct teaching of school pupils and students, or as indirect instruction of adults who like learning, even though they may not be aware of it. This means that in either case educational programming requires the services of specialists: either professional teachers who combine broadcasting with their normal teaching duties, or others (often ex-teachers) who devote their lives to writing, lecturing and broadcasting about, say, the humanities or certain practical skills. The educational field is enormous both in radio and television but with this qualification. Whereas in radio it is widely accessible to freelances, in television freelancing is severely restricted and mainly confined to consultancy—a point discussed on p. 292.

Bearing in mind the commanding control of radio exercised by the BBC, and the fact that every advance in fees has had to be fought for from the beginning from a position of weakness, it is a tribute to the skill of generations of writers' representatives and to their insistence, in latter years, on annual negotiations, that the rates in one or other category of radio scripting and broadcasting have been kept on the move. Whereas 20 years previously the rate for a scripted talk by an established broadcaster had been one and a half guineas a minute, while a 90-minute radio play earned at best about 150 guineas, the following examples of minimum rates in force with the BBC in 1980–81 show what was achieved in the difficult circumstances described, and in the face of inflation that at one time approached 30 per cent per year.

1980–81

	Established	Beginners
Radio Drama (specially written)	£15 per minute	£9.50 per minute

A 60-minute play, taking say six months to write and produce, would yield respectively £900 and £570.

For a *Schools* programme	£10.50—£11.50 per minute	£9.50 per minute

Radio Talks and Features (per minute)
Script and reading £8.20, reading only £6.05, illustrated talks £6.35, features £9.50 (with a minimum of £66.50). Interviews (all radio rights contract) £22.60 (talks requisition contract), £20–£28 according to duration up to 15 minutes, fully negotiable thereafter.

Use of Published Material (per minute)
Plays £4.95, prose £4.65, poems £4.95 (per ½ minute), prose for dramatisation £3.80.

Repeats were generally remunerated at 75 per cent of the original fee.

At times agents have made excellent terms for their clients, while individual writers of eminence have on occasions done no less well for themselves alone; but as regards collective negotiations, the main burden has fallen on the Society of Authors,[36] joined in 1968 by the Writers' Guild[37] for radio drama negotiations. In that year the Society attempted unsuccessfully to form a consortium in order to negotiate with one voice over a large part of radiowriting. But the BBC was adamant in its opposition. By only recognising separate organisations (singly or in small groups) for separate categories of broadcasting (the Society and the Guild for radio drama; the Society, the Association of Broadcasting Staffs (ABS) and the National Union of Journalists (NUJ) for talks, features and documentaries;[38] the

Society and Publishers Association for the use of published material), the Corporation retained its commanding position in every negotiation. Categorisation induces fragmentation—and weakness.

Like most other forms of authorship, radiowriting was and remains a highly vulnerable activity. With a very few exceptions, no writer could expect to make a living out of it. At the rates quoted, he or she would have to write and have produced, for example, six one-hour plays a year to make a modest income—a practical and spiritual impossibility. Further, however 'established' he might be, no radiowriter could ever rely on continuing employment, in contrast, say, to a producer or other member of the BBC staff with an assured salary, regularly increased, and who enjoyed occupational pension rights and the hidden benefits of office services. Radio remains a part-time medium, even for the expert.

CHAPTER ELEVEN

Screen–Cinema

Early films and film makers. USA gains early lead. Copyright protection. Cecil Raleigh's advice. Investigations by sub-committee of Society of Authors in 1914. Rex Beach on writing for films in USA in 1918. Film rights and film deals in the 1920s. Scott Fitzgerald's experience as a screenwriter. American dominance of British market in 1920s. Films Act, 1927. Rise of British 'verticals'. Impact of the 'talkies' after 1927. Boom in British film industry in 1930s. Alexander Korda and others. Slump in 1938. Films Act, 1938. Salaried screenwriters in Hollywood. US writers' fight for recognition. Screenwriters' Association founded under Society of Authors' auspices in 1937. Screenwriting in 1939. Documentary films in Britain. British film making in the Second World War. Rise of Arthur Rank. Reports on the film industry. Currency restrictions on film imports in 1947. Anglo-American Agreement, 1948. Films Act, 1948. National Film Finance Corporation. Reports on production, distribution and exhibition. Some British films post-war. Ealing Studios. Balcon, Danischewsky, Tibby Clarke. US anti-trust legislation in 1948. Emergence of conglomerates. Drastic fall in cinema attendances. New patterns of film making by end of 1950s. 'New wave' of British films. Woodfall and others. Film censorship. Williams Report, 1979. Further Films Acts. Steep drop in British film production by 1981. Film finance, film rights and remuneration of screenwriting in early 1980s.

Already by the early 1900s, the cinema was becoming a force in entertainment both in America and Europe. Britain produced some notable pioneers: William Friese-Greene, a controversial figure, who had patented a primitive movie camera in 1889 but who did not—it is generally agreed—fulfil the claim of being 'the inventor of kinematography'; Robert Paul, a scientific instrument maker who, in 1895, began making films in his own workshop—both he and Birt Acres, another cameraman, filmed a number of public events (including the Derby, and the opening of the Kiel Canal), and produced numerous 'shorts'; while W. K. Dickson (Thomas Edison's assistant) and E. J. Muybridge, both Englishmen, were active in the United States. The first films were curiosities, lasting only a few minutes (action or trick shots etc.) and appeared as items in music hall programmes, in shows organised at skating rinks and fairgrounds, and in converted shops. Their attraction however was powerful, since it cost only a few pence to see them, and they provided novelty, glamour, and frequent changes of programme.[1]

It is not surprising therefore that, by about 1908 (just over a decade after the first public film show), custom-built 'picture palaces' were being put up, presenting full-length programmes of films. At the same time the tripartite structure of the industry was fast taking shape, namely, the film maker or producer, the renter or distributor, and the exhibitor or cinema owner. By this time too the practice of hiring out films was beginning to replace that of outright sale, and reflected the growth of full-length feature films which, by reason of their cost, had become too expensive for an exhibitor to buy, and needed new measures to finance them.

Before the First World War a number of British film firms were already making their mark: for instance, the London Film Company, and the Hepworth Film Company. Cecil Hepworth was a prolific and inventive producer who re-created classics (Dickens was popular) on the screen, and tried to establish a corps of native film stars (Alma Taylor and Stewart Rome, among them). But although Hepworth survived the war as a film maker, likewise George Pearson, another notable pioneer,[2] already by 1914 it was clear that America had begun to lead the field. Thereafter, thanks partly to the absence of competition from war-torn Europe, partly to the abundance of money, natural energy and talent, and partly to the domination of the industry by a handful of powerful entrepreneurs, this lead was soon transformed into a near-monopoly of the world market.

It was a development that, only partially for reasons of a common language, was felt most severely in Britain and other

English-speaking countries; but there were other factors. One was the need to keep British cinemas (already about 4,000 of them) supplied with feature films once or twice a week, a demand that only large-scale American production could satisfy. A second factor arose out of the first. Because of demand, exhibitors found themselves in thrall to distributors who insisted either on 'block booking' (i.e. reserving screen time for months ahead), or, worse still, 'blind booking' (i.e. reservation, but without knowing which films were being booked, indeed some of them had still to be made). A third factor was that British cinemagoers were becoming so conditioned to American film entertainment that they were coming to prefer it—the stars, the life styles, Westerns, epics and fantasies of luxurious living and purple romance. Such was the background of events until the late 1920s, before the advent of sound and the introduction of a quota for British-made films,[3] which helped generate a revival of the native film industry.

What of the writers? Most early scripts or scenarios were no more than story outlines or notes for a sequence of shots; likewise the captions or titles essential to dialogue and continuity in a silent film. These were often worked out on the spot, sometimes by the producer or director himself (who might well be the same individual),[4] or contributed by an outside writer and paid for outright on an output basis.[5] However as films lengthened, and as audiences began to demand something more sophisticated than engaging tricks and crude drama, producers began to adapt published material for the screen, usually classical or popular fiction.

For a time, copyright owners felt threatened by a number of court decisions affirming that the cinema performance of a work did not infringe dramatic rights. In other words, although there was an element of risk, film makers were free to make use of original material without licence or payment. This anomaly was corrected in Britain by the 1911 Copyright Act which defined film rights and placed them firmly under the protection of the law. In the United States it formed the subject of an important case that went through the courts in 1911–12 and again in 1916 and concerned a film version of General Lew Wallace's novel, *Ben Hur*.

The defendant [the Kalem Company] employed a man to read

Ben Hur and to write out such a description or scenario of certain portions that it could be followed in action . . . It then caused the action to be performed, and took negatives for moving pictures of the scenes, from which it produced films suitable for exhibition . . . It advertised them under the title 'Ben Hur'. 'Scenery and Supers by Pain's Fireworks Co. Costumes from the Metropolitan Opera House. Chariot Race by 3rd Battery, Brooklyn. Positively the Most Superb Moving Picture Spectacle ever Produced in America. In Sixteen Magnificent Scenes, etc'.[6]

In both instances the case went against the film company, so that thenceforward authors or other owners of published works in copyright felt reasonably safe, although plenty of trouble lay in store as to the security of scenarios and the plagiarism of ideas.

By this time the new medium was becoming respectable and attractive to the writing profession. Frequent articles appeared in *The Author*, and in trade papers such as *The Bioscope*, encouraging authors to write for the cinema and advising them how to do it. For instance Cecil Raleigh, actor and dramatist, outlined practically every aspect of film making and presentation.[7] After describing film as a 'long piece of celluloid gelatine, 100 to 2,000 feet in length, covered with photographs . . . passed very rapidly through the camera', he warned that 'set words for the characters to speak are useless. The facts should be written out in exactly the same way that a ballet is written. The *facts* and the *emotions* only should be stated.'

Gretchen is sitting Centre reading her lover's letter by the aid of a candle. Suddenly the door Right is thrown open, and her father enters. Gretchen springs up in surprise, holding her lover's letter in her left hand, which she hides behind her. Her father eyes her sternly. He throws down his rifle, flings from his shoulder the dead chamois that he has brought from his hunting, and casts aside his cape. He comes down stage and for a moment eyes her critically. He holds out his right hand as though to say 'Show me what is in your hand'. She holds out her right hand before him. He shakes his head and demands the other hand. Very reluctantly she holds out her left hand from which, with a quick gesture of anger, he snatches her lover's

[243]

letter. He reads it and turns fiercely upon his daughter who falls back to the table Left.

'The moving picture story is told,' he concluded, 'not by beautiful and well-chosen words, but by dramatic and expressive gestures.'

Raleigh then speculated on what an author might expect to earn from a film. There were several alternative methods of payment: so much (1s?) per foot run of the film (this had obvious disadvantages, as length was no criterion of quality), outright sale of rights, or best of all some scheme comparable to publishing practice, i.e. a royalty on gross income with an initial advance.

It will be found that . . . £400 on account of 10 per cent [of the gross] is rather high, and can only be secured by authors with very well-known names. £100 down on account of five per cent is quite fair remuneration either in this country or America . . . In America it is said that everybody writes moving picture plots, and that their price is $2. In this country endless plots have been written for £2 and £3 a piece. But this period is passing away . . . I know of several instances in which dramatists have sold moving picture rights of their plays for £200. That looked like becoming a standard price, but competition luckily brought an advance. Not long ago an author received £500 for the entire rights in a play, and more recently an author with a worldwide reputation received £750 on account of a percentage of the gross.

One film contract dated 27 June 1914 between Zenith Films and Nita Morris, concering what was described as 'the Prehistoric Play' entitled *Before our Time*, offered rather less favourable terms to the author, who was required:

1. to write a complete scenario of the play, assist in the production, and grant all rights worldwide to the company.

2. to provide free of charge eighteen pretty girls and six young men to take part in the said production and 'positively travel' to Portland or any other suitable place selected by the company by train on July 4th or 5th. Surprisingly, the company was

willing to pay the rail fares and provide food, and would 'if possible find accommodation for all, but, in the event of suitable accommodation not being found . . . one and all will have to camp out as best they can and regard the conditions in the light of a picnic holiday outing'.

3. to accept an advance of £20 and a royalty of 10 per cent of the *net* profits.

And Ms Morris actually signed the agreement!

In October 1914 the Society of Authors appointed a Cinema Sub-Committee[8] consisting of R. C. Carton, Basil Dean, James B. Fagan, W. L. George, Max Pemberton, and Dr Marie Stopes, with Edgar Jepson as Chairman. This group instituted an enquiry into film fees and contracts, while in 1915 Marie Stopes undertook to circularise members of the Society about educational films. The response was disappointing; but one respondent (a professor of surgery) stated that he used film regularly for research purposes. This elicited the further question as to why an author should not make his own film and hire it out, rather than write a paper for a professional society or journal with a limited circulation and indeterminate results. Most members favoured the idea of using films for communication, or as an aid to teaching, but in all cases cost was found to be prohibitive. A few considered that even serious films on scientific subjects ('the examination of the stomach under X-rays') would do harm by 'forestalling mental effort'; while one writer (Ivy Low) thought that films were replacing reading and accounted for a great increase in the use of spectacles. She also doubted whether there was any real demand for the 'picture palace', ascribing the habit to a lack of alternatives.

I think people go to the 'movies' simply because there is no other way of filling in odd half-hours, nowhere else to take their girls.

As to the degrading atmosphere of many of the picture palaces, the ugliness of the whole thing, not even the frequent use of such words as 'clean', 'refined', 'wholesome', by a certain firm, not all the cant talked on the yellow posters in all the tube stations in London, can slur over this shame to our towns.[9]

Attacks of this kind, and Marie Stopes's conclusion that the cinema 'is in the main a power prostituted', were vigorously rebutted by the editor of *The Bioscope*.

The marvel to most people is not that there have been so many bad films, but that there have been so many fine ones.
    For example, *Cabiria, The Birth of a Nation*, and *Quo Vadis*.

As to the cinema as an educational force, the editor quoted Bernard Shaw:

The cinematograph begins educating people when the projection lantern begins clicking, and does not stop until it leaves off. Whether it is showing you what the South Pole ice barrier is like through the films of Mr Ponting, or making you silly and sentimental by pictorial novelettes, it is educating you all the time. And it is educating you far more effectively when you think it is only amusing you than when it is avowedly instructing you in the habits of lobsters.[10]

Acceptance of the cinema's potential, artistic and academic, was clearly neither automatic nor immediate, despite its undoubted fascination as a medium of entertainment. To break this barrier, film companies published lists of well-known authors whose works they had adapted for the screen. As early as 1915, for example, the Famous Players Company (later Paramount) listed the names of James Barrie, Hall Caine, Henry Arthur Jones and Thomas Hardy; and similar lists were issued by other companies. Yet it was a common criticism, both in the USA and UK, that far too many producers relied on a staff of hacks to cobble up plots, and that whenever they relied on a freelance writer of repute, they so mutilated his adaptation that it seriously damaged the original.

This led Rex Beach, chairman of the Motion-Picture Committee of the Authors' League of America, to review the whole business of writing for films, as matters stood towards the end of 1918. He spared neither authors nor producers.

> The first mistake of authors has been in refusing to treat the industry seriously and in considering motion-picture money as a mere side issue and as an easy pick-up ... There are few writers who do not understand in a general way what it costs to publish a book and what a successful sale means in copies and in dollars and cents. There are few playwrights who cannot tell you what it costs to produce a play and what constitutes good box office business, also how royalties are computed ... but there are not more than half-a-dozen writers who can form even an approximate estimate of the cost of making a five- or seven-reel photoplay, the cost of advertising, exploitation and distribution, or the average earning capacity of a successful feature: or who know whether, in case of a royalty contract, the author's royalty is based on gross box office receipts, gross film rentals, or gross receipts of the producer.
> How can you ask or get a fair price for your goods if you don't know what they are worth?

He then turned to the producer.

> I refer to the theft of ideas, to the systematic and well-organised piracy that goes on in some offices. If a producer fails to pay over your royalties, you can hale him into court ... But when he steals your story and rewrites it ... you face a different proposition ... To the average motion picture producer all the vast realm that lies between the covers, whether magazine or book, is a no man's land into which he can send his picked squads of scenario editors and continuity writers to mutilate the living and despoil the dead.[11]

The fact was that film rights were a commodity that had to be bargained for in a market where, in most instances, the buyer was the stronger party. Even so, while many writers parted with their properties for a miserable sum or, as Rex Beach complained, were robbed of them altogether, a minority with established reputations did good business: thanks usually to a shrewd agent and their own ability to stand their ground financially.

In 1920, for example, Somerset Maugham sold a script to Jesse Lasky and Samuel Goldwyn for $15,000, a deal that prompted him to comment, 'I look back on my connection with the cinema world with horror mitigated only by fifteen thousand dollars.' He changed his opinion later. In 1923 his short story, *Rain*—dramatised by other hands and staged on Broadway the previous year—fetched $150,000, of which Maugham received 25 per cent. Three films were subsequently made of this famous tale, which eventually earned more than a million dollars.[12]

Another example concerned Ibañez's *The Four Horsemen of the Apocalypse*, filmed in 1921

> . . . the competitive bidding between companies ended with Ibanez accepting $20,000 and a 10 per cent royalty from Metro. An expert screenwriter, June Mathis, was put on to the work of scripting a film which some members of the company felt would be a flop because war-subjects were at this period supposed to be unpopular. When the film was discovered to be an outstanding success, the 10 per cent royalty proved an embarrassment, and Ibañez was persuaded to sell his interest outright for a further $170,000. Had he stuck to his contract he would have earned $400,000.[13]

Films played an important part in the life of another well-known fiction writer. For about a dozen years after 1920, F. Scott Fitzgerald depended mainly for his living on short stories contributed to the *Saturday Evening Post, Scribner's*, and other popular American magazines, and on a handful of novels. During this time his agent forced his fees up from $40 to $4,000 per story, so that at his peak Fitzgerald was earning $30,000 a year from this genre alone. Some of the stories were turned into films, and in 1926 the rights of his best known full-length work, *The Great Gatsby*, fetched $16,000. In the same year he received an offer from Hollywood of $12,000 for a ten-week assignment to work on scripts. The deal foundered, as did another in 1932, but five years later he completed an 18-month stint as a scriptwriter for Metro-Goldwyn-Mayer which provides a vivid illustration of the human pressures and problems involved.

Fitzgerald's job lasted from July 1937 to January 1939, and he was paid an initial salary of $1,000 a week.

His first job was the relatively easy one of polishing up the script of *A Yank at Oxford*, soon to be filmed in England with Robert Taylor in the title role. He contributed several new scenes, made some changes in the rest of the dialogue, and then devoted the rest of July to reading over the scripts of some recent M-G-M hits and having them shown in the studio theater. In August, he was given his first major assignment, the preparation of a 'treatment' of Erich Maria Remarque's recent novel, *Three Comrades*. In a treatment, the writer was expected to reduce to straightforward expository narrative the main story line that he felt should be followed in making the film. Metro was notorious for its practice (introduced by Irving Thalberg) of hiring several different writers to prepare independent treatments of the same film. Afterwards, at a series of conferences, they would all get together with the film's producer, and the best parts (presumably) of each treatment would be salvaged. Then a team of writers (not necessarily the ones who had written the treatments) would be ordered to weave this material into a final script. Suspecting that some such system was being used for *Three Comrades*, Fitzgerald begged Joe Mankiewicz, the producer, to let him go ahead on his own and turn his treatment into a full-dress script. He felt, quite rightly, that the expository form of treatment would not do justice to his ideas, and that only a script of his own, complete with dialogue and detailed descriptions of settings, could convey adequately the kind of film he had in mind.

But Mankiewicz refused and 'ordered him instead to collaborate on the final script with a veteran M-G-M author, E. E. Paramore, Jr'.

Paramore knew a great deal more than Fitzgerald about the technical problems of film making. They differed radically in their views as to how the script should be written . . . and soon were quarrelling over every scene. Nonetheless, Fitzgerald restrained himself as best he could until January, when his contract was renewed at the new figure of $1,250 per week. Then he blew up, flew off angrily for a holiday . . . and sent

[249]

Mankiewicz a bitter letter . . . 'I think you now have a flop on your hands.'

On his copy of the final script, Fitzgerald noted '37 pages mine, about ⅓, but all shadows and rhythm removed' . . . Fitzgerald's treatment was original and unconventional, but it would have required an unusually talented director to turn it into a good film. The Mankiewicz–Paramore version was a much more predictable box-office success in every way.[14]

And so it proved. Fitzgerald's contract was not renewed in January 1939, and although it was not the end of his career as a scriptwriter, from then on he went rapidly downhill until his death in 1941—the victim of a disastrous marriage, alcoholism, and the destructive forces surrounding his profession.

Meanwhile no one in Britain was more aware of the value of film rights than Bernard Shaw. As early as 1922 he had told the AGM of the Society of Authors[15] how vital it was not to let them go as part of a package of all subsidiary rights. In the old days, he said, subsidiary rights were worth perhaps £50. Now, the 'cinema rights' alone of a story might be worth £10,000. He himself had been offered £20,000 a year for five years on condition that he delivered two film stories a year.

> When you are dealing with speculators in works of art there is no definite standard of honesty. An honest price for a table or a chair is its cost of production plus so much per cent profit. But there is no honest price for copyrights. When a man bargains with you for them he gambles, you gamble—and he makes the best bargain he can . . . That is not dishonest: it is the only way in which the commercial game can be played.

He had once talked 'to a great film producer who declared, probably quite sincerely, that he had no mercenary motives, and wanted to elevate people'.

'I said to him, "The difficulty is that you care for nothing but art, and I care for nothing but money".'

The producer was Samuel Goldwyn.

We must now return to considering the state of the industry. The first period of domination by Hollywood lasted until the end of 1927. During that time American films ruled the British market for the reasons already stated, and also because they were able, increasingly, to rely on a large home market to absorb most, if not all, their initial outlay, so that—once the relatively low distribution costs had been met—income from films exported abroad was additional rather than essential to the economics of the enterprise. Nor was it necessary for American producers to own British cinemas or circuits, since distribution alone gave them all the control they needed, thanks to their ability to guarantee supply and offer more attractive terms to exhibitors than their few British competitors.

Already by 1923 only about 10 per cent of feature films shown in the UK were British made; and the figure soon dropped to five per cent. It was obviously an intolerable situation from every point of view, economic, cultural and social; and although an attempt was made by the trade to correct the imbalance by voluntary action, it failed, and it was left to Parliament to pass the Cinematograph Films Act in December 1927. Familiarly known as the 'Quota Act', it required all films to be registered with the Board of Trade before being offered for hire; it abolished 'blind', and reduced 'block' booking by exhibitors; it compelled both distributors and exhibitors to accept an annual quota (on a rising scale) of British-made films based on footage; and it set up a committee to advise the Board on the administration of the Act.

The consequences of the Act were mixed. By guaranteeing an outlet, it galvanised the production of British films; and by encouraging the investment of capital in UK producing companies, it stimulated development in all sections of the industry— in film making and renting, in the construction of studios and cinemas, and in the employment of actors, actresses, directors, scriptwriters, editors, and technicians, thereby generating a boom that lasted until 1937–8.

Of significance was the rise in Britain of three large vertical combines, involved through subsidiaries and interlocking interests in all levels of the industry. These were the Gaumont-British Picture Corporation, British International Pictures (Associated British Picture Corporation), and the Odeon Group (which eventually became one of the principal planks of the Rank empire). These multipurpose organisations—making and renting films, and owning together about one-fifth of all the cinemas in the country—constituted a counterblast to Hollywood and a move towards rationalisation, although competition was never eliminated, either with the small groups and independents, or indeed with the American 'majors'.[16]

On the debit side—by making no provision as to quality or the minimum cost of producing a film, and by concentrating on length (thus omitting short films such as documentaries), the Quota Act give birth to a plethora of 'quickies'; in other words, inferior cheaply-made films produced solely to satisfy quota requirements. British examples were as bad as the American ones made in British studios, which was one way in which US interests retained a hold on the British market, additional to the fact that they continued to provide the majority of non-quota films. Another way was by financial penetration of the British 'verticals'; and yet another by the advent of a revolutionary new technique, the sound film or 'talky' in 1927. This demanded an immense outlay in new production apparatus, conversion of studios, re-equipment of cinemas, replacement of numerous silent players, and a change in the system of film hire whereby the old flat-rate charge gave way to a division of box office takings between distributor and exhibitor, much to the advantage of the former. On top of it all, patents for the new sound equipment mainly benefited the Americans.

Despite these changes and commitments, the 1930s witnessed—as explained—a vigorous revival in all departments of the film industry in Britain, which owed much to close contacts with the theatre—writers and others working in both areas. Moreover the rising reputations of directors such as Anthony Asquith and Alfred Hitchcock; the excellence of a bevy of British actors and actresses playing both in the UK and the USA, not least the popularity of comedians such as George Formby, Will Hay and Gracie Fields; the sequence of successful films produced, for example, by Michael Balcon, Victor Saville and Herbert Wilcox; above all the resounding international success of Alexander Korda's *The Private Life of Henry VIII*,[17] with Charles Laughton in the name part—all roused the hope that British films would find a permanent place in the world market.

Alas, the honeymoon did not last long.

In 1928 there were 19 stages in British studios with a total area of 105,200 square feet. By 1938 this had increased to 70 sound stages and 777,650 square feet: nearly four times as many stages and seven times as much floor space. The value of production in 1937 was just over £7 million as against £500,000 in 1928.

The peak of production was reached in the year ended March 31, 1938, when 228 British feature films were registered, but before the last film had been completed the slump had started and production during the following year was cut by more than a half . . . The chief cause of the slump was over-investment . . .[18]

And, it should be added, inflated costs of production, an excessive share of the 'take' going to the distributors, and inability to capture an adequate share of the American market, which ultimately undermined the confidence of investors.

Parliament then had to step in again with a fresh Cinematograph Films Act, 1938, which revised the quota percentages and calculations, found a place for short films, and introduced a minimum cost test of £7,500 per film based on labour charges. In short the Act maintained the principle of protection though without finding—by means of a subsidy or other alternative—any stable system of financing film production, which had hitherto depended on City backing, with ultimately fatal results. An early outcome of the Act was to extend American film production in British studios; but the year was 1938 and money in Britain was wanted for next year's war.

What had happened to the screenwriter?

Whatever the merits of silent scripts, the introduction of sound to film making created a new category of imaginative writing.[19] In the first flush, sound was exploited for its sheer novelty; hence the success of popular stage plays (plenty of dialogue), of action-packed stories about gangsters and cowboys, and of musicals directed by men like Ernst Lubitsch. But that was only the beginning. Although it was proudly announced that it was now possible to transfer 'the full flavour of great works to the screen', it was in fact no longer a case of simply transferring a work from one medium to another, but of developing a technique specifically suited to the requirements of both sight and sound, whether the plot was an original or an adaptation. And that, in turn, demanded intimate collaboration between writer and director throughout all the component stages: basic plot, treatment, screenplay, shooting script, and ultimate editing in the cutting room. Notwithstanding everything contributed by everyone else (producer, players, technicians, *et al.*), the writer and the director had of necessity to be the prime creators of the identity and quality of any film.

In Hollywood in the early days a script department of salaried writers was attached to each studio; hence the origin of the term, 'the writers' row' or 'the writers' block', i.e. a team of scripters sitting like secretaries in their offices from nine till five, inventing plots, adapting novels and plays, adding incidents and dialogue, and concocting alternative endings—all in virtual isolation. It was this system that Scott Fitzgerald fell foul of and which, at a later date, John Mortimer vividly described in his autobiography, *Clinging to the Wreckage*:[20]

Writers, in the first days when I visited Hollywood . . . were put in small, similar offices in the studio and were not supposed to go 'off the lot'. Nothing, I found, stifles creative endeavour more quickly than a desk in an air-conditioned cell, piles of yellow pads and stacks of sharpened pencils with a secretary waiting eagerly to type out 'the pages'. Every twenty pages had to be shown to the producer who first read it with deeply sincere admiration, and then having shown it to his wife, a number of old friends, three or four guys from the front office, his children and his devoted grey-haired secretary, found that it was sadly lacking in drama, was too literary, contained too many words, contained characters who were flat as a pancake and many another fatal flaw . . .

Another great handicap for a writer was the 'story conference' where as many people as possible were supposed to sit round joining in the discussion, with the result that the plot, out of sheer boredom, crept away and died . . . Successful fiction writing, which depends on privacy, secrecy and a writer's occasional ability to take himself by surprise, was impossible under these conditions . . .

With all this to contend with I was surprised to find my fellow-prisoners in what was appropriately called 'The Writers' Block' reasonably contented. As producers didn't read books they had to have scripts written in order to find out that no one wanted to make the movie. So a handsome and extremely safe living could be made from writing films that never went into production. There were also writers who had perfected the art of remaining on the pay-roll of a film which was, in fact, being written by someone else.

Indeed, at this point, it was often the director (rather than the producer) who took charge and exercised a free hand, not only in interpreting the script by the way he shot it, but frequently in re-writing the script himself. He was the big name and got all the credit; so much so that, in many histories still being written, past films are discussed in terms principally of the director, sometimes of the producer, sometimes of the actors, rarely of the writer, without whom of course even the most megalomaniac director had nothing to work on.

In the USA however writers fought hard from the first for recognition and succeeded in many instances, either by fruitful collaboration with prominent directors or by directing their own films. Examples include Ben Hecht who wrote numerous scripts from the earliest days of sound, ranging from Noël Coward's *Design for Living*, directed by Lubitsch in 1933, to Ernest Hemingway's *A Farewell to Arms*, directed by Charles Vidor in 1957. Or Nunnally Johnson, who became both a director and a producer in his time, notable for his version of John Steinbeck's *The Grapes of Wrath*, directed by John Ford in 1940. Or Preston Sturges who both wrote and directed a number of films, including *Sullivan's Travels* in 1942, and *The Miracle of Morgan's Creek* in 1944. Thus the role of the scriptwriter came gradually to be accepted, at any rate in the trade, as a distinct and valued craft, and strengthened the work of the US Screenwriters' Guild, founded in 1933.[21]

In passing, mention may be made of some of the British writers attracted to Hollywood. R. C. Sherriff never made his mark, but Aldous Huxley—paid at the rate of $1,500 a week—wrote a pleasing adaptation of Jane Austen's *Pride and Prejudice*, while Hugh Walpole had several successes. In 1933 MGM bought the film rights of his novel, *Vanessa*, for $12,500, and in the following year invited him over to make a screen version of *David Copperfield*. He also adapted *Vanessa*—all at a salary of £200 a week. In 1935 he returned for another stint, but he had become tired of the 'unreality' of the place. 'Nothing,' he wrote, 'is real here but salaries.' A much younger British writer, Christopher Isherwood, migrated—as is widely known—with the poet, W. H. Auden, to America in 1939. Isherwood's ability to write dialogue attracted the notice of Berthold Viertel, an Austrian Jewish film director, who had settled in California. Thus it was thanks to Viertel (and Gottfried, son of Max Reinhardt, the leading stage producer in Germany before Hitler) that Isherwood broke into films and picked up one scripting commission after another, though much of his work never reached the screen until after the war.[22]

Meanwhile a parallel process in screenwriting, although on a much more modest scale, was taking place in Britain. Recognition of the art, even by the writers themselves, was a problem from the start. As late as 1939, Margaret Kennedy, author of *The Constant Nymph*, wrote in the spring issue of *The Author*:

The born screenwriter, one who conceives a story from the beginning in terms of the screen and has no desire to expose himself to any other medium, is only just beginning to emerge.

In consequence screenwriters today fall into two groups. There are those to whom it is a whole-time profession, whose ambition and future are entirely bound up with the development of the film industry. They regard themselves as a part of that industry and, in the course of continual work for different companies at various studios, are brought into contact with technicians of all kinds, and come to know a good deal about film production as a whole. And there are those whose main profession is outside the industry, who, on the strength of their particular skill or reputation, are engaged to work for it occasionally, but who do not depend on it and may know very little about the work of experts in other branches of it.

This state of things tends to make the position of the screenwriter somewhat anomalous ... The screenwriter has not half the prestige of a playwright, not because his work is less important but because his status is negligible.[23]

James Bridie, already established as a dramatist, vigorously opposed this view in the summer issue.

A Screen Writer is either a dramatist or he is not. If he is not he ought to be. If he is, his interests ought to be fully protected by the League of British Dramatists.

Miss Kennedy replied:

Does Mr Bridie mean, by a dramatist, a writer of stage plays? Because, if he does, he might as well say: A harpist is either a violinist or he is not ... The screen, as a medium for story telling, differs as radically from the stage as a harp differs from a violin. It is possible, but not obligatory, for one man to play both these instruments, and either requires a perfectly distinct technique.

Ability to write stage plays does not necessarily imply aptitude or experience of the kind needed for film scripts ... In fact, a dramatist who takes screen writing seriously generally finds that he has to forget all that he has ever learnt about acts, curtains, entrances, exits, 'building up a scene', and the placing of comedy lines. His stage experience is a hindrance rather than a help to him.[24]

Bridie was not satisfied.

A dramatist is a person who writes dramas, and whether his dramas are acted by peasant actors on a village green or by American Film Stars in front of a camera is a purely technical matter.[25]

But Bridie had been left behind by events. Two years earlier the Screenwriters' Association had been formed under the aegis of the Society of Authors. I am indebted to Frank Launder, first Honorary Secretary and later President of the Association, for the following information about the early days of the Association.

Gathering in the winter of 1935 in flats in Bayswater, Baker Street and Notting Hill (we most of us seemed to live north of Hyde Park), we fulminated about the lowly position of writers in films, the inadequate screen credits we received, and the pitiful rewards.

These private 'demos' were greatly influenced by Christopher Mann, the artistes' and writers' manager, and his partner Alan Grogan, both of whom held the highly unfashionable view—heresy then in Wardour Street—that writing was important in films . . . There already existed an organisation calling itself 'The British Screenwriters' Association' which was formed in the twenties. Its members appeared to be mainly producers and directors. Its notepaper bore the address of a film studio, and its president was a well-known film director. To us an organisation so constituted seemed to be acquiescing in one of the very injustices we were complaining about—the sharing of screen credits with directors and producers. There were even directors who demanded payment from writers in return for giving them screen credits. In any case the old association seemed to us to be moribund.

The problem was how to form a true filmwriters' guild. There were few professional screenwriters in Britain then, and being paid little, we could not afford much. We decided to approach the Society of Authors, and a handful of us . . . met the Society's Secretary, Denys Kilham Roberts, together with Benn Levy representing the League of Dramatists. We found them only too anxious to help, and it was agreed that we could operate autonomously under the wing of the Society.

On 2 March 1937 a meeting was held at the Society's offices at which a provisional committee was appointed, consisting of Lajos Biro, Roger Burford, Ian Dalrymple, Sidney Gilliat, Michael Hogan, Margaret Kennedy, Angus MacPhail, Miles Malleson, Clemence Dane, Wolfgang Wilhelm, J. B. Williams, and Frank Launder himself. The first Committee meeting proper took place six days later.[26] Launder continued:

Naturally our first consideration was to gather members . . . The response surprised us, and we were hardly geared to deal with it. Among the first to join were Bernard Shaw, Somerset

Maugham, James Bridie,[27] L. A. G. Strong, G. B. Stern and Monckton Hoffe. Shaw paid us ten years' subscription in a lump sum, but when the time expired and the Treasurer applied for further payment, he replied that he regarded the first sum as a life subscription, and the fact that he outlived the ten years was our misfortune and not his.

A. P. Herbert accepted an invitation to become our first President and Fred Bellenger [later Secretary of State for War] our first Vice-President. These illustrous names were our window dressing, calculated as we fondly thought to strike terror into the hearts of the cinema moguls—but they come tough in Wardour Street and the battles ahead needed a good deal more than impressive notepaper as ammunition. We found it in a strong go-ahead working committee drawn in the main from full-time screenwriters present at those first meetings.

There was much to be done. A host of individual complaints, e.g. allegations of plagiarism, claims for breaches of contract, late payments and non-payments, arguments over screen credits, etc., in all of which we were ably advised first by Stanley Rubinstein and later Arnold Goodman, which entailed a great deal more legal and clerical work by the Society than had been anticipated; but where nonetheless we owed a great deal to the wise counsels of Denys Kilham Roberts, and his principal assistant, Elizabeth Barber.

One of the first and most important collective actions of the fledgling Screenwriters' Association concerned the Cinematograph Films Act, 1938, which, as already mentioned, revised the quota system. At the Bill stage a campaign was led by J. B. Williams, described by Launder as a 'highly talented writer, who was reputed to have taken a law examination while directing, by night, one of the first British sound films'.

Jim, who possessed all the fiery intensity of a Welsh preacher ... evolved an ingenious plan which he called 'The Separate Quota Scheme'. In effect it would have doubled the number of British films to be made by law, by having one quota for the Distributors, and another for the Exhibitors ...[28]

The campaign culminated in a mass meeting of film

[259]

employees at the Victoria Palace where the scheme met with general acclaim. It was endorsed by the trade unions, the film producers, and many other worthy bodies. As a result an amendment embodying it received majority support at the Bill's first reading in Parliament; but just when it seemed likely to become the key-stone of the new Act, the Government changed its mind for reasons not entirely dissociated, our Committee felt, from the American distributors' dislike of the plan. The Whips were put on, and the 'Separate Quota Scheme' vanished overnight.

Another casualty was A. P. Herbert's attempt to have two authors—specifically screenwriters—appointed to the Films Council, set up under the Act to monitor the progress of the industry and advise the Board of Trade. Yet these rebuffs, as often happens, benefited the Screenwriters' Association in that, thanks to all the publicity, it attracted a number of new members who were already making a name in films, among them, Walter Greenwood, T. E. B. Clarke, Paul Rotha, Eric Ambler and Ted Willis, who was later to play a vital role in shaping the destiny of the Association.

One of the changes incorporated in the 1938 Quota Act was the recognition accorded to short films. This had a bearing on a distinct and essentially British innovation in the art of film making that took wing during the 1930s—the documentary. Although factual films had been made long before, it is generally agreed that the genre was established by the pioneer work of John Grierson who, in 1929, made *Drifters*, a silent film about the Scottish herring fleet. The history of the documentary film has been amply recorded in books and articles,[29] and I do not propose to enlarge on the subject here, beyond observing that a documentary was more than mere film journalism. In Grierson's words:

> . . . the documentary idea, after all, demands no more than that the affairs of our time shall be brought to the screen in any fashion which strikes the imagination and makes observation a little richer than it was. At one level, the vision may be journalistic; at another it may rise to poetry and drama. At another level again, aesthetic quality may lie in the mere lucidity of its exposition.[30]

The introduction of sound added fresh force both to the impact made by the documentary film and to its purpose: namely the interpretation of reality by, for example, portraying the techniques of different jobs in industry and exposing social conditions—conveyed for the most part in the speech and actions of the people involved, replacing dialogue spoken by actors. This imposed a considerable burden upon the film maker who, in early days, might have to write the script, direct the shooting, and edit the film himself, which meant that he had not only to be a creative technician, but so identify himself with the subject as to be capable of communicating it from the *inside*. This was Grierson's *forte*, but after *Drifters* he concentrated as a producer on planning and supervising films, on training directors, and on expounding his ideas.

The documentary was important also for other reasons. First, in contrast to feature films which paid high wages and salaries only during production, documentary film units offered lower remuneration in exchange for steady employment and exciting prospects of innovation and experiment. Secondly, the films did not depend solely on the trade system of distribution and exhibition, although a number were in fact booked by commercial cinemas. Many were shown in halls hired by sponsors, in schools, institutes, canteens, etc. This method of non-theatrical distribution was greatly enlarged during the Second World War. Lastly, the success of the documentary had a profound effect on the nature of British feature films produced during and after the war.

The Second World War did not extinguish the British film industry—on its heels after the slump of 1937–8—as had been feared. Despite all the difficulties deriving from staff shortages, studio closures, war damage, the restriction of financial and many other resources, and a panic decision at the outbreak of hostilities to close all cinemas, the industry made a remarkable recovery.

The conditions of wartime provided the film industry with a proper role to play in national life, and the challenge was taken up, producing a miraculous transformation in content, style, subject matter and aesthetics. At last British film had matured and could pass into its golden age of the forties.[31]

Much of this success was due to the war itself: to making films, wholly or partly documentary in character, that told the story of Britain's war effort and way of life. At one end of the scale, ten-minute 'shorts' commissioned by the Ministry of Information and inserted into every cinema programme; at the other, full-length features such as Harry Watt's *Target for Tonight* (1941) about an RAF raid on Kiel; Noël Coward's *In Which We Serve* (1942) about the life and death of a destroyer; Thorold Dickinson's *Next of Kin* (1942) that dealt more effectively with the consequences of careless talk than much official propaganda; Humphrey Jennings's *Fires were Started* (1942) about the Auxiliary Fire Service; *Desert Victory* (1943), produced by the Army Film Unit and directed by Roy Boulting about the Alamein campaign, which—like *Target for Tonight*—made a great impression upon American audiences; and Carol Reed's *The Way Ahead* (1944) about the conversion of civilian recruits into fighting soldiers. These and many other films served the dual purpose of telling a story and imparting information in factual and fictional form, to such good effect that the medium of the film played a vital part in sustaining national confidence at home and abroad.

Not all British wartime films fell within this category. Indeed there was a wide range of the kinds of films familiar in peacetime. For example comedies (Will Hay, George Formby, Tommy Handley, *et al.*); a 1941 version of H. G. Wells's novel, *Kipps*; costume pieces such as *The Man in Grey* (1943); a melodrama, *Fanny by Gaslight* (1944); a love story, *Brief Encounter* (1944). Such films helped audiences forget the drab realities and, as the war went on, reflected a reaction in taste, highlighted by the lavish production in colour of Shakespeare's *Henry V*, starring Laurence Olivier who also directed.

By the end of the war British film makers—producers, directors, actors, writers and technicians—had gained an international reputation for the quality of their work, which compared favourably with anything emanating from the USA or the rest of the world, and generated great hopes for the future of the industry. The record of output was also improving. Some 4,000[32] cinemas up and down the country showed 67 British feature films produced in 1945 and 83 in 1946, while the annual total of American films had been limited to 400 or less. Admissions had risen from 19 million to 30 million per week; thus the war was the heyday of film attendance. At the same time box office receipts had trebled, though profits were diminished by successive increases in Entertainments Duty and the imposition of Excess Profits Tax.

The structure of the industry had also undergone one important change, due to the expansion of the empire of J. Arthur Rank who, by adding Gaumont-British to his Odeon Group, controlled over 500 cinemas, or two out of the three main circuits. The third, and Rank's main competitor, was Associated British in which Warner Brothers had secured a 25 per cent interest. These developments were so significant that already in 1944—at the request of the Board of Trade—the Film Council had published a searching report[33] on the state of the industry, examining the growth of monopoly and exposing a variety of abuses inherent in the way that films were made, distributed, exhibited and financed. No action was taken before the end of the war, but the report influenced much that took place in the following years. Meanwhile the euphoria of peace was reflected in the sharp rise in the production of British feature films—from 83 in 1945–6 to 170 in 1947–8—though ultimately these three years ended in disaster, illustrated predominantly by the experience of Rank, by far the most prolific British manufacturer of films and, as has been shown, the most powerful distributor and exhibitor as well, with apparently inexhaustible sources of finance.

There were two causes. One was the attempt, begun during the war, to ensure success by means of extravagant productions. An extreme example was Bernard Shaw's *Caesar and Cleopatra*, another was *London Town* (with Sid Field, as the star comedian), each of which cost £1 million more or less and failed financially.[34] Rank also invested heavily in cinema circuits overseas, in the production of animated cartoons and children's films, in a rival to the US news documentary *March of Time*, and in the Independent Frame system devised by David Rawnsley.[35] The second cause was related to the first, namely an attempt to break into the American mass market with British films and so create a source of overseas income, essential if home-produced films—at least of the 'prestige' sort—were to show a profit.[36] However the effort failed, and by 1947–8 heavy losses resulted.

By this time too the country was in the throes of the post-war balance of payments crisis. Imports and remittances abroad had to be cut, films included. In August 1947 a customs duty of 75 per cent was imposed on the value of all imported films, which caused an immediate reaction, not only in the USA, where the Motion Picture Association suspended all shipments of films indefinitely. Fierce criticism was also expressed by the British exhibitors who relied on the USA for 80 per cent of their screen time and who foresaw—after the current stock of American films had been exhausted—a point when audiences, tired of re-runs and extended runs, would stay at home and seek alternative forms of entertainment. If cinemas closed, then film making itself would be affected; and although the 75 per cent duty seemed to offer British film producers a heaven-sent opportunity to capture the market, the gap left by the Americans was too large to fill in terms of either quality or quantity. In the event further losses were incurred by British companies, especially by Rank.

The opportunity was too sudden and too fleeting for yet another reason. Thanks largely to the initiative of Harold Wilson, then President of the Board of Trade, the crisis of supply was shortly dispelled by the Anglo-American agreement of March 1948, which repealed the 75 per cent import duty and permitted American companies to remit $17 million[37] per annum of their British earnings, a figure to be increased by a sum equal to the annual earnings of British films in USA. However British film producers had already accepted the challenge and were committed to making many more films. By the time most of these were ready for release, American films were ready to come into the country again, and so the two streams collided, the British coming off worst.[38]

Wilson's action in March 1948 heralded the third occasion in twenty-odd years on which the Government had intervened in the film industry, the previous two being the Films Act of 1927 and 1938, the latter now coming to the end of its legislative life. The 1948 Act introduced several important changes. It retained the exhibitors' but abolished the distributors' quotas, and fixed the percentages of British films to be shown (on an annually reviewed basis) at 45 per cent for 'first features' (formerly 'long films') and

25 per cent for the 'supporting programme' (formerly 'short films')—unrealistically high figures as events proved. The Act also reflected the Government's desire to help the independent producer by restraining the expansion of the three main cinema circuits, and by insisting that a proportion of screen time be reserved for independent films.

Action did not stop there. Wilson had already set going an enquiry into studio space , a problem however that soon solved itself, and then appointed two committees, one (chaired by Sir George Gater) on film production costs, the other (chaired first by Lord Portal, then by Sir Arnold Plant) on distribution and exhibition. These two committees reported in 1949.[39] In addition Wilson formed the National Film Finance Corporation (NFFC) in October 1948, with an initial grant of £5 million, to lend money to film producers, particularly the independents. In the end the Government decided against altering the existing structure of the industry and rejected a proposal by the principal union, the Association of Ciné and Allied Technicians (ACT, later ACTT when television came in), for a nationalised cinema circuit, linked to a state distributor, to compete with Rank and ABC. Instead, in 1950, it introduced the so-called Eady plan,[40] whereby Entertainments Duty was reduced, seat prices raised, and directed that—out of the savings effected—a levy of a farthing per ticket sold be paid by exhibitors to producers. In the event it was not possible for this ingenious device, even when augmented and made compulsory, by itself to bridge the gap between producers' costs and earnings; nor was overseas revenue sufficient. But while Rank and ABC were able to set distribution/exhibition profits against production losses, not so the independent film makers who had no such alternatives and remained at greatest risk. They had therefore to turn to the other source of Government aid, the NFFC, which, as noted, had been founded in 1948 primarily for their benefit—but, ironically, only to fulfil a *temporary* need, i.e. until investors regained confidence in the industry. However, like some other 'temporary' institutions, the NFFC is still (1982) with us; indeed its powers to lend money have recently been extended up to 1985. Although, early on, the Corporation took the extraordinary decision to lend over half its original capital to Alexander Korda of British Lion—and never got it back—its record reads quite well. By 1980 it had helped finance over 750 features and 170 'shorts' during the previous thirty years, and had advanced £32,239,700 against repayments of £19,946,195: a relatively respectable record in the light of the enormous investment required for films and the equally enormous risks. But, although the NFFC did useful service in simplifying some of the financial procedures, it never had sufficient money to pull its weight as intended, and was forced to reduce support of innovative and independent ventures.

It is not possible in this one chapter to list or discuss the numerous films, many of them memorable, that—despite recurring financial crises—were produced in Britain in the first decade after the war. For a succinct survey of the scene, I refer the reader to the several histories available, notably George Perry's *The Great British Picture Show*, chapters 12–18 (Paladin, 1975);[41] and draw attention to the fact that after 1948 American companies found it increasingly advantageous to make films in Britain, partly to use up blocked earnings, and partly because—as in the 1930s—their films qualified as British for the purposes of Quota, with the Eady money added. Instead, I propose to glance briefly at the career of one British company, Ealing Studios, as master-minded by Michael Balcon, who stamped his personality on a series of films that 'projected Britain and the British character'.

Balcon never directed an Ealing film himself but—as an inspired boss with a remarkable flair, albeit with a strong streak of paternalism—he was the moving spirit behind a team of writers, artists, actors, administrators and technicians, many of whose names and deeds appear in Charles Barr's history of the enterprise,[42] and whose association with him are vividly recalled in his own life story.[43] Here is an impression of what it was like working for Balcon in the words of two close friends and associates, both involved partly or wholly at script and other stages, and whose varied experiences impart the flavour of working in films at that time.

Monja Danischewsky, known as 'Danny', was born in Russia in 1911, left the country with his family in 1919 and settled in England where he has lived ever since. At the age of 20 he started work in the London office of MGM as a junior in the publicity department at £3 a week, writing for the company magazine. Quite soon he was doing a variety of similar jobs for other firms and contributing to trade papers. He also began freelancing as a reviewer, and writing plays and short stories. In 1938 he landed the job of Director of Publicity at Ealing, which he held for ten years and which, through the cultivation of his contacts in Fleet Street, helped materially to make Ealing a household name. In his book (1966),[44] he described his career and some of the mysteries of film making:

> I have often been asked by laymen to describe the relative functions of a film producer and film director. It is not easy to find a simple definition because nowadays there are different kinds of directors and producers, the functions have merged, eminent directors very often produce their own films, working with a figure-head or purely administrative producer, and the producers themselves vary from the creative technician to the strictly business man . . .
>
> In principle, it is the film producer who chooses the subject, nurses the script through its stages, appoints the director, chooses the cast and, during the production of the film, plays the dual role of being responsible for the film keeping to its schedule and budget, and supervising the director's work. The director it is who decides on the camera movements, has the technical control on the studio floor and directs the actors. In point of fact, there is the tendency nowadays for the producer and director to collaborate closely through all the stages of film-making. The director's status has risen, in general, and the producer's has declined.

Danny emphasised that 'more senior film technicians in Britain today owe their careers to being spotted and encouraged by Mick Balcon than by any other man'.

The late Robert Hamer, who directed *Kind Hearts and Coronets* and also collaborated on the script, came to Ealing to work in the cutting rooms. Charles Frend (*Scott of the Antarctic* and *The Cruel Sea*), Charles Crichton (*The Lavender Hill Mob*), Henry Cornelius (*Passport to Pimlico* and *Genevieve*), all came up through the cutting rooms. Basil

Dearden, who made *Sapphire*, among other successful films, started in Ealing as an assistant director, and his collaborator, producer Michael Relph, worked as a designer in the art department. Alexander Mackendrick, who was my director in *Whisky Galore* was employed as a visualiser—drawing camera set-ups under the guidance of established directors. Harry Watt, who made *The Overlanders* in Australia, was picked out by Balcon when a young maker of documentaries for the wartime Ministry of Information. All of us young fellows were given our break in Mr Balcon's Academy for Young Gentlemen . . . 'I'm sticking my neck out,' he said to me before my departure to the Isle of Barra to make *Whisky Galore*—and appealed: 'For God's sake, don't let me down, dear boy.'

Danny added that 'if Mick was the father figure, Cavalcanti ("Cav") was the Nanny who brought us up . . . A stimulating colleague, he was an influence on us all, and fortunately for us he was a natural if inarticulate teacher.'[45]

Cav recognised in me the desire to do something more than publicise the exciting things that were now happening in Ealing, and with Balcon's ready agreement, he allowed me to become involved in them. While continuing my normal job, I was allowed to work with him on the wartime documentaries he was making for us. I persuaded Frank Owen and Michael Foot to write the commentaries, and Frank to speak them, and so I had a hand, for the first time, in actual film-making.

It was in 1948 that Balcon (who had just been knighted) gave Danny his big chance by appointing him producer (technically his associate producer) of the film *Whisky Galore*, scripted by Angus MacPhail and Compton Mackenzie from the latter's novel, itself based on a true incident. The film was to be made on location, using all the accommodation and other (restricted) resources of the Island of Barra, although in the end some of the scenes had to be shot at Ealing. The total cost was £107,000 (some £20,000 above budget) but the film proved a great success artistically and financially and 'sold more Scotch in the United States than the advertisements for the product'.

Danny was paid on the basis of his previous salary as publicity director (£80 a week), but without the generous expenses that went with it or any additional fee for his contribution to the script! He was in fact that familiar phenomenon in the film world, a 'hyphenate', i.e. someone who combines at least two jobs—the commonest perhaps being director-writer. In his case, apart from publicity work, it was producer-writer, as will be illustrated shortly.

Danny's colleague and close friend, T. E. B. ('Tibby') Clarke, the star comedy scriptwriter at Ealing, was also a journalist by trade and training. He had had plenty of excitement in his youth (including nearly being shot in the Argentine revolution of 1930), and he did duty as a wartime policeman before being recruited to Ealing by Danny. When Balcon asked, 'What films has he written?' Danny replied, 'None—but he's lived plenty.' Tibby paid tribute to Balcon 'for his readiness to acknowledge that the story was a film's most important ingredient—and, what was more, to act on that belief'.

> The average producer, in choosing a subject, needs the assurance of knowing it has already succeeded as a book, a play, or a TV series. Not so Balcon: if he could 'see' a film in a suggestion that might cover half a page of typescript, then its instigator would be authorised to develop it until its worth could be fairly judged by himself and others.[46]

A high proportion of Ealing successes came, therefore, from original stories written for the screen. Tibby's contributions included *Hue and Cry*, *Passport to Pimlico*, *The Lavender Hill Mob*, and *The Titfield Thunderbolt*.[47] As a scriptwriter he was worried at first by his lack of technical knowledge, knowing nothing for example about 'when a long shot should be cut to a medium shot, camera panning with one character and another moving into close shot'. He soon made up his mind not to bother, never meeting a director who expected the writer to tell him his business, although that did not exclude fruitful collaboration and interchange of ideas with directors like Cavalcanti (whose English was anyhow 'a bit shaky'), or Charles Frend with whom he worked on *Johnny Frenchman*.

Among other peculiarities of the job was the fact that three or four scripts—often more—would be written for every one accepted for filming. While a novelist with a name could rely on his work continuing to reach the public, not so the screenwriter, however successful. Nor would he necessarily be remembered once the film had had its run.

A writer may be responsible for all that goes into a screenplay—original idea, story, characters, plot construction, dialogue—up to the moment it goes before the camera. After that nobody remembers or cares who did the preliminary scribbling, it is the director who takes every bow.

Write a play for the stage and you will be treated with respect. Your advice on its production will be sought, no other writer will be hired behind your back to change what you have written; when your play is presented you will receive due credit as its creator, and you will be paid royalties every time it is performed thereafter. Write it for the screen and you will be lucky if your name is mentioned in connection with it; you will be even luckier if you have the minutest share of any profits it might make.

And he illustrated the point with the following anecdote:

I once attended a luncheon with one of Hollywood's leading scriptwriters, the late Harry Kurnitz. Seated between us was a tycoon of industry. 'It is strange', he said, 'that never before to my knowledge have I met a screenwriter, yet now I find myself with one on each side of me. Tell me of your work, I know nothing about it.'

'Do you know anything about breeding thoroughbred horses?' Harry inquired.

A little surprised, the business man confessed he was almost equally ignorant on that subject.

'In every racing stud,' Harry explained, 'they keep a rugged old horse known as a "teaser". They use him for titillating a mare who's about to be mated. Once he has gotten her into the right mood of excited anticipation, he is whisked away and the stallion is brought in to do the job. Well, sir, we screenwriters are the teasers of the film industry.'

Tibby never bothered much about his contract at Ealing,

calculating that working for Balcon on salary compensated for the loss of large sums he might have made elsewhere on other terms.

> My most successful screenplay, *The Lavender Hill Mob*, won me an Oscar, a writing award at the Venice Festival and the annual award of the US National Board of Review. The film has been shown countless times in cinemas and on television the world over. I should like to have had royalties bringing me in just a fraction of what others have made out of that picture. In fact I was paid some £1,500 at the time I wrote it and have had nothing since . . . Though my Ealing comedies brought me little in the way of hard cash, it was wholly due to my work on them that I was later employed to write inferior Hollywood pictures at $5,000 a week.

Tibby spent sixteen years at Ealing. After Balcon left in 1955 and the company was taken over by Associated British, he got himself an agent who advised him to secure release from his contract by paying over the penalty of £1,000 demanded. 'All,' he said ruefully, 'I had managed to save in those sixteen years.'

To return to Danny for one further illustration of the economics of scriptwriting and producing during this period, which also throws light on the complex and exaggerated world of film finance and politics—inseparable it seems from the industry at any time.

The success of *Whisky Galore* encouraged Danny to go independent and set up a company, 'Sirius', with Henry Cornelius. Together they made a comedy, *The Galloping Major*, which yielded Danny a fee of 'not less than £5,000 and not more than £7,500'. Unable to find another suitable subject, the two men parted amicably and Danny sold his shares at a profit. At Balcon's invitation he then returned to Ealing for a two-picture deal on a salary of £5,000 a year, producing *The Love Lottery* and *Meet Mr Lucifer* in 1951–2. He wrote part of the script of the latter picture, but most of it was the work of Harry Kurnitz.

Over the next fifteen years he wrote and/or produced a dozen films, not all of which reached the screen. Those that did included *Rockets Galore* (1958), *Topkapi* (1964) and *Mr Moses* (1965); but I refer here to *The Battle of the Sexes* (1960), based on James

Thurber's short story, *The Catbird Seat*, which several other writers, including Tibby Clarke, had earlier adapted without success. In Danny's words:

> My contract for the script was with the firm Hecht, Hill and Lancaster, which in turn was financed by United Artists. Hecht had been an agent and scriptwriter, Hill was an exscriptwriter, and Lancaster was and is Burt Lancaster, the big star. They made a number of successful and 'important' films—blockbusters with huge budgets and expensive stars, directors, etc. Then Hecht fell in love with a delightful TV play called *Marty*, and decided to make a film of it . . . It made a tremendous profit—a fortune. Hecht . . . then decided to make a group of moderate cost films based in Europe. *The Catbird Seat* was to be one of this group, and another was to be an updated version of Turgenev's lovely novella, *First Love*—an enterprise about which I had my doubts.
>
> My contract was to involve me in both subjects. I was to get £15,000 for the script and producing *The Catbird Seat*, as well as for producing, but not writing, *First Love*. Hecht, Hill and Lancaster had the option, however, to break off after I had delivered the script for *The Catbird Seat* with a payment of £7,500 only. I also received 350 dollars a week subsistence allowance, and Brenda (my wife) and I were flown by them first class to and from Los Angeles.

As it turned out the script pleased Hecht but not his colleagues, and when United Artists withdrew their backing Danny's contract was terminated—but the day was not yet lost. Back in Britain, Michael Balcon had become chairman of Bryanston Films.

> It was an attempt to make another Ealing type operation. There were a number of the old 'Ealing boys' who, like myself, had bought themselves into the company. We all had to pay £1,000 in cash and put another £4,000 on ice at Lloyds Bank, for which we were given 5,000 £1 shares. This, together with money from the Rank Organisation and British Lion, gave us a revolving credit of £1 million.

In the event Bryanston bought Danny's script of *The Catbird Seat* from the Americans for £20,000 plus 15 per cent of the producer's profits.

> This was a very cheap buy since they had to lose what they had spent on previous scripts for the same subject. Normal practice is to cover the cost of previous rejected scripts (past mistakes) by adding them to the final sum asked for a film subject.[48]

Danny had already received £7,500 for writing the script and, as producer, he was paid a further £8,500 (approximately) plus 10 per cent of the producer's profit. The film, re-titled *The Battle of the Sexes*, with Peter Sellers, Robert Morley and Constance Cummings in the principal roles, was released in 1960, having cost £133,000; it duly netted a profit of £58,000. Danny concluded:

> My economics are not the easiest to illustrate . . . I muddle the issue by getting involved on both sides of the fence. For straightforward commissioned scripts my fees were established at £10,000 to £12,000 for the script (generally 10–12 weeks' work) made up to £20,000 as and when the script reached production. Subsequent to the success of *The Battle of the Sexes* I had several such commissions from United Artists. But of these commissions only two reached production stage, and as they were both negotiated as 'doctoring' existing scripts, and with restricted time to deliver, I received only the first stage. These were *Topkapi* (1964) and *Mr Moses* (1965), the latter yielding TV residuals.
>
> The fees I received for scriptwriting by no means put me in the front rank of screenwriters, but halfway up the ladder.

The fact that Tibby Clarke felt cheated of his due and failed to benefit from the continuing success of his Ealing films emphasised the inadequacy of the studio system, at any rate as it affected scriptwriters. The situation had already altered in the USA where many writers had gone independent and were making their own terms with the producing companies, an example followed in Britain during the 1950s. Indeed no period in the history of the screen saw more changes than in the twenty years following the end of the Second World War. In America the power of the 'movie majors' was abruptly undermined, after 1948, by anti-trust legislation directed against monopoly, which ruled that film production and distribution must be divorced from ownership of cinema chains. Although many changes consequently took place in the composition and control of the dominant corporations, new concentrations eventually emerged with the centre of power located as before with the film distributor, without whose backing few producers would dare start work on a new film. As indicated, the old studio system came to an end, independent producers multiplied, while leading writers and actors also set up on their own. Some of the best talent left America for political reasons, as a result of the 'Hollywood Ten' hearings instituted in 1947 to investigate Communist infiltration of the film industry. But the most serious development was the alarming fall in cinema attendance, while costs of film making soared. One reason was that the return of peace offered many alternatives for spending money, backed by an enormous expansion of hire purchase. Another was the arrival of television which, almost overnight, brought the screen into the home.

The film companies fought back with a variety of technological innovations—wide screens, improved colour, stereoscopic sound and vision, even smells released through the air circulation system of the movie houses! However, after their initial impact, none of these devices succeeded in saving the situation, although some were permanently adopted for film showing. Film production in the USA continued of course. Not only that, it continued to dominate world markets outside the Soviet bloc and China; but in so doing it underwent a basic economic change. Whereas in the past an American film could count on making a profit from exhibition in home cinemas alone, by the late 1950s that era had passed and, ten years later, most American features depended heavily upon income from foreign showings, mainly in the UK and Europe. This influenced film making in several ways. First it meant that producers had to take account of foreign, or at least of international, taste, so that a film had to be tailored to appeal to audiences on both sides of the Atlantic. Secondly it prompted US companies to open offices and set up production units abroad. This applied particularly to the UK, at a time when costs were relatively low and the sterling–dollar exchange operated strongly in the latter's favour. Naturally a stream of American directors and players accompanied these moves.

The policy paid off for additional reasons. An American backed film, made in Britain, not only benefited from guaranteed distribution in the world market (including, most importantly, the USA), but—as already mentioned—it qualified as 'British' for the purposes of the Quota and Eady income. Moreover, even when earnings abroad were blocked, the Americans showed great ingenuity in converting local currency into merchandise and services of various kinds—timber, shipping, real estate, etc., and thereby retaining the profits made by their films.

Behind these manoeuvres a yet more significant movement was taking place. This was the process whereby the old film companies were penetrated by television and other communications concerns or, as particularly in the case of RKO,[49] were absorbed by conglomerates for whom film making was but one of many disparate interests. One by one the familiar names suffered a sea change of this sort—Columbia, MGM, Paramount, Twentieth Century Fox, United Artists, Warner. But, although as one writer put it, some of these conglomerates were 'more interested in funeral parlors and life insurance than films',[50] film making in the USA proved remarkably resilient, ranging from low cost productions aimed primarily at young audiences in 'drive-in' cinemas, to a 39-episode TV series such as Rockford, or a blockbuster such as The Godfather released in 1972 by Paramount (itself part of Gulf and Western), for which NBC two years later paid $10 million for TV showing. The Godfather II proved no less successful.[51]

In Britain the history of film making after the Second World War followed a parallel course, although on a far smaller scale and with important variations. As in the USA weekly cinema attendances dropped drastically[52] and for similar reasons, i.e. alternative outlets for spending and the arrival of television although, in the latter case, the full impact was not felt until after 1955 when a dramatic expansion took place in the sale of TV licences and sets to working-class families, formerly the principal patrons of films. Those hardest hit were the small circuits and independent cinema owners who were less able to invest in the new exhibition equipment (wide screens, etc.), and were generally at a disadvantage in reacting to recession by comparison with the two biggest operators, Rank and ABC. With some 900 houses, these two owned most of the best buildings and locations, and they could afford to dispose of unprofitable properties, often making money out of the re-development of the sites.[53] Also, as the biggest distributors, linked to American interests, they usually secured the most popular films and priorities for exhibition, an important consideration when cinemas depended on US films for 70 per cent of their screen time.

Despite these advantages, even Rank and ABC were unable to stem the decline. Whereas profits were generally sustained by increases in the prices of admission and by the repeal in 1960 of Entertainments Duty (offset later by the imposition of VAT), the effect of cinema closures, the extension of runs and re-runs, and the attraction of alternatives, all combined to discourage the habit of film going and put an end to the halcyon days when the local cinema was an integral part of community life. Inevitably these factors, taken in conjunction with the steep rise in production costs, had a radical effect on film making in Britain. The situation was clearly set out in an article by the film critic, Stephen Watts, published in the winter 1959 issue of *The Author*.

> British feature films come about in a number of ways which can be defined fairly simply. They may be made by one of the major British companies, or by an American production company, or by either of these in conjunction with an independent producer, or by an independent producer in association with a British or American distributor.
>
> The days are past when Rank or Associated British lined up each year a programme of pictures of their own, sufficient to keep their production companies fully occupied, their studios in constant use, and their distribution companies supplied with enough films (plus the contributions of their American associates) to keep the mills of distribution grinding steadily. More and more the pictures made by the two major groups have an 'independent' element, with the independent producer either in the role of the studio tenant or committed to deliver his finished product to the group's distributing company. It is

not uncommon for the independent producer to offer a 'package' to the big company, the producer having mounted his proposed production to the point where he has script, director, stars and part of the required finance. Negotiations then result in the big company deciding what its participation is to be—merely landlord, co-producer, distributor guaranteeing 70 per cent or more of the total cost against an agreed percentage of the receipts, or an adaptation or combination of these.

As has been made abundantly clear, the presence of American companies making 'British' films was an important part of the scene. Their studio operations and other investments were welcomed by those who faced the fact that, without American money and outlets, the output of feature films made in Britain would have dropped well below the annual average of 150 or so during the 1960s, and unemployment in the industry would have been severe. At the same time the emergence of independent producers opened the door to a number of British writers and directors, generally associated with the 'new wave' in drama and fiction that began to beat against the emplacements of society in the late 1950s.

One such production unit was Woodfall Films, formed in 1958 by Tony Richardson and John Osborne of the English Stage Company. Between 1959 and 1963 Richardson directed films of Osborne's *Look Back in Anger* and *The Entertainer*, Shelagh Delaney's *A Taste of Honey*, and Alan Sillitoe's *The Loneliness of the Long-Distance Runner*. Like Ealing, Woodfall and other independents produced films of a genuinely native character but, unlike Ealing, they were concerned not with transmitting the flavour of British traditions and tilting kindly at them, but with dealing starkly with contemporary problems: criminal behaviour, psychological disturbance, and social breakdown at all levels. Critical acclaim however did not always match box office returns and highlighted the fact that the appeal of most of these films was limited primarily to home audiences, at a time when export income had become ever more necessary to run into profit. By contrast, Woodfall's outstanding success with *Tom Jones*— Henry Fielding's robust 18th century comedy, directed by Richardson, scripted by Osborne, with Albert Finney in the name part—was enjoyed as sheer entertainment the world over.

The 1960s, when most of the 'new wave' films appeared,[54] constituted *par excellence* the period of permissiveness when social attitudes to sex and other conventions, as reflected in performance (stage, films, broadcasting), radically changed. Just as Osborne's *Look Back in Anger* fired the stage revolt, so—it is suggested—Jack Clayton's direction of John Braine's novel, *Room at the Top*, detonated the films explosion in 1958. The new situation was recognised, notably, by John Trevelyan, Secretary of the British Board of Film Censors (BBFC), who was personally responsible for liberalising the Board's policy. Film censorship had had an odd pragmatic history in the UK. The first Cinematograph Films Act of 1909 did not bother about morals, but authorised local authorities to license premises in order 'to safeguard the public from the danger which arises from fires at cinematograph entertainments'. In 1913—nine years before the inception of the Hays office in the USA—the industry set up its own voluntary body, the BBFC, to examine films for offensive material and classify them either as U (universal exhibition) or A (not recommended for children). The Board had no legal standing, nor has it today, but it was useful to the local authorities who generally, though not invariably, accepted its film categories. In 1932 the H certificate was introduced to denote 'horror' films unsuitable for children, but was replaced in 1951 by the X certificate which, while excluding the under-sixteens, opened the door wider to films on adult themes and subjects, mainly sex. In 1970, by which time it was clear that X had been abused, a new category, AA, came in, excluding children under fourteen. At the same time the age of admission to X films was raised to eighteen, but children were allowed to attend A films, if permitted by their parents.

Meanwhile censorship had long been overtly sidestepped by the existence of film clubs that needed no certificates, either from the Board or the local authorities. Not all such clubs existed to show 'blue' films. A number served the perfectly respectable purpose of screening subjects of specialised or minority interest, or foreign language films. Nevertheless many club cinemas, notoriously in Soho, were 'porn palaces' and as such made nonsense of the system. The total abolition of stage censorship in 1968 strengthened the view that film censorship should be abolished too, and that exhibitors of 'blue' films should simply be liable to prosecution for obscenity, as with publications. Indeed the difficulty of discriminating between art and dirt was underlined by the report of the Committee on Obscenity and Film Censorship published in 1979. Out of a welter of observations, largely favouring permissiveness, but which emphasised the need to protect children and penalise the gratuitous display or delivery of offensive material, the Committee condemned the 'pornography of violence' as strongly as it did the 'pornography of sex', and commented on their close connection. No action has as yet (1982) been taken to implement the report, and the subject is unlikely ever to be settled unequivocally by law, since social attitudes are divided and constantly shifting. Writers however cannot avoid the issue because it is they, principally, who have influenced—and must continue to influence—public opinion, whether writing for the screen or any other medium, simply by the way they treat sex and violence in their work. It was his willingness to think clearly and constructively on this subject, as on others, that distinguished A. P. Herbert; and so I refer the reader to his remarks, quoted on pages 115–16.

To return to the 1960s and the independents. Woodfall was one of the units associated with Bryanston Films.[55] Headed by Michael Balcon, it represented a brave attempt to establish a kind of co-operative, finding finance without reliance on the two principal film distributors. In this instance distribution was in the hands of British Lion,[56] which released nearly a hundred films between 1955 and 1970. Unhappily the impetus of the 1960s faded during the 1970s,[57] so that by the end of 1981, the annual output of British feature films had fallen to a mere 27[58]—a decline that rendered the Quota (standing at 30 per cent and extended by the Films Acts of 1960, 1970 and 1980) virtually irrelevant. Reasons included the familiar one of the shrinking of the home market, the disinclination of the public to go to cinemas and its undoubted preference for screen entertainment at home on the TV; also the fact that even British companies making high-cost films were spending their resources in America, the market which yields some 50 per cent of all film revenue in the Western world.

The outlook was not however totally without hope. Although Rank had stopped making films altogether; although EMI (even after its merger with the Thorn Electrical Industries group) contributed only two films in 1981; and although a handful of American companies continued to make use of British production facilities and personnel, so long as the pound sterling remained weak in relation to the dollar—yet some new film makers had appeared. Among the largest was Goldcrest, a subsidiary of Pearson Longman, the publishing empire, which found 60 per cent of the money for Richard Attenborough's epic, *Gandhi*, and paid for the scripting of *Chariots of Fire*,[59] both films scoring major international successes. Among the others, notably those making low-cost films (i.e. less than £1 million) there were interesting ventures backed either by the NFFC or by the British Film Institute (BFI), and, significantly, by certain television companies with an eye on both TV and theatrical exhibition.[60]

The relevance of this information is obvious. Without a viable film industry in Britain, not only would there be no work for writers or anyone else engaged in film making, but the position would soon revert to that pertaining in the early 1920s, when native talent was forced to emigrate *en masse*. That is one of the penalties of allowing market forces to dictate terms, although far more is at stake than 'mere' money. *Force majeure* in film finance has often led to the sapping of confidence in indigenous culture and enterprise, and in a situation where for us British, a common language with America is a dangerous disadvantage. Moreover, as is well known, film finance belongs to the realms of fantasy. Huge sums are invested and expended, and market risks are so high that only about one film in ten makes a profit; yet, when successful, that one film can earn so much that more money can always be found for fresh ventures. Ironically only a small proportion reaches the writer of the script or the novelist or playwright whose work has been turned into a screenplay. Since the last war, film rights of works by well-known British authors[61] have certainly been sold for large sums—large, that is, when considered in isolation; but when related to the film budget, let alone the ultimate cost of production, outlay on the original material would rarely exceed three per cent, the percentage reacting in inverse proportion to the size of the budget. Essentially the price is a matter of bargaining, the producer aiming at the lowest price obtainable, the author or his agent at the highest.

For most authors, film rights are a mirage. Even if an option is taken up, the odds against a story filtering through all the stages and reaching the screen are heavy. Hazards of production are such that 'get-out' clauses, incorporated in the contract, can be acted upon to cancel out weeks of work and obliterate thousands of pounds spent on preliminary development. Even at a time of comparatively high production, experienced writers would complete as many as a dozen screenplays, commissioned and paid for over a period of five years, but only one would reach production stage. Likewise a play would be worked and re-worked by four or five writers in succession, and still not be filmed. Almost always a film property is sold outright and for the full term of copyright; and so, once the deal has been made, that is virtually the end of it for the author, at any rate so far as theatrical exhibition is concerned. Participation in subsequent profits is exceptional, but even if a microscopic percentage is conceded, it may not materialise if the producer or distributor takes refuge in 'creative accounting'.

A very few top-line authors have broken through this barrier. The case of *Godfather* Puzo in the USA has already been mentioned in Note 51, and there have been others less vertiginous. Nearer home Frederick Forsyth was quoted in *Now* (21 November 1980) as saying that, while he had sold the rights outright of his first bestseller, *The Day of the Jackal*, he had since made other arrangements for *The Dogs of War*. Without revealing the size of the initial payment, 'The film cost nine-and-a-half million dollars and I get a percentage after it has recouped three times its negative costs. I think it should do that easily.'

The writer of the script is even more at risk, be it an original story or an adaptation. Although negotiations over basic terms for feature films between the Writers' Guild and the producers' representatives broke down in 1982 (but have since re-started), an experienced professional writer would expect to receive at least £15,000 for a treatment and first draft, and a further £10,000 for a final draft which would usually include a payment on the first day of shooting. In the past, such sums have traditionally included all residuals (overseas exhibition, television screening, etc.), in contrast to the USA where, for example, the writer would be paid additionally for any film he had scripted for the cinema, if shown on television.

[281]

CHAPTER TWELVE

Screen—Television

Television in the 1930s. Re-started in 1946 after Second World War. Advent of independent television in 1954–5. Television flourishes late 1950s to early 1980s. Huge demand for written material, especially original scripts. Screenwriters' Association becomes independent of the Society of Authors, and resists take-over by ACTT. It registers as a trade union and adopts title of the Writers' Guild of Great Britain. Fears of American invasion of British television programmes. Terms available to scriptwriters in 1957. Collective agreements. Comparative rates for teleplays in 1971 and 1982. Writing for educational television. The precariousness of freelance TV scriptwriting. Advent of videograms and cable television; their impact on television and future possibilities. Direct broadcasting by satellite. How to protect creators' rights?

Public television had begun with a daily half-hour transmission in 1932 and, within a few years, the BBC was operating regular evening programmes from Alexandra Palace. The service closed down at the outbreak of war, but re-opened in 1946. In contrast to the USA, however, progress was relatively slow, and in 1952 radio still outnumbered TV licences by about 11 to 1. But, with the arrival of independent or commercial television in 1955, following legislation in the previous year, the pace so accelerated that, by the summer of 1957, 85 per cent of the country had been covered for viewing; and by the following January there was a nightly audience of 20 million.

During the next 25 years—late 1950s to early 1980s—television became and flourished as the principal source of information and entertainment for the nation as a whole, partly at the expense of existing media, but partly and more positively because it generated a large additional audience for whom a television set had become a necessary adjunct to living. This is not the place to attempt any historical account of television in terms of politics or organisation, or of the immense range of its programmes, rather to comment on its impact upon the profession of writing, the opportunities and rewards, and the reactions of some of the writers involved.

The first and obvious fact was the huge quantity of written material demanded by TV, particularly for dramatic scripts. Whereas the cinema continued to rely, to a large degree, on film versions of novels and plays, in television original scripts far outnumbered adaptations. Exceptions such as Colin Welland's original script of *Chariots of Fire*, written for the cinema, and John Mortimer's adaptation for television of Evelyn Waugh's novel, *Brideshead Revisited*, though memorable, do not disprove the point. Secondly, it was the *immediacy* of television in practically every department that influenced the character of the programmes; with the day-to-day emphasis on news, weather, sport, current affairs; on debates, interviews, quizzes, panel games and light entertainment, where contemporary fashions and events were an essential part of the subject matter; and even in interpretations of history, science, society and human character, conveyed factually as in *Life on Earth*, wholly or semi-fictionally in *Coronation Street* and *Cathy Come Home*, or fantastically in *Dr Who*. In these and many other instances, television fell, or seemed to fall, within the category of documentary—'this is what happened', or 'this is what might happen'. Thirdly and contingently, television programmes had to be shorter and more condensed than either feature films, stage plays or print, owing to the quantity and variety of transmissions during a day's viewing. Thus a teleplay was unlikely ever to be longer than 90 minutes, while 30 to 40 minutes were considered long enough for most other types of programme. What was lost in individual length was made up in output, by the running of series and serials to give full rein to a serious subject or popular programme, and by the fact that, even before the arrival of Channel Four in 1982, the two BBC channels and ITV alone were transmitting over 250 hours a week.

This was, by any yardstick, a staggering figure, especially in terms of scriptwriting; but the prospect had been apparent from the very beginning of the period and had altered the whole horizon for screenwriters and their representative organisation, the Screenwriters' Association, referred to earlier. The foundation of the Association in 1937 and subsequent separation from the Society of Authors is described in Chapter Six of Part One of this book, but the relevant extract is repeated in Note 1 of this Chapter for the sake of clarity.[1]

After the war the SWA moved fast to establish its own identity before the campaign over television began. For example it negotiated the first ever Screen Credits Agreement with the British Film Producers Association, set up a separate office,[2] formed an asssociate membership group, and elected J. B. Priestley to succeed A. P. Herbert (after a long and arduous stint) as President. In Frank Launder's view, Priestley was 'a man of abounding energy, and if he was to be President he was going to be a working one'.

> His views on the rights of writers in films and television were nothing if not definite. He wanted a royalty system for us similar to that enjoyed by the dramatists. He wanted screenwriters to have their names in lights outside cinemas, and to receive a share of the gross box-office takings . . . These things for us were distant horizons . . . but Priestley wanted it all to happen at once, or at any rate in the forseeable future. Perhaps he was right. Perhaps the time was ripe then, but we had neither the power, nor the influence to make it possible. I think the truth of this dawned on him, for gradually his interest in us waned, and after a lapse of time he tendered his resignation.

This led to Launder himself being elected President and to his becoming involved in a domestic crisis arising out of a move by the writers' section of the film union, ACT (later ACTT), designed to take over the Screenwriters' Association. There were certain positive advantages—the backing of a paid administration, a stronger platform for negotiation, and a fair measure of autonomy. After a series of fevered debates, however, SWA members voted by a large majority to retain their independence and, in order to safeguard the future, to change the status of the Association. This was the moment, therefore, when, at one stroke as it were, SWA made a formal break with the Society of Authors, resisted a take-over by ACT, and confirmed its own separate existence and strength by registering as a trade union in 1956.

Neither these events, nor the intrigues and in-fighting arising out of them, concealed or dispelled wider issues. The great fear in the late 1950s was that, just as US interests had long dominated the production of films for the cinema, so a similar pattern might develop in television. It was well known that the Americans had been stockpiling TV films, not to mention old feature films unloaded by Hollywood on the US networks. Screenwriters therefore pressed for a Quota, similar to the one in force for the film industry: in this case they wanted 80 per cent British, 20 per cent imported; but no such demand was ever conceded—only the assurance that the 'tone and style of the programmes' would be 'predominantly British'.

In those early days negotiations for basic terms and conditions for television writing were arduous and protracted; and initial progress was due as much to individual writers who could afford to stand their ground, or to their agents, as to collective bargaining. An indication of what a TV dramatist might earn for a one-hour play in 1957 was offered by Donald Bull, then drama script editor of Associated-Rediffusion Ltd, one of the independent programme contractors.

> For the right to transmit his play over the entire Independent Television Network, a writer may expect to receive between £200 and £300. Usually he allows the originating company a licence that may be from 6 months to 2 years, in which to produce his play once for the given fee and providing for extra fees in the event of repeats, but . . . at present the chances of repeat performances are virtually nil, owing to the lack of a satisfactory system of telerecording.
>
> In theory, in foreign TV markets the writer can do very well. America will pay from $1,250 upwards for a major network run of his play . . . Canada will pay from $450 to $1,000 . . . Australia is a rising young market and there are further possibilities in Germany, Italy, France and Spain, but what does all this amount to financially? Taking average figures: a *certain* £250 from the UK; a *possible* £150 from Europe; a *doubtful* £30 from Australia; a mouth-watering but *unlikely* £1,000 from the Americas.[3]

Even allowing in these figures for the pre-inflation value of the pound, the fact remained that—as in the early days of films—the television script was regarded as a minor item compared with the cost of production, transmission, promotion and overheads, although without it none of the rest followed. A familiar story. In such a situation experience was to show that, in negotiating with a limited number of employers—as was the case with television—trade union status was necessary if writers were to secure basic terms and conditions comparable to those guaranteed to performers and technicians. Further, that whatever the objections to the concept of the 'closed shop'[4] as applied to the arts, the possibility of collective withdrawal of labour by writers had to be considered if all else failed. No such situation, it should be pointed out, prevailed in the world of books, owing to the multiplicity of publishers, whose principal representative organisation (the Publishers Association) had no mandatory powers over members, and to the practical impossibility of 'organising' or even identifying all book writers. In the event other courses of action had had to be followed and fair contracts evolved as a result of competition among publishers in the market, and by pressure and publicity exerted over many years by the authors' organisations and agents.

As it turned out, the Writers' Guild only occasionally instructed its members to refuse their services, and then not always successfully. Nevertheless, thanks to forceful negotiations in the years following its formation, the Guild not only gained recognition as the main body in Britain representing the collective interests of screenwriters, but succeeded in signing a series of minimum terms agreements with the film and television employers, such agreements defining the categories and stages of scriptwriting, with basic scales of remuneration and methods of payment. In short a framework was constructed, within which individual writers or their agents were free to bargain for the best terms they could extract from the market, resting upon the foundation of agreed minima.

At first it was a slow business. Writing in *The Screenwriter* of summer 1963, Allan Prior[5] reflected:

What is a writer worth?
I'm not thinking of the Rattigans, Ustinovs, Mankowitzs, or

Bryan Forbes—we know that ... golden boys of that carat comprise less than three per cent of the Guild's membership, and that the financial gulf between them and the rest is enormous.

Nor am I thinking of the dynamos, the extraordinary prolific and professional writers like Ted Willis ...

I'm thinking of the Average Joe. The bloke whose job in life is to supply workable, competent scripts which entertain millions. He may write second feature films, and occasionally a first feature. Or, more likely, he may work solely for TV—on original plays, on episodes for series, live or filmed.

He earns annually about half the income of the average television staff producer or director, and he has considerable professional expenses which do not trouble the staff man ... And, of course, he has no shred of security, no pension scheme or royalties 'nest egg'.

Prior then cited two cases. One was a highly experienced writer who had been working for thirty years in all the performance media. His annual income was about £1,500. 'Sometimes it tops the £2,000 mark, sometimes it drops out of sight.' The other was a young man with about five years' experience, then writing for ABC's *The Avengers* series. He currently earned £1,000 p.a.[6] On the same page Elizabeth Taylor, the actress, was reported as receiving £100,000 for a one-hour TV film, *Elizabeth Taylor in London*, being made that summer.

Over the next twenty years rates and benefits improved substantially. For example, the minimum for an original 60-minute teleplay by an established writer rose from £650 (BBC) in 1971 to £3,450 (BBC) and £3,800 (ITCA) in 1982, by which time the concept of the minimum had been replaced by that of the 'going' rate, defined as 'the actual payment which a writer should realistically expect to receive', exclusive of repeats, royalties on overseas sales, and a pension scheme to which both writer and employer contributed. Similar improvements applied to other categories of scripted programmes—series, serials, dramatisations, educational drama, etc.—but on a lower scale for new writers or beginners, who might expect to receive about one third less than the going rate. It was to the credit of the Guild that these increases did more than keep pace with inflation and represented a real financial gain for the writer, particularly when account was taken of the returns and benefits additional to basic fees.

Yet, despite these improvements, television was widely regarded as a jungle, even by those who regularly wrote for it, and as almost impenetrable by those trying to get in. The following quotations from two experienced writers were typical. In 1978 Robert Wales wrote:[7]

There are two principal methods of writing for television— with an agent or without one. Without one, you are likely to spend more time writing letters than scripts. And you will do a lot of travelling . . . trying to befriend producers and convince them that your script, or your idea of one, is the greatest happening since sliced bread . . . With an agent, it is much simpler. All you have to do is never leave your doorstep, sit close by your telephone and wait for the angel to ring. And wait. And wait. Getting more paranoid by the month.

For the newcomer into British TV, however, agencies are a Catch 22 situation. Unless you already have TV credits, very few agents, if any, would want to know about you . . . You quickly discover that, apart from single plays, almost all else is commissioned—through agents . . . Only one in a thousand of unsolicited plays offered to British TV is ever considered.

TV is very much writing to order. Do not imagine for a moment that most TV writers set out to create gratuitous violence, for instance. If it is required by the TV company or the BBC for reasons of ratings or whatever, it is dictated by the producer and the writer obliges. Again, it is doubtful if any author would tolerate the complete mangling of his manuscript without any reference back to him . . . But it is something that happens to TV writers. On occasion they have been so horrified by what has been done to their scripts that the only recourse open to them is the demand to have their name removed from the credits.

Perhaps attitudes such as these spring from the fact that, for the most part, TV is a one-night-stand affair. One performance, and it is all over . . . It is entirely transient . . . Now you see it, now you don't. There, gone, forgotten.

In 1979—when rates were substantially lower than those quoted for 1982—John Bowen wrote:[8]

'Aha,' you say. 'Easy to make a living. Three plays a year by an established writer for independent television make him £5,445, which is over £100 a week before tax: *that's* more than a lorry-driver's basic wage.'

But consider, the independent companies between them only produce 39 plays a year, the BBC not so many more, if one excludes classic revivals. If every playwright wrote three, there'd be only thirteen writers writing plays for ITV. Since there are already many more than thirteen established playwrights, how would the new ones get a showing?

'Very well,' you say. 'One play and two episodes of a series; it's still £5,115.' You reckon without the compartmentalisation of television. A few writers cross the line (I've done so myself), but in general the producers of series require a known product. They do not require either depth of characterisation (since the main characters are already provided) or felicity of dialogue. They do require the ability to write to a budget, a deadline and locations often already set, and to manipulate familiar situations in a familiar way, and a readiness to allow one's work to be messed about in any way the producer wishes.

'Serials, where the writer provides the storyline. One play and three episodes of a serial—£5,815. Or a play and three dramatisations—£5,115. It can still be done.'

But how many serials, where the writer provides etc., are transmitted in a year? Since such a serial will only use one writer, how much work does that leave for other writers? How many dramatisations are transmitted in a year?

Television is a closed market . . . It is difficult for new writers to enter it, but they should, they must, and they do and at a faster rate than the existing ones die off. The writer of a successful comedy series may make a lot of money over a short period. The small pool of series writers exists on its own, its members comparatively affluent but perpetually fearful of falling out with the even smaller pool of series producers. For most of the rest, slim pickings.

All the comments and statistics quoted here must be treated as samples, i.e. indications only of some of the problems confronting TV writers at different times. They cannot of course be comprehensive, even in drama to which they mostly refer and which is a distinct genre attracting the highest rewards, where playwrights such as John Hopkins, Dennis Potter and David Mercer made their names, and where others writing for one or more of the performance media enhanced their reputations. Sampling in other categories of scriptwriting, e.g. commentaries on facts and events, would yield parallel results: namely, that, during the late 1970s, the writer of a popular and continuing programme could usually command fees well above the minima and earn, say, £20,000 in a year, when all the spin-offs had been calculated. However there was never any guarantee that, once the subject had been exhausted, a fresh commission would come along. As with acting, typecasting could be a danger, and there were other pitfalls too. To quote Robert Wales again:

> To categorise you is comforting to agents and producers alike. They need the security. It worries them if you suddenly switch from re-writing the Bible to cops and robbers, and you then suggest you'd like to do a romance. They don't know where they stand even if you do. However, if you prefer to restrict yourself to dramatised adaptations of books, for example, and write only for the confines of the electronic studio, there is danger. If the TV moguls decide that this vein has worn out and call a halt, you are likely to find yourself unemployed for quite a while.

In the 1970s the names most familiar to viewers were not those of the scriptwriters, nor even of the directors or producers. They would appear in the credits, but often flashed so fast at the end of the programme that you could barely read, let alone remember, them. It was the presenters and entertainers that stole the screen—newsreaders, reporters, political, sports and other commentators, actors, singers, disc jockeys, and participants in panel games. In only one area did the scriptwriter make his mark, and that was when he personally presented a programme or series that he himself had written or researched. David Attenborough was an outstanding example, with his vivid evocations of evolution; or Robert Kee unravelling Irish history; or Bamber Gascoigne tracing the origins and growth of Christianity. In these and other instances the writer came into his own, not merely because of a pleasing personality or because he happened already to be a well-known broadcaster, but essentially because the script was an integral part of the presentation.

As in radio, television has played an important role in the area of education. In 1981–2 the BBC, for example, provided 70 TV programmes (plus 113 radio) for primary and secondary schools over the whole of the UK; also '116 broadcast services aimed at viewers at home or in formal and informal learning environments as part of its commitment to the education of adults'.[9] Although on a smaller scale, ITV's services for schools and colleges were considerable, and included 35 series produced by four of the major companies—Central, Granada, Thames and Yorkshire. The advent of Channel Four in November 1982 promised a considerable increase in provision and coverage: notably in collaboration with the Manpower Services Commission, with plans for better training and learning facilities for school leavers. All these programmes—whether from the BBC, ITV, or Closed Circuit Television authorities—required an adequate amount of equipment for reception; and it was significant that an estimated 90 per cent of primary and secondary schools were able and willing to incorporate what was offered as part of their curriculum.

Finally, a word about the Open University, which many regard as the most important single advance in adult education this century, and which went on the air in January 1971. It opened its own broadcasting centre at Milton Keynes in May 1982, described as 'virtually self-contained . . . with its own programme service areas for film, visual effects, studio and graphic design'.[10] Through the medium of the BBC, it transmitted in 1981–2 some 35 hours a week (mostly at the weekend, also in the early morning, with one programme each weekday evening), in addition to 20 hours of radio, all of which was integrated with a comprehensive service of correspondence tuition, aimed at enabling students to work at home and qualify for degrees in their spare time.

Most Open University and many other educational programmes are prepared by professional teachers and academics, operating as members of a team assigned to a particular course or series, which means that copyright is normally vested in the commissioning authority. But where an individual writer is employed as a consultant or is in a position to write a complete programme, educational or otherwise, then copyright remains his property and he grants a licence for a limited period (two and a half to five years according to circumstances), after which time he regains his rights. This is important for several reasons. One is the need to defend the concept of a freelance as a writer 'who retains essential control of the material he has created'.[11] Another is that, however ephemeral a programme may appear to be, there is always the chance of a repeat or a re-make after the licence has run out—and this is particularly relevant with the development of video and cable. A third and related reason concerns the tendency, especially in television, to favour staff writing. This is frowned on by the unions as poaching on the preserves of the freelance, and because self-commissioning is all too easy to justify on technical grounds (e.g. where background knowledge is essential for a long-running serial). Yet there is no doubt about the value of staff experience.

Reading, assessing and tailoring scripts, researching a subject, and taking part in the production itself, are all effective ways of learning the writer's craft; and of course they provide useful contacts when an editor or producer turns freelance. The leap from a safe well-paid job on the inside of broadcasting to the cold competitive world of scripting outside is always a difficult decision. Yet it is commonly done by those who feel that independence sharpens effort and originality, while an indefinite spell of security tends to induce somnolence. Yet however he starts, and however successful he becomes, the television scriptwriter must always operate as part of the production team. A good programme depends as much on fruitful collaboration between creator and producer as on the inherent value of the script; and no clause in the contract can make certain of that.

The screen, both large and small, has probably offered writers more scope for their talents, more opportunities, and more money, than any other medium;[12] yet it is the most fickle in its fashions and exerts the briefest impact upon the audience. The rate of loss among writers has always been high. Writing in March 1980,[13] Eric Paice, then President of the Writers' Guild, questioned how long the lifestyle of a television writer could last.

He estimated that, over the previous twelve months, the cost of working as a freelance had so increased that he would have to earn about £20,000 gross to clear £8–10,000 before tax. As television budgets had escalated, so the proportion allocated to the script had shrunk.

> Twenty years ago it was around $5\frac{1}{2}$ to 4 per cent of the total budget on an *Armchair Theatre* play or an episode of *The Avengers*. Now it is down to below 2 per cent, sometimes only a little over 1 per cent.

He quoted Allan Prior as saying:

> Of the original group of a hundred-odd writers who came into the business in the late fifties and early sixties, 20 per cent have disappeared without trace. Fifty per cent of the rest are either dead or dead drunk.[14]

The inference is that only a small minority of freelances writing for the screen can expect to sustain a successful output all their working lives. For the majority the artistic demands alone prove too exacting, which means that sooner or later their earning power will decline and die. It means also that, as in other kinds of authorship, unless a writer has managed to conserve and re-animate some of his copyrights (unlikely), or has succeeded in using his gifts abroad (e.g. in Hollywood), or has scraped enough from a wildly fluctuating income to pay for a private pension in addition to state retirement contributions, or has saved some real money during an affluent spell (difficult, even with the help of a first-class accountant), he has at some point to abandon his profession. Thereafter he has either to try to sell work in a different medium, or find a job outside writing altogether: not easy after middle age; impossible in a recession. But that is the price that most freelances have to pay.

When I was finishing this book in the spring of 1983, television as we knew it seemed to be reaching its apogee, after a generation of unprecedented popularity and prosperity. The Fourth Channel, intended primarily as an outlet for independent producers but widely regarded as ITV2, had begun transmitting in November 1982, and television at breakfast time early in 1983. The future seemed boundless. In fact there were already signs of transition, if not decay. The introduction of videograms (video recorders and cassettes, and video discs) had already taken place and was making breakneck progress. The number of VCRs in British homes had risen from c. 15,000 in 1976 to c. 675,000 in 1982 and was expected to exceed 3 million by the end of 1983. You could as easily buy or rent pre-recorded cassettes or acquire blank tapes to capture favourite TV programmes for convenient showing at home, as obtain gramophone records or books. The video disc, a miracle of condensation and long life, was not capable of recording off-air, but its other advantages promised enormous possibilities in world markets. As noted earlier, all forms of video reproduction were and are, however, bedevilled by piracy on a rocketing scale, not to mention the trade in video pornography. Until this problem has been mastered, or at least controlled, e.g. by taxation on software and exemplary fines or imprisonment, the future looks dark for manufacturers and copyright owners alike. Even then, the solution ultimately depends on the ability to 'convince the public that there is anything immoral or illegal in video theft'.[15]

In October 1982 the Hunt Committee had recommended the extension of cable television in Britain. The advantage lay in freedom from interference, better reception, and the capability to communicate a large number of channels simultaneously. The main disadvantage was the high cost of installation, though offset by the relative cheapness of maintenance by comparison with the present systems of broadcasting. In theory[16] cable could replace these systems altogether, so that viewers could simply pay for the programmes of their choice out of catalogues offered them by the cable companies. However the Government was expected to ensure[17] that, in Britain, cable would have to carry the national networks as well as the items available on subscription. Nonetheless the advent of almost limitless choice, however attractive at first sight, might in practice—as American experience seems to indicate—generate grave disadvantages. The sheer cost of providing such a volume and variety of programmes might mean that no commercial company could afford to produce good plays, good documentaries, good educational work or music, of the kind we now enjoy by selection from among the four channels available on television. In short, instead of polarising choice so that you could pick and pay for a subject of special interest (from gardening and DIY to classical jazz), cable might—as the Annan Report of March 1977 suggested—erode audience figures for any single programme of worth, to the extent that we would be flooded with fill-ins, repeats, advertisements, and an endless assortment of rubbish.

Cost apart—does programme material on such a colossal scale actually exist? If not, abundance could be a myth.

Whatever happens, the writers' organisations will have to lobby hard to ensure that there is a fair quota of British-made programmes, and that foreign material is properly paid for.

Ironically, even the heyday of cable might be cut short since, technically, it could be replaced by direct broadcasting by satellite (DBS).

> It is now possible to bypass control by placing a 'dish antenna', about four feet in diameter, on your roof and tune in directly to programmes reflected by satellites. However, direct satellite broadcasting to the home is unlikely to spread very fast. Some countries have prohibited the use of domestic receivers altogether, but a more effective form of control will be the encoding of all satellite signals, so that they need to be unscrambled before viewing.[18]

Assuming that the process of unscrambling will be contracted to authorised reception points for re-transmission, or possibly by a device attached to the screen, then everyone should be kept in business.

To conclude. The potential of growth in visual communication is enormous; and by the time this book appears much more, no doubt, will have happened or been projected. In any event it follows that opportunities for origination will be almost as large.

How do we safeguard creators' rights in what promises to be a sea of saturation?

Notes

Abbreviations: V.B-C, Volume One = *Authors by Profession*, Volume One: published by the Society of Authors, 1978. SoA = The Society of Authors. Guild = The Writers' Guild of Great Britain.

PART ONE:
WRITING FOR PRINT

CHAPTER ONE

1 V.B-C, Volume One, p. 98.

2 V.B-C, Volume One, p. 216. Two points should be noted by way of qualification of this statement: 1. If an author sold his copyright, then the powers quoted in the Act passed to the new owner. 2. The Act incorporated a curious restriction whereby, after 25 years following the author's death, the reproduction of any of his works was not deemed to be an infringement of copyright, if a statutory royalty of 10% was paid to the then copyright owner. This provision was abolished in the 1956 Copyright Act.

3 In its early days the BBC claimed that sound broadcasting was not covered by the 1911 Copyright Act, but this contention was fortunately disproved.

4 See *The Net Book Agreement 1899* by Frederick Macmillan, Robert Maclehose, 1924.

5 England and Wales only. Scotland and Northern Ireland followed later.

6 Miscellaneous paper dated 17 May 1948.

7 That is, apart from the activities of a handful of reputable authors' agents in business at the time, who had not formed any representative association of their own.

8 Quotation from p. 57 of *The Publishers' Association 1896–1946* by R. J. L. Kingsford, CUP, 1970. This book also provided the statistical information quoted in the rest of the paragraph.

9 *The Author*, April 1917, p. 172.

10 *Experiment in Autobiography*, Volume Two, by H. G. Wells, pp. 670–1. Gollancz and the Cresset Press, 1934.

11 Miss Braddon was the mother of W. B. Maxwell, himself a novelist, who became chairman of the Society of Authors' Committee of Management and of the National Book Committee in the 1920s.

12 See p. 131 of *D. H. Lawrence's Nightmare. The Writer and his Circle in the Years of the Great War* by Paul Delany, Harvester Press, 1979.

13 SoA archives.

14 *The Author*, February 1917, and SoA archives.

15 Published in *The Author*, March 1912.

16 Published in *The Author*, July 1913.

17 *The Grievances between Authors and Publishers*, 1887, *The Cost of Production*, 1889, *The Methods of Publishing*, 1890. See V.B-C, Volume One, pp. 134–5 and 148–9.

18 It was an expensive victory since Kyle was unable to pay, and the Society had to ask members for a special contribution to settle the bill. As Ian Hay Beith, Chairman of the Committee of Management at the time, said: 'To extinguish Galloway Kyle, the Society has temporarily extinguished itself.' Subsequently the Society set up a Fighting Fund in order to finance large-scale actions in defence of principle.

19 See *The Publishing Unwins* by Philip Unwin, Heinemann, 1972. Also *The Truth about a Publisher* by Sir Stanley Unwin, George Allen & Unwin, 1960. Unwin was also concerned, from an early date, with the Society of Bookmen, founded in 1921 by Hugh Walpole 'for the advancement of knowledge and the appreciation of good literature', from which sprang the National Book Council (forerunner of the National Book League) formed in 1925, of which Unwin was the founder.

20 From p. 360 of *The Time Traveller: The Life of H. G. Wells* by Norman and Jeanne Mackenzie, Weidenfeld & Nicolson, 1973. In recounting this incident I have relied both on the Mackenzies' work and read the original documents that now form part of the SoA archive at the British Library.

21 *Ibid.*, p. 361.

22 *Ibid.*, p. 363.

23 Thring left the Society of Authors with a generous testimonial subscribed by the membership, but a disappointed man. On 14 February 1930 he had written to Shaw:

Dear Mr Shaw,
    No doubt you saw in the January *Author* a note to the effect that I had been superannuated and that I leave the Society's office on March 1st. I am still retained as 'Consulting Secretary' on a salary.
    I am very upset as I had no reason to think that while I was physically and mentally sound that I should be asked at three months' notice to leave an office that I have held for 37 years. In the

matter of salary the Committee have treated me very fairly, but they have a veto on whatever work I take up.

As it is impossible for me with my present financial responsibilities to make both ends meet I am now on the look out for something to do that will bring me an assured income. I hope therefore you will excuse my writing to you to inquire whether you would allow me to refer to you. Your name is a valuable one to conjure with, and I may be sadly in need of such backing.

However I have not left the office yet. I have had two refusals from very likely sources and my difficulty lies in the fact that the market for my special knowledge is very restricted and lies to a great extent with the enemy, i.e. Publishers and Managers.

I have endeavoured during my term here to safeguard Authors.

> Believe me
> Yours sincerely
> Herbert Thring

Shaw forwarded Thring's letter to Wells and wrote on 21 February:

My dear H.G.,

This will end with our having to get up a subscription for Thring. You know, don't you—or do you?—that the unhappy man is down and out? We have superannuated him (he dates from the days of Walter Besant) without giving him a sufficient pension or having ever paid him enough to enable him to save. He has been domestically unlucky too; but I need not put all that on paper.

Two years ago or so we took on a gentleman named Roberts [Denys Kilham Roberts] to assist him and be trained to succeed him; and this succession has now occurred, Thring being retained as 'consulting secretary' at £200 a year: the best the Society can do for him officially by way of a pension.

I enclose a letter which I have received from T. himself, which is rather pathetic, as he does not seem to see that 37 years' service is a reason for superannuation, not against it, and that his difficulty in finding employment is simply that he is too old. Of course he has no notion of why, with his start in life, he has not earned £20,000 a year as a family solicitor . . . But as we have had him cheap, and he has been devoted to the Society, incorruptible and hardworking, we cannot leave him in the soup merely because his method of taking up cases included fixing his teeth in the calves of both parties.

Note. This deplorable situation was partially corrected by the decision of the Committee of Management, at the insistence of Galsworthy, to increase the pension from £200 to £500 p.a., by the gift of a testimonial which reached a total approaching £800, and by the presentation of a portrait by William Rothenstein which now hangs in the Society's offices.

24 *The Time Traveller*, pp. 363–6. Another less serious, indeed hilarious, copyright case of a rather different though odd character occurred at this time, and was reported in *The Author*, October 1926. The paintiff was a medium, Miss Geraldine Dorothy Cummins, who claimed the copyright in 'automatic writing' produced by her hand while her mind was in a dream state. This writing, known as the 'Chronicle of Cleophas', was deemed to emanate from a medieval monk laying information as to the whereabouts of certain undiscovered buildings at Glastonbury Abbey, which in the event proved true. The Chronicle was passed to Frederick Bligh Bond, Director of Excavation at Glastonbury, who edited the manuscript and converted it into a book. He claimed that no copyright existed in the work (other than his own) as far more than 50 years had elapsed since the death of the original author. The learned judge (Mr Justice Eve) thought otherwise and said that, if the psychic source of these writings was admitted, it would seem as though they were the joint product of Miss Cummins and a gentleman who lived some 1,900 [sic] years ago. His jurisdiction, however, was confined to people in this world and from the earthly standpoint of the Copyright Act, 1911, there could be no doubt that Miss Cummins was the sole author and sole owner of the copyright.

CHAPTER TWO

1 Denys Kilham Roberts edited, alone or in collaboration, *The Year's Poetry, The Centuries' Poetry, Penguin Parade*, and *Orion*. He also compiled *The Authors Handbook* 1935–40. (see p. 51).

2 The sale of Virginia Woolf's books contributed materially to the profits of the Hogarth Press, but I have omitted these from the Woolfs' returns from writing. Leonard was of course the business head.

3 By Leonard Woolf in *Downhill all the Way*, Hogarth Press, 1967, and *Journey not the Arrival Matters*, Hogarth Press, 1969. By John Lehmann in *The Whispering Gallery*, Longman, 1955, and *I am My Brother*, Longman, 1960; also in *Thrown to the Woolfs*, Weidenfeld, 1978.

4 *Journey to the Frontier* by Peter Stansky and William Abrahams, p. 77.

5 Bodley Head gave Lehmann £60 per issue 'to cover all editorial expenses and translators' fees, as well as contributors'. Lehmann often had to supplement this amount and offered 'each contributor (of prose more than 3,000 words in length) at least £4 on account of royalties'.

6 *C.Day-Lewis. An English Literary Life* by Sean Day-Lewis, Weidenfeld, 1980.

7 *Revolution in Writing* by C. Day-Lewis, p. 11, Hogarth Press, 1935.

8 Sean Day-Lewis, *op. cit.*, p. 96.

9 Gorell's Bill contended that liability in libel should not lie where 'there was no intent to defame the plaintiff . . . or no knowledge of the existence of the plaintiff . . . or no want or due care in failure to know or recollect the existence of the plaintiff . . . or no failure to take steps to prevent the alleged libel being so read or understood'. The Special Committee of the House of Lords however rejected the Bill on the ground that 'the evidence adduced did not justify the proposed changes in law'. Another Bill of a similar nature, introduced in November 1938 in the House of Commons by Sir Stanley Reed, MP, and A. P. Herbert, MP, met a similar fate. See *The Author*, spring 1939, p. 83.

10 Gorell gave a graphic account of his part in the affair in his autobiography, *One Man . . . Many Parts*, Odhams, 1956. He described the Council meeting called on 19 March 1930 as 'surely the most unusual gathering of celebrities of the English literary world in this century'. See pp. 249–55 of his book.

11 Both letters were reproduced in *The Author*, January 1930.

12 I am indebted to Caterina Gilardino (Mrs Monaghan) who joined the Society's staff a few months after Elizabeth Barber, and who has recorded a great deal of information on tape for me about events and conditions at the various offices. At Mortimer some of the staff lived at Briarlea, DKR's house, others found lodging in the village where Margaret Storm Jameson, Chairman of the Committee of Management 1941–2, was also living at the time.

13 As Kingsford points out, and as everyone in the trade knows, Book Tokens Ltd has done a great deal for the common good by subsidising various schemes of book promotion and by charitable donations.

14 *The Bookseller*, October 1934.

15 Kingsford, *The Publishers' Association, 1896–1946*, p. 126.

16 The SoA has published—free to its members, but on sale to the public—a series of 'Quick Guides' on *Copyright, The Protection of Titles, Libel, Your Copyrights after Your Death, Income Tax, V.A.T., Authors' Agents*, and *Publishing Contracts*. Also 'Bulletins' on *Teachers as Authors, Translators as Authors, Guidelines for Authors of Educational Books*, and *Guidelines for Authors of Medical Books*.

17 SoA archives.

18 *Journey from the North*, Volume Two, Collins and Harvill Press, 1970.

1 *The Author*, spring 1945. By permission of the Estate of H. E. Bates. Hilary St George Saunders was librarian of the House of Commons 1946–50. He wrote *The Battle of Britain*, 1941, *Per Ardua*, 1944, *The Green Beret*, 1949, *The Red Beret*, 1950.

2 The Diamond Jubilee, celebrated on 22 June 1945 with a Conversazione at Grosvenor House, London, 'was a most impressive and distinguished literary gathering' attended by John Masefield, the Society's President, and Osbert Sitwell, Chairman of the Committee of Management. 'Perhaps its most significant feature, however, was the presence of a much larger proportion of younger writers of both sexes, many in uniform, than is usual on such occasions.' *The Author*, winter 1945. This Conversazione had been preceded on 14 May by a poetry recital organised by the Society at the Wigmore Hall. In his biography of his father, Sean Day-Lewis wrote (p. 162):

> It was a notable occasion attended by Queen Elizabeth [wife of George VI] and her two young daughters, and starting with a prologue written and delivered by the Poet Laureate, John Masefield. Among others who read from their own work were Walter de la Mare, T. S. Eliot, Edith Sitwell, Louis MacNeice and Dylan Thomas (who at one stage in the proceedings was seen to flick his cigarette ash in the Queen's lap).

It was about a similar occasion in the ballroom of the Dorchester Hotel, that Elizabeth Barber recorded:

> I can see Masefield now. Poetry was to be read and Masefield wanted to be sure that acoustics were good. There he was, with hotel staff scurrying hither and thither arranging tables, standing first on one chair and then on another and then trying out a little podium, in morning coat, white hair and moustache, declaiming the first lines of *Paradise Lost* over and over again:
>
> Of Man's First Disobedience and the Fruit
>
> His voice could have been absurd in its sing-song quality (Dylan Thomas's was the only other voice I ever heard that slightly resembled it). But it never seemed absurd, always movingly beautiful. Later that afternoon, as he read the last lines of his *Everlasting Mercy*
>
> > O lovely lily clean,
> > O lily springing green,
> > O lily bursting white,
> > Dear lily of delight . . .

even the waiters stopped clattering and stood starry-eyed.

3 In his will Shaw had directed the Public Trustee (his executor and trustee) to see to the publication of a more efficient 'British Alphabet' of at least 40 letters. This requirement was subsequently declared invalid in the High Court, but the three beneficiaries—the British Museum, the Royal Academy of Dramatic Art, and the National Gallery of Ireland—agreed to pay a certain sum (over £8,000) towards the preparation of the Alphabet; and a prize of £500 was offered for a new alphabet complying most nearly with Shaw's wishes. See report in *The Bookseller* of 24 November 1962. All three beneficiaries received regular and substantial income from Shaw royalties, as did the Society of Authors in its capacity of agent to the estate, especially after the production of *My Fair Lady*, the musical version of *Pygmalion*. This made it possible to subsidise the membership subscriptions and keep them at an artificially low level for a number of years.

4 See V.B-C, Volume One, chapters 7 and 8.

5 They included John Farquharson (1919), A. M. Heath (1919), A. D. Peters (1924), Raymond Savage (1924), Rupert Crew (1927), Stephen Aske (1929), Eric Glass (1932), Savoy Writers Agency (1932), Margery Vosper (1932), Pearn, Pollinger & Higham (1935).

6 SoA Quick Guide, *Authors' Agents*.

7 See *The Author's Empty Purse and the Rise of the Literary Agent* by James Hepburn, p. 98, OUP, 1968.

8 *Ibid.*, p. 85.

9 *Literary Gent* by David Higham, pp. 130–1, Cape, 1978.

10 Since work at the Society has always been so large and varied in character, each senior member of staff has had to take on several jobs. The following examples, related to 1971–8 (the period of the triumvirate), are at best an approximation in shorthand of the duties involved:

Advisory Service (contract vetting, legal and other business advice to members): Philippa MacLiesh, with John Coleby then Ian Rowland Hill.

Archives: Victor Bonham-Carter.

The Author (SoA quarterly journal): Editor, Richard Findlater. Production, Victor Bonham-Carter.

Awards, Prizes and Welfare Funds: George Astley and Julia Jones.

Broadcasting: John Coleby, then Ian Rowland Hill.

Children's Writers Group: Diana Shine.

Collection Bureau and Literary Estates: Anne Munro-Kerr* with Roma Woodnutt and Julia Jones.

Educational Writers Group: Philippa MacLiesh.

Finance: George Astley and Margaret Smith.

League of Dramatists: Julia Jones.

Membership: Diana Shine.

Public Lending Right: Victor Bonham-Carter, then John Coleby, then Ian Rowland Hill.

Publicity and Publications: Victor Bonham-Carter.

Permissions: Frances Hickson.

Translators Association: George Astley.

*Anne Munro-Kerr was the longest serving member of the staff, having joined the office in 1946 and experienced a variety of jobs, including Broadcasting (she was Secretary of the Radiowriters Association after Helen Lehmann).

11 *The Author*, October 1909. See also V.B-C, Volume One, p. 210.

12 Charles Garvice, 1833–1921, novelist, journalist and dramatist.

13 For a list of business expenses deductible before tax, see SoA Quick Guide, *Income Tax*.

14 SoA Archives.

15 The taxation sub-committee consisted of Compton Mackenzie (Chairman), A. P. Herbert, H. E. Bates, John Moore, Raymond Postgate, John Pudney and E. P. Smith.

16 Most of the problems affecting business expenses, spread-back and spread-forward etc., were clarified by consolidating legislation, viz., the Income and Corporation Taxes Act, 1970.

17 Ralph Hammond Innes explained further: 'It was a test case. If I had lost, any doctor who treated his mother for free after being mugged, would have had to pay tax on the fee he might have charged but did not.'

CHAPTER FOUR

1 See SoA Quick Guide, *Publishing Contracts*.

2 *The Author*, winter 1950.

3 A possible exception occurred in the mid-19th century during the heyday of the great Victorian novelists such as Dickens, Thackeray, George Eliot, Trollope, *et al.*; and when literary magazines such as the *Cornhill* paid liberally for serials.

4 *The Author*, spring 1951.

It is relevant at this point to refer to a scheme launched in 1957 by Robert Lusty, head of Hutchinson, and 'cooked up in his bath', he told me. This was the experiment of New Authors Ltd., described as:

> an attempt to reconcile the difficulties and frustration of the new writer with something of importance to say with the harsh economic climate of publishing as it is today. There can be no complete answer to the problem facing the young creative writer and his potential publisher. The writer writes to be read; the publisher publishes to make—if he can—a reasonable return on what is, at the least, a considerable financial investment.

The scheme made a considerable impact and attracted a large number of first-book writers, some of whom went on to make their names in the literary scene, e.g. Alan Clark, Prudence Andrew, Stanley Middleton, Elizabeth Mavor and Julian Mitchell. The terms offered were a standard advance of £150 against royalties of 10 per cent to 5,000 copies, 12½ per cent to 7,500, 15 per cent thereafter in the home market, with appropriate arrangements for overseas sales. The company was designed to be run on a profit-sharing basis, i.e. after meeting the costs of production plus a management fee of 25 per cent of its turnover payable to Hutchinson & Co. to cover overheads, the audited profit remaining was to be 'divided among the contributing authors in the proportion of their individual total sales in the relevant year'. Whether any such profits ever eventuated, Lusty could not remember; but the idea was visionary and stimulating.

5 *The Author*, autumn 1951.

6 The sub-committee included Walter Allen, Nigel Balchin, Richard Church, Jacquetta Hawkes, Noel Streatfeild and Francis Williams.

7 Another interesting question arising out of the survey, answered by Findlater, was, 'How on earth do all the primaries get by, who earned less than £500 a year?'

> *Reply.* The answer lies of course in non-literary or 'unearned' income. They depend on pensions. They spend their savings or legacies. They get allowances from parents. They are supported by husbands, or sometimes by their wives. If they are young enough, they take odd casual jobs, washing up, sitting in, portering. What is luridly clear is that if Britain's authors had to depend for a living *on their books alone*, most of them would be on National Assistance.

8 For income from books alone, the figure was *c.* 25 per cent.

9 *The History of Public Lending Right, 1951–82* by Victor Bonham-Carter. Unpublished.

CHAPTER FIVE

1 Its members were A. P. Herbert (Chairman), Walter Allen, H. E. Bates, David Carver (Secretary of PEN), Professor Guy Chapman, W. B. Clowes, W. A. R. Collins, Joseph Compton, Rupert Hart-Davis, Roy Jenkins, A. D. Peters, V. S. Pritchett, John Pudney, Herbert Read, Denys Kilham Roberts, Norman St John Stevas, and W. E. Williams. The honorary secretary was C. R. Hewitt (C. H. Rolph of the *New Statesman*). Most of the information about the obscenity campaign is taken from the account written by Hewitt for the Society of Authors, dated May 1968, and from his article in the autumn 1968 issue of *The Author*.

2 Article in the *Daily Telegraph*, 27 July 1959.

3 *Ibid.*

4 Article in *The Times*, 26 August 1970.

5 Elizabeth Barber left this note about APH's last illness:

> When he was very nearly dying, I used to drop in to see him on my way down to the country on Saturday mornings. One such day he could not lift his hand to hold mine. His teeth had long ago been discarded, but his eyes were still beady bright and his eyebrows as gymnastic as ever. He managed to stick a foot out from under the bedclothes with an unspoken invitation to hold it. And thus we sat while he discoursed with as clear a mind as ever on the ways and means of reducing the price of books. The last words I heard him say were, 'Come and tell me what the Publishers Association have to say about that one.'
>
> He, like many of the other great fighters I have known, had a dogged capacity for attention to detail—too much sometimes. He would ring me up at all times of the day—so often when I was just about to have a bath that he used to say, 'Here's a thought for the bath and mind you take your log tables in with you.' Many are the calculations he made me do with him and if ever I said, 'But, my dear Alan, this is honestly a waste of time', he would reply, 'Nothing is wasted. Never forget that.' At his Memorial Service at St. Martin-in-the-Fields on 6 December 1971, Vivian Ellis's settings of APH's poem on that theme was sung:

> Nothing is wasted, nothing is in vain:
> The seas roll over, but the rocks remain.
> They can break man's happiness but not man's will:
> Little lamps of liberty will smoulder still,
> Till the trumpet sounds and we break the chain
> And the wings of the spirit ride the free air again.

6 *Report by the Working Party set up by a Conference on the Obscenity Laws convened by the Chairman of the Arts Council of Great Britain*. July 1969.

7 John Montgomerie, solicitor and partner of Lord Goodman, chaired the Arts Council Working Party.

8 *The Author*, summer 1972.

9 To ascertain members' views, the Society of Authors circulated a questionnaire to which over 700 replied. On the basis of this response, a sub-committee consisting of Michael Scammell, C. R. Hewitt, and Francis Bennion prepared a document for submission to the Home Office and approved by the Society's Committee of Management. See the summer 1978 issue of *The Author*.

10 Among sources drawn on for this section are *The Lessons of PQ 17* by Michael Gilbert in the summer 1972 issue of *The Author*, the Society of Authors' Quick Guide on *Libel*, and the report, *Learning*

about Libel, by Philippa MacLiesh in the summer 1982 issue of *The Author*.

11 In the case of a defamatory statement about a dead person, successful libel proceedings can be brought by a descendant only if the statement by implication constitutes a libel on himself, e.g. by imputing to the dead an inheritable mental disease. See Quick Guide on *Libel*.

12 Author of *SOE in France*. HMSO 1976.

13 In March 1966 the Society of Authors submitted a memorandum to over 30 historians inquiring into the working of the 50-year rule, and received replies from almost every correspondent. Subsequently two representatives of the Society—Captain Stephen Roskill, RN, the naval historian, and Victor Bonham-Carter—gave evidence before the Advisory Committee.

14 Respectively Chairman and Deputy Chairman of the Society of Authors' Committee of Management at the time.

15 Scammell was also founder director of Writers' and Scholars' International, to which *Index* belonged. For his account of the origins of this organisation see his article in the winter 1978 issue of *The Author*.

16 From *Closed Shops and Charters* by Michael Scammell in the summer 1977 issue of *The Author*.

17 One example was the campaign waged against illustrators by the National Graphical Association (NGA) and the Society of Lithographic Artists, Designers, Engravers and Process Workers (SLADE) when they blacked art work at printers from non-union sources. This threatened the livelihood of certain illustrator members of the Society, including children's book writers who illustrated their own works. By extension it was feared that a similar attack might be made, e.g. by print workers, against writers who either did not belong to a trade union or belonged to no representative organisation of any kind.

18 Quoted in V.B-C, Volume One, p. 194.

19 From V.B-C, Volume One, p. 195.

20 See the *Times Literary Supplement*, issues of 21 and 28 July; 4, 11, 18 and 25 August; 8 and 29 September; 13 October 1978.

21 Happily, Lady Antonia Fraser later rejoined the Society.

CHAPTER SIX

1 Since the Second World War, the Society of Authors has formed the following specialist groups in order to concentrate on the particular business problems of the *genre* or market, but all of them ultimately responsible to the Society's Committee of Management: Translators' Association, Educational Writers' Group, Children's Writers' Group, Medical Writers' Group, Technical Writers' Group; also the Broadcasting Group which absorbed the Radiowriters' Association

(formed 1947). The League of Dramatists (formed 1931) was dissolved in 1975.

2 See Part Two, Chapters Eleven and Twelve of this book.

3 It is often invidious to list names but, by way of example, mention should be made of John Coleby and Ian Rowland Hill, successive Secretaries of the Radiowriters' Association. In addition Coleby succeeded in working harmoniously with WAG and the Guild over PLR, while Rowland Hill went on to become Secretary of the Writers' Guild itself. Philippa MacLiesh, head of the Society's advisory service, was also a strong influence, respected by all parties for her legal expertise and grasp of many complex issues.

4 An important part of the Act dealt with the 'television exhibiting right' conferred on the BBC and the Independent Television Authority, in respect of the visual images broadcast by way of television and any sounds broadcast with those images. This new right was 'subsidiary to the right of the composer or author of a copyright work'. See p. 79, summer 1955 issue of *The Author*.

5 *The Author*, summer 1977.

6 Henry Cecil (His Honour Judge H. C. Leon), author of *Brothers in Law* and many other works, served a term as chairman of the Society's Committee of Management, and of the Executive Committee of the British Copyright Council.

7 See the summer 1974 issue of *The Author*.

8 *The Author*, autumn 1981.

9 Sources of information for this section include the article on ALCS by Denis de Freitas in the winter 1978 issue of *The Author*, announcements under 'Front Line' in the autumn and winter 1981 issues, and statements by the ALCS itself. Philippa MacLiesh and Denis de Freitas represented the Society on the working party with the ALCS.

10 Machin's article was extensively quoted in *Publishers' Weekly*, the principal American trade journal, used as a front page news story in the *Sunday Times* of 13 January 1980, and re-published in *The Author*, spring 1980.

11 See report in *The Author*, spring 1981.

12 See report in *The Author*, spring 1982.

13 See article on Microform Publishing by Charles Chadwyck-Healey in *The Author*, spring 1978.

CHAPTER SEVEN

1 Reported in *The Author*, April 1920.

2 Information from Nigel Cross and Alec Harrison. See also the NUJ Freelance Fees Guide.

3 One guinea = 21 shillings.

4 *The Author*, summer 1967.

5 Information and quotations by permission of Curtis Brown Associates Ltd. © 1970 by Jessica Mitford.

CHAPTER EIGHT
1 See V.B-C, Volume One, p. 12.
2 See 'Civil List Pensions' by Nigel Cross, published in *The Times Literary Supplement*, 19 December 1980, from which I have drawn most of the information on this subject.
3 A. J. Balfour, Conservative Prime Minister, 1902–6.
4 H. H. Asquith, Liberal Prime Minister, 1908–16.
5 For example, the Contingency Fund, and the Francis Head Bequest, both sources of aid for authors, administered by the Society of Authors.
6 See *Government Patronage of the Arts in Great Britain* by John S. Harris. University of Chicago Press, 1970.
7 Since 1983, transferred to the Office of Arts and Libraries.
8 I served on the literature panel of the Arts Council from 1967 to 1972.
9 *The Arts Council of Great Britain* by Eric W. White, Davis-Poynter, 1975.
10 Arts Council Annual Report 1980–1, p. 22.
11 Quoted from 'The Meritorious and the Needy' by Nigel Cross, published in *The Times Literary Supplement*, 21 August 1981.

PART TWO:
WRITING FOR PERFORMANCE

CHAPTER NINE
1 Founded in 1899.
2 See *The Unholy Trade* by Richard Findlater, Gollancz, 1952. I rely heavily on this and other publications by the same author, notably *The Future of the Theatre*, Fabian Society, 1959; 'The Playwright and his Money', *Theatre Quarterly*, October–December 1972; and various articles published in *The Author*.
3 Phrase borrowed from *The Other Theatre* by Norman Marshall, John Lehmann, 1947. An important source of information.
4 *Collected Letters of George Bernard Shaw*, Volume One, 1874–1897, edited by Dan H. Laurence, Max Reinhardt/Dodd Mead & Co., 1965.
5 'It was generally believed, though the belief seems to have had no clear legal support, that if a play was published before it was performed, the performing right in it was irretrievably lost. Actors were therefore hired to give what amounted to public readings of manuscript plays. Normally no costumes were worn and no scenery used.' *Oxford Companion to the Theatre*, pp. 202–3, OUP, 1967.

6 St. John Ervine said that the only good play he was able to see in the West End in 1918 was Barrie's *Dear Brutus*.

7 *The Unholy Trade*, Richard Findlater, *op. cit.*

8 *Op. cit.*

9 Formed in December 1929 out of the Actors' Association and the Stage Guild.

10 Information from *Banned: A Review of Theatrical Censorship in Britain* by Richard Findlater. MacGibbon & Kee, 1967.

11 The Playhouse in Beaumont Street was built in 1938. Earlier, Fagan had made use of a converted museum building in Woodstock Road.

12 For a fuller account and discussion of these 'other' theatres, see Norman Marshall's book, *The Other Theatre, op. cit.*

13 In the course of time, emphasis was switched from the amateur to the professional theatre, and was reflected in the change of name from the British Drama League to the British Theatre Association, with effect from 1 November 1972.

14 Another amateur enterprise of note, and known to me personally, was the Citizen House Theatre, Bath, managed by Consuelo de Reyes who produced, among others, some of Laurence Housman's short plays. As a child I attended one of these performances and sat behind G. K. Chesterton whose bulk filled two adjacent seats in the tiny theatre above a shop. When he laughed, as he readily did, the whole row shook.

15 *The Author*, July 1927.

16 *The Author*, April 1923.

17 Shaw's letter was originally addressed to Percival Wilde, Secretary of the Drama Guild of the Authors' League of America and published in *The Author*, July 1928. Wilde replied in similar Shavian vein—see *The Author*, October 1928.

18 *The Author*, July 1928.

19 Dakers, 1951.

20 Quartet Books, 1979.

21 Hamish Hamilton, 1953.

22 Letter dated 1 April 1927.

23 SoA archives. Verbatim report of the meeting on 15 June 1931.

24 *Ibid.*

25 Those who served on the League's executive committee during the first two decades or so included Anthony Armstrong, James Bridie, Harold Brighouse, Ernest Denny, Douglas Furber, A. P. Herbert, Ronald Jeans, Getrude Jennings, Benn Levy, Esther MacCracken, Miles Malleson, Edward Percy, J. B. Priestley, Terence Rattigan, R. C. Sherriff, Dodie Smith, Peter Ustinov, Emlyn Williams. The next two decades brought in Robert Bolt, Wynyard Browne, John Chapman, James Forsyth, Willis Hall, N. C. Hunter, William Douglas Home, Ann Jellicoe, John Mortimer, John Osborne, Jack Ronder, Ted Willis.

26 '1983 marks Ted Willis's 40th year as an author. Apart from novels, he has written 22 stage plays, 25 screenplays and, we are told, holds the world record for creator of the most television series, 24 to date.' *The Bookseller*, 18 December 1982.

27 SoA archives.

28 John Mortimer's subsequent successes as a television playwright, quite apart from his career as a critic and a barrister, hardly need to be mentioned. See his autobiography, *Clinging to the Wreckage*, Weidenfeld, 1982.

29 See p. 204.

30 See p. 191 about early aid to the Old Vic and Sadlers' Wells.

31 Entertainment National Services Association and the Army Bureau of Current Affairs.

32 Council for the Encouragement of Music and the Arts. CEMA was the brainchild of Lord de la Warr, President of the Board of Education, Thomas Jones, Secretary of the Pilgrim Trust, and the latter's chairman, Lord Macmillan, who happened also to be Minister of Information. Finance was initially provided by the Trust with a grant of £25,000, matched pound for pound (through the Board of Education's financial vote) by the Treasury. Various honorary directors took charge of arts activities—among them, Lewis Casson for professional drama, and L. du Garde Peach for amateur drama, while Ivor Brown, then drama critic of *The Observer*, was made responsible for publicity. When CEMA was replaced by the Arts Council of Great Britain in 1946, Lord Keynes was appointed first chairman, but unhappily died before he could take up the appointment.

33 For authoritative accounts of this period, see *Off-Stage* by Charles Landstone, Elek, 1953, and Richard Findlater's *The Unholy Trade*, *op. cit.*

34 See *Government Patronage of the Arts* by John S. Harris, University of Chicago Press, 1970. *The Arts Council of Great Britain* by Eric Walter White, Davis-Poynter, 1975. Also Richard Findlater's publications as listed in Note 2; *The Set-Up* by Ronald Hayman, Eyre Methuen, 1973; *Theatre Inside Out* by Kenneth Hurren, W. H. Allen, 1977; and *The History of the National Theatre* by John Elsom and Nicholas Tomalin, Cape, 1978. Also the annual reports of the Arts Council and special publications, e.g. *The Theatre Today in England and Wales* issued by the Council in January, 1970. Another relevant source is *Scottish Prospects* by Trevor Royle published in *The Author*, spring 1970.

35 Quoted from *Money for Playwrights* by Richard Findlater. *The Author*, winter 1975.

36 For a note on the Stoke scheme, where Peter Terson was appointed resident dramatist in 1966, see *The Stoke Experiment* by Irving Wardle in *The Author*, spring 1967.

37 The Octagon Theatre, Bolton, has a flexible auditorium with a basic 318 seats, increased to 430 when opened up 'in the round'.

38 Quoted from *Post-War British Theatre* by John Elsom, Routledge, 1976. For the history of the English Stage Company and the work of George Devine, see *The Set-Up* by Ronald Hayman, Eyre Methuen, 1973; *Playwright's Theatre* by Terry Browne, Pitman, 1975; *The Theatres of George Devine* by Irving Wardle, Cape, 1978; and *At the Royal Court*, edited by Richard Findlater, Amber Lane Press, 1981.

39 A parallel agreement was concluded with the Independent Theatres Council, representing about 70 fringe theatres (including the Bush Theatre, Shepherds Bush, London, about which John Elsom wrote in *The Author*, spring 1980). The Writers' Guild and the Theatre Writers' Union also announced that they would endeavour to agree terms, first with the rest of the subsidised theatres, and then with the commercial theatre managers of the West End. After a lot of jockeying, the Society of Authors was excluded from negotiations with the Theatres National Committee, mainly because at the outset it was not a trade union and because the TNC decided to deal only with union representatives. The Society, which became a union soon after, continues to represent its dramatist members and literary estates individually.

40 The rates quoted in the 1979 Agreement have since been re-negotiated and improved.

41 *Saint's Day* and *A Penny for a Song*.

42 *The Living Room*.

43 Quoted from *The British Theatre: a personal view* by Edward McFadyen, National Book League, 1977.

44 Osborne's play not only made the author's fame and fortune, put the English Stage Company on the map and salved its finances, but it continued to earn so handsomely from subsidiary rights that the Arts Council's subsidy to the company did not exceed £8,000 p.a. for the first six years.

45 Quoted from *Drama in Britain 1964–1973* by J. W. Lambert, British Council and Longman, 1974.

46 *Drama in Britain 1951–1964* by J. C. Trewin, British Council and Longman, 1965 and J. W. Lambert *op. cit.* Also more recent works by John Elsom, Richard Findlater, Ronald Hayman, Arnold P. Hinchcliffe, Kenneth Hurren, John Russell Taylor, and others.

47 Lambert, *op. cit.*

48 *Drama*, quarterly journal published by the British Theatre Association, 9, Fitzroy Square, London W.1.

49 An article in the same issue of *Drama*, entitled *Where Angels Fear to Tread* by Antony Wilson, gives an interesting insight into the business of backing commercial shows.

50 See Findlater's article, *The Playwright and His Money op. cit.*

Although published in 1972, so that some of the statistics may need updating, the article is highly relevant and authoritative. See especially the sections entitled 'For Richer or Poorer?' and 'What Does a Dramatist Earn?'

51 *Playwrights: An Endangered Species?* available from the Theatre Writers' Union, 9, Fitzroy Square, London W.1. For a detailed and critical commentary on this report, see the article, 'New deal for playwrights?' by Richard Findlater, published in the spring 1983 issue of *The Author.*

CHAPTER TEN

1 For the preliminaries to these events, and for a full account of the early years of the BBC, see *The History of Broadcasting in the United Kingdom: Volume 1* by Asa Briggs, OUP, 1961. I have drawn on this and subsequent volumes for much of the information about the BBC.

2 Reith was succeeded by F. W. Ogilvie, Vice-Chancellor of Queen's University, Belfast, in 1938. Reith then became chairman of Imperial Airways.

3 It is of historical interest that the BBC's first literary critic was John Strachey, soon succeeded by Desmond MacCarthy. The first drama critic was Archibald Haddon, followed by James Agate. The first play specially written for radio was by A. R. Burrows and broadcast in Children's Hour, a highly successful programme from its inception, but see the reference to Richard Hughes on p. 213.

4 Frank Robert Benson, 1858–1939. Actor-manager of repute, who toured the country with his own company and gave numerous performances of Shakespeare.

5 Letter dated 30 January 1924 addressed to Herbert Thring.

6 Letter dated 24 November 1924 addressed to Herbert Thring.

7 Reproduced in *The Author,* April 1926, and reprinted here by permission of the Estate of A. A. Milne. In contrast to this incident, I quote from a letter written to me by Leslie Baily, a regular radio writer whose first script was an adaptation of Dickens's *Christmas Carol,* transmitted from Belfast at Christmas 1924 and produced by 'another unknown young man, Tyrone Guthrie'. Baily wrote:

Rates of pay were low, but in that period for the very good reason that the BBC simply hadn't the cash. Its friendly officials did their best to spread the butter to us few writers: often they were programme-makers themselves . . . I myself joined the BBC as its first London-based writer in 1937, and the Reithian Corporation was not at all the starchy place that it is often painted.

Baily gained great popularity as the compiler and broadcaster of the annual *Scrapbooks.*

8 Minimum terms for a full-length stage play, for example, rose from 6 guineas in 1923 to 25 guineas in 1942.

9 *The Author*, winter 1930.

10 *The Author*, spring 1931.

11 L. du Garde Peach (1890–1975) wrote 400 radio plays broadcast by the BBC, and was first chairman of the Radiowriters' Association founded by the Society of Authors in 1947.

12 Published by the Society of Authors in 1978.

13 It was only logical that the Society should assist in the formation of the Composers' Guild in 1944, and transfer its musician members to that body.

14 *The Author*, summer 1933.

15 *The Author*, summer 1936.

16 Relations between the PRS and SoA improved when they combined in the campaign to defeat the Musical Copyright Bill, 1929, which sought, *inter alia*, to impose a maximum fee of 2d per copy of any copyright work to be performed in public. The Bill was eventually negatived after a considerable collective effort by music interests, backed by public statements by leading members of SoA, including Bernard Shaw, A. P. Herbert, Frederic Austin, and Lord Gorell (then chairman of SoA's Committee of Management).

17 Ashley Dukes 1885–1959. Author, dramatist and translator. Director of the Mercury Theatre, Notting Hill Gate, London: home of ballet and *avante-garde* drama.

18 The increase conceded by the BBC was from £2 to 4 guineas. In the case of excerpts from full-length plays, the BBC would often allocate a consolidated amount of money to cover salaries of artistes as well as authors' fees. The League of Dramatists recommended all its members in such cases to stipulate a minimum charge of 10 per cent of the total sum so allocated. See *The Author*, autumn 1937, p. 30.

19 The parties to the agreement were the BBC, and the Society of Authors/League of Dramatists/Publishers Association. See *The Author*, spring 1942.

20 *The Author*, spring 1945.

21 The Society was represented by Osbert Sitwell, St. John Ervine and Kilham Roberts (Secretary-General of SoA): The BBC by Lord Simon of Wythenshawe (Chairman of BBC Board of Governors), Sir William Haley (Director-General), and R. J. F. Howgill (Acting-Controller of BBC Entertainment Division).

22 Other producers at Bristol included Gilbert Phelps, the novelist (who had succeeded Geoffrey Grigson, shortly before my arrival); Kenneth Hudson, specialist in industrial archaeology; and Vivian Ogilvie, historian of the public schools. Frank Gillard was the forceful director of the station for most of my time.

23 See *Dartington Hall: the formative years 1925–1957* by Victor Bonham-Carter, with an account of the School by W. B. Curry, Phoenix House, 1958; re-issued by the Exmoor Press, 1970.
24 Members in the early years included Dennis Arundell, A. L. Bacharach, Leslie Baily, Robert Buckland, Arthur Calder-Marshall, Mabel Constanduros, Henrik Ege, Lionel Gamlin, Geoffrey Grigson, Ted Kavanagh, Rosamond Lehmann, L. du Garde Peach, Roy Plomley, Dilys Powell, V. S. Pritchett, E. Arnot Robertson, L. A. G. Strong, Peter Ustinov, John Watt and Ted Willis.
25 Helen Lehmann, elder sister of Rosamond, the novelist; Beatrix, the actress; and John, publisher and man of letters.
26 The first members of the panel were—Radiowriters' Association: Lionel Gamlin and Helen Lehmann; BBC: R. G. Walford and Miss Candler.
27 *The Author*, winter 1949.
28 *Ibid.*
29 Radio/TV licences, 7,898,247. Radio licences alone, 6,743,027.
30 See Helen Lehmann's remarks in the summer 1960 issue of *The Author*, p. 83, in which she enumerated some of the pettifogging objections she had had to contend with. One example gives the flavour: 'the notion that a broadcast talk was worth less than the current rate when it was a "religious" talk'.
31 This principle was confirmed in 1970 in a lecture on 'Radio in the Seventies' by Ian Trethowan, then Managing Director of BBC Radio, when he said:

> The BBC . . . has a clear role in sustaining a range of cultural speech programmes . . . BBC radio has a cultural function which, in whatever form, should be nourished . . . We should provide for established culture, but we should also provide opportunities for new developments, for new writing, for new ideas, and by no means last, for experiment in the use of radio itself as an art form—for programmes which push at the frontiers of the medium.

Quoted by Konrad Syrop in the autumn 1980 issue of *The Author*.
32 See *Drama on Capital Radio* by Anthony Cornish in the May 1981 issue of *Broadcasting Bulletin* (Society of Authors).
33 Committee on the Future of Broadcasting, appointed 1973.
34 See *Radio Drama*, edited by Peter Lewis, Longman, 1981, and *Radio Drama* by Ian Rodger, Macmillan, 1982.
35 See *Crisis in BBC Radio* by Konrad Syrop. *The Author*, autumn 1980. Also the Hearst Report published in January 1981.
36 As explained the Society of Authors formed the Radiowriters' Association in 1947 to represent its radio interests, but this was absorbed into the Society's Broadcasting Committee in 1978 to cover both radio and television.

37 The Writers' Guild was the eventual successor to the Screenwriters' Association set up by the Society of Authors in 1937. See under *Writing for the Screen*.
38 The ABS and the NUJ are principally recognised for negotiations on behalf of BBC staff. They also have freelance branches which enjoy observer status in the talks and features negotiations, for which the Society of Authors is the recognised union.

CHAPTER ELEVEN

1 See *The History of the British Film 1896–1906* by Rachel Low and Roger Manvell, Allen & Unwin, 1973.
2 Hepworth went bankrupt in 1924. Pearson became 'the leading inspiration as producer-director connecting the best in British film making in the period *c.* 1914–30 to the young film makers coming up in the 1930s. He was highly literate (having been a headmaster) and published his autobiography, *Flashback*, Allen & Unwin, 1937.' Information from Roger Manvell.
3 Cinematograph Films Act, 1927.
4 Charles Chaplin, notably, made his films—dialogue and all—'off the cuff'.
5 I refer the reader to the section on Screenwriting, contributed by Roger Manvell to *The International Encyclopedia of the Film* (Michael Joseph, 1972), a work which he also edited. He records, for example, that 'a journalist called Roy McCardell was hired in the 1900s at the considerable salary of $150 a week to create ten good scenarios weekly, while pressmen and story-writers could get from $10 to $25 for stories acceptable for shooting'. He also refers to the work of three women screenwriters in the USA—Anita Loos, who 'joined D. W. Griffith's studio as a staff-writer after *The Birth of a Nation*'; Jeannie MacPherson, who worked with Cecil B. De Mille and wrote the film script of Barrie's *The Admirable Crichton*; and June Mathis, who became 'the administrative head of the large scenario department of the Goldwyn Studios'.
6 *The Author*, June 1912 and December 1916.
7 *The Author*, May 1913. Cecil Raleigh died on 10 November 1914. He was a man of prescience as well as practicality. He foresaw, for instance, the addition of sound to films, though not the ultimate technique. He suggested that improved gramophone recording would provide the means, and that newsreels would supply same-day coverage in sight and sound. 'A speech in Liverpool at twelve o'clock in the morning will be heard and seen at the Palace on the same evening.'
8 Previously all film business at the Society had been looked after by the Dramatic Sub-Committee.
9 *The Author*, October and November 1915.

10 *The Author*, November 1915.

11 Published in the *Bulletin* of the Authors' League of America and reprinted in *The Author*, December 1918.

12 Information from *Somerset Maugham* by Ted Morgan, Cape, 1980. Maugham worked very rarely on any film scripts of his own works.

13 Quoted from Manvell, *op. cit.*

14 Quotations and information from *F. Scott Fitzgerald: A Critical Portrait* by Henry Dan Piper, Holt, Rinehart & Winston, 1965. See also Scott Fitzgerald's own book, *The Last Tycoon*, a fictional but penetrating study of Hollywood based on his own experiences.

15 24 May 1922.

16 For a description of the complex financial structure of these three organisations, see *Money Behind the Screen* by F. D. Klingender and Stuart Legg, Lawrence & Wishart, 1937; also *The British Film Industry*, PEP, 1952.

17 Alexander Korda was a gifted Hungarian, who combined in a high degree the abilities of artist, financier, technician and administrator. He founded London Film Productions in 1932 with his brothers Vincent (art director) and Zoltan (director), and Lajos Biro (story editor). His production of *The Private Life of Henry VIII* (script by Biro and Arthur Wimperis) not only took Britain by storm and established him as a film maker of world stature, but induced the Prudential Assurance Company to finance the building of Denham Studios and encouraged Korda to make more films designed to challenge the American 'majors'. As stated in the text, Korda's initial success and the 1930s film boom in Britain were short lived. In 1940 however Korda went over to America where he made a number of films, including a highly successful one about Lady Hamilton, Nelson's mistress. For this and for certain undercover work on behalf of British Intelligence, he received a knighthood. He returned to Britain before the end of the war, reactivated London Films and bought a controlling interest in British Lion, an independent distributor. He then rivalled Rank in making a series of expensive prestige films aimed at breaking into the international market but, like Rank, failed in the attempt. Ironically some of Korda's less ambitious and less expensive films did very well. Examples: *The Fallen Idol* and *The Third Man*, both written by Graham Greene; *The Small Back Room* and *Mine Own Executioner* by Nigel Balchin; and *The Winslow Boy* by Terence Rattigan. Despite his financial failures, Korda's contribution to the British film industry was of very great importance. See *Alexander Korda. The Man Who Could Work Miracles* by Karol Kulik, W. H. Allen, 1975.

18 Quoted from pp. 67–8 of *The British Film Industry*, *op. cit.*

19 In his book, *The Long View*, published by Secker & Warburg in 1974, Basil Wright wrote:

. . . The eventual solution of the problem had to be *photography* of sound, so that picture and sound could be married on the same piece of film and be projected simultaneously through the same machine . . . Thus the synchronous film, based on the amplifier triode valve, must have been perfectly possible from, say, 1912, if not earlier, had anyone wanted it enough to press on with its practical development . . . But apparently no one did.

In the event it was for economic reasons—the fact that they were being squeezed out of cinema circuits—that Warner Brothers took the necessary step in November 1927 with *The Jazz Singer* in which Al Jolson 'spoke a few words and sang a few songs . . . Nothing was ever the same again'.

20 Weidenfeld & Nicholson, 1982. In a chapter, 'The Film on Paper', contributed to another book, *Of Screen and Audience*, in the series 'Film To-day Books' published by the Saturn Press in 1947, Mortimer illustrated no less vividly the point about collaboration, in reference to the script of *Oliver Twist*, which David Lean both co-scripted and directed:

> David Lean's filming of Dickens gives an admirable example of the different problems and possibilities which face the novelist and the screenwriter. The novelist can afford to digress and stop to admire the view, he can afford to be verbally amusing in descriptive passages. In the cinema all action must be simplified . . . The scriptwriters—in this case David Lean and Stanley Hayes—see us . . . crowded together in a warm, darkened cinema, gazing half-hypnotised at a bright screen fixed a certain distance from our eyes. They know that time is short, at most only two and a half hours. They know we don't listen patiently to long explanations on the sound-track, but that we react instantly to powerful images on the screen. They must have simplicity. They want us to feel at once the misery of Oliver's heritage, the wretchedness to which he is doomed, and so they write a strong introductory sequence . . .

See also an interesting account of writing and directing in *The Log of a Film Director* by Norman Lee, Quality Press, 1949.

21 See *Talking Pictures* by Richard Corliss, Overlook Press, N.Y., 1974 and Penguin Books, 1975. Also *The Twenty Best Film Plays*, edited by John Gassner and Dudley Nichols, Crown, N.Y., 1943.

22 Geoffrey Household told me: 'In 1939 Korda placed a small stable of writers, including myself, Graham Greene and one or two others whom I forget, under an indefinite contract to work for him. I have no longer any record of the terms. When we all went to war and Korda departed for Hollywood and MGM, he carried the contract with him as an asset. Thereafter I was paid a retainer—if I remember—of

£16 a week during the war which certainly came in mighty handy . . .
After the war MGM had no work to offer Korda's team whom, I
believe, they never wanted.'

23 *The Author*, spring 1939. Reprinted by permission of the Estate of
Margaret Kennedy.

24 *Ibid.*, autumn 1939. Permission as above.

25 *Ibid.*, winter 1939.

26 This Committee replaced in effect the Society's old Cinema
Sub-Committee, first formed in 1914. The Screenwriters' Association's first officers were Miles Malleson, Chairman; Frank Launder,
Secretary; Roger Burford, Treasurer. The first general meeting took
place on 14 July 1937. The annual subscription was agreed at three
guineas, payable to the Society for office accommodation, printing
and typing services, and legal advice. The drafting of the constitution
was assigned to Denys Kilham Roberts, General Secretary of the
Society.

27 Bridie's objections, as expressed to Margaret Kennedy in *The Author*
in 1939, must have come as an afterthought.

28 Partly achieved in the 1948 Quota Act.

29 See *The Factual Film* published by PEP and OUP in 1942 on behalf
of the Arts Enquiry, a survey sponsored by the Trustees of Dartington
Hall, Devon. Also a number of other publications listed in the
bibliography available at the British Film Institute.

30 Quoted from *The Story of the Documentary Film* by John Grierson
and published in *The Fortnightly Review*, August 1939. By way of
illustration, young creative artists such as the composer Benjamin
Britten, and writers such as W. H. Auden, Louis MacNeice, and Cecil
Day-Lewis, were all employed on documentaries.

31 Quoted from *The Great British Picture Show* by George Perry,
Paladin, 1975, to which I am indebted for much information in this
chapter.

32 Only about 10 per cent of the total of cinemas went out of business by
reason of bombing or other wartime causes.

33 The report was produced by a committee chaired by Albert Palache.

34 Even *Henry V* took five years to recover its cost.

35 For a description of this system, see *The Great British Picture Show*
op. cit., p. 119.

36 A similar policy was pursued by the British Lion Group, into which
Alexander Korda had bought his way on returning from America.
This Group was mainly concerned with production and distribution,
but had no cinema circuit of its own.

37 Since at this time $50 million per annum was being remitted to US film
companies, the annual saving was reckoned at $33 million.

38 In his statement to members of Odeon Theatres Ltd. about the
financial year ending 25 June 1949, J. Arthur Rank said:

Unfortunately many of the films we produced were not of a quality to ensure even reasonable returns. It can now be seen that our plans to meet an unexpected and critical situation were too ambitious, that we made demands on the creative talent in the industry that were beyond its resources, and that as a result we spread our production capacity, in which I still have unshaken faith, too thinly over the films we made.

39 The Gater Committee (or working party) had some difficulty in finding out facts, but did its best to analyse and comment on the intricate variety of items that composed the final bill for a film. Obvious points of criticism included high salaries of the stars, disproportionate cost of location and materials, restrictive practices, and excessive 'waste' associated with what might be called the 'artistic' element (scripting, acting, shooting, set construction, etc.), all of which militated against strict budget control and efficient planning. Despite these defects, the committee was convinced that the producer received far too small a share of box office receipts—only about 3½ per cent. This conclusion coincided with the Plant Committee findings, which considered that the existing distribution/exhibition system, as controlled by the combines, was too rigid and ought to be altered to allow a greater degree of competition.

40 Named after Sir Wilfred Eady of the Treasury. Entertainments Duty was abolished in 1960, while the levy—voluntary at first—was made compulsory by the Films Act, 1957. The 1980 rate was one twelfth of the ticket price, net of VAT, the cash being collected by Customs and Excise and paid over to the British Film Fund Agency, which was responsible for administration.

41 My own choice of notable films, produced immediately post-war would include the following, listed under producer or director:

Anthony Asquith: *The Winslow Boy* (1948), *The Browning Version* (1951), both scripts of plays by Terence Rattigan.

Sidney Box: *Quartet* (1948), adaptations of four short stories by Somerset Maugham.

The Boulting Brothers: *Brighton Rock* (1948), script by Graham Greene. *The Guinea Pig* (1948) adapted from the play by Warren Chetham Strode.

David Lean: *Great Expectations* (1946) and *Oliver Twist* (1948), scripts of Dickens's novels.

Frank Launder and Sidney Gilliatt: *London Belongs to Me* (1948), script of the novel by Norman Collins.

Laurence Olivier: who acted and directed *Hamlet* (1948) in black and white.

Michael Powell and Emeric Pressburger: *A Matter of Life and Death* (1947), *The Red Shoes* (1948) and *The Small Back Room* (1948), the latter scripted from the novel by Nigel Balchin.

Carol Reed: *Odd Man Out* (1947) script of the novel by F. L. Green. *The Fallen Idol* (1948) and *The Third Man* (1949), both scripts by Graham Greene.

Peter Ustinov: who wrote and directed *Private Angelo* (1949).

Herbert Wilcox: *The Lady with a Lamp* (1951) and *Odette* (1950), both vehicles for his wife, Anna Neagle.

42 *Ealing Studios* by Charles Barr, Cameron and Tayleur (Books) in association with David & Charles, 1977. See also 'The context of creativity: Ealing Studios and Hammer' in *British Cinema History*, edited by J. Curran and V. Porter. Weidenfeld & Nicolson, 1983. Also John Ellis's contribution to *Screen*, Vol. 16, No. 1, 1975.

43 *Michael Balcon presents . . . A Lifetime of Films* by Michael Balcon, Hutchinson, 1969.

44 *White Russian—Red Face* by Monja Danischewsky, Gollancz, 1966. All other information has been given me by the author in conversation and correspondence.

45 Alberto de Almeida Cavalcanti, Brazilian film maker.

46 This and other quotations in this section are taken from *This is where I came in* by T. E. B. Clarke, Michael Joseph, 1974.

47 Not all Clarke's scripts were original stories. He adapted, for example, Ted Willis's play, *The Blue Lamp*, a story of the London police in which Jack Warner played the lead, filmed in 1950. It was the forerunner of Willis's highly successful TV series, *Dixon of Dock Green*, in which Warner was also the star.

48 In Hollywood the proportion of unused scripts was always high. Their cost, in relation to the total film budget was usually so low, that it paid to commission several for each film. It is of incidental interest that Alexander Korda made a practice of buying up unused scripts which figured afterwards as valuable assets in the annual accounts of London Films.

49 The fate of RKO vividly illustrates the intricacies of film business in the 1950s. After a short period of sole ownership by Howard Hughes, it passed in 1955 to General Teleradio Inc., a subsidiary of the General Tyre and Rubber Company, 'a huge conglomerate whose far-flung interests included tyremaking, chemicals, plastics, rockets, guided-missile controls, submarines and even tennis balls'. The new owner wasted no time in selling off RKO's back stock of some 740 feature films and 1,000 shorts for TV distribution—a highly profitable deal both for the seller and the buyer, C & C Television, since the latter's showings of the RKO stock earned an estimated $25 million inside two years. Meanwhile RKO itself went on making new films, but unsuccessfully, and in 1958 it closed down for ever.

See *The Celluloid Empire. A History of the American Motion Picture Industry* by Robert Stanley Ph.D., Hasting House, N.Y. 1978—an important source of information.

50 See Chapter 21 by David Gordon in *The American Film Industry*, edited by Tino Balio, University of Wisconsin Press, 1976.

51 The film rights of the novel by Mario Puzo were bought originally for $10,000. However this 'oversight' was soon put right and Mr Puzo is said to have netted a total of *c.* $500 million from both the *Godfather* films, *Earthquake* and *Superman*, in the form of down payments plus a percentage of the gross takings.

52 Between 1950 and 1960 the number of cinemas in Britain fell from 4,500 to 3,000, and weekly attendances slumped from 30 million to 10 million.

53 Although the Gaumont and Odeon circuits both belonged to Rank, they operated separately until 1958 when the Board of Trade withdrew its opposition to their being combined. This was a necessary preliminary to rationalisation. Within a short time Rank had closed 125 houses, and ABC 59. Later the rationalising process continued by means of 'twinning', i.e. converting a large cinema into two or more auditoria.

54 For detailed information I must again refer the reader to the relevant film histories, but the following is my own selective list, offered by way of example only, of films which—by virtue of the quality of their scripts or direction—reflected the 'new wave'.

SOCIAL REALISM

(Stories concerned with industrial and racial tensions, sexual permissiveness, and family attitudes, with emphasis on working and lower middle class surroundings)

Room at the Top (1958) script of John Braine's novel, directed by Jack Clayton.

The Angry Silence (1960) script by Bryan Forbes, directed by Guy Green.

A Kind of Loving (1962) script by Keith Waterhouse and Willis Hall from the novel by Stan Barstow, directed by John Schlesinger.

This Sporting Life (1963) script by David Storey, directed by Lindsay Anderson.

The Knack (1965) script by Charles Wood from the play by Ann Jellicoe, directed by Dick Lester.

COMEDY AND SATIRE

(Incorporating some of epithets attributed to Social Realism)

Lucky Jim (1957) script of the novel by Kingsley Amis, directed by John Boulting.

Entertaining Mr Sloane (1969) script of the play by Joe Orton, directed by Douglas Hickox.

Loot (1970), script by Ray Galton and Alan Simpson from the play by Joe Orton, directed by Silvio Narrizano.

PYSCHOLOGICAL STUDIES

The Innocents (1961) script of Henry James's novel, *The Turn of the Screw*, directed by John Clayton.

The Caretaker (1963), script by Harold Pinter, directed by Clive Donner.

Lord of the Flies (1963) script of the novel by William Golding, directed by Peter Brooke.

HISTORY

Lawrence of Arabia (1962) script by Robert Bolt, directed by David Lean.

A Man for All Seasons (1967) script by Robert Bolt, directed by Fred Zinneman.

CLASSICS

Far from the Madding Crowd (1967) script of the novel by Thomas Hardy, directed by John Schlesinger.

Jane Eyre (1970) script of the novel by Charlotte Brontë, directed by Delbert Mann.

55 Bryanston Films lasted only four years and was sold in 1963 to Associated-Rediffusion, one of the television programme companies.

56 At this time British Lion was the third most important producer/distributor in the UK, despite a difficult career. Under Korda (see Note 36) it had received a loan of £3 million from the NFFC, which it was unable to repay and faced bankruptcy in 1954. Next year it became virtually a state enterprise with the NFFC holding the majority of shares, but in 1958 it was given fresh stimulus with a board of directors appointed from inside the industry. Eventually, after a complex series of manoeuvres, the company was disposed of to EMI.

57 I have omitted highly successful popular series such as the adventures of James Bond, adapted from the novels of Ian Fleming, first filmed in 1962 and recreated by fresh hands from 1980 onwards; also the *Carry On* stories (first backed by NFFC) of which no less than 27 films had been completed by 1975. The former were international bestsellers, the latter probably incomprehensible outside the UK.

Also omitted is the name of the American producer, Joseph Losey—a refugee from the McCarthy witch hunt—whose British films overlap the period and were remarkable for their insight into native character and atmosphere, e.g. *Accident* (1967) and *The Go-Between* (1971), both scripted by Harold Pinter, the former from the novel by Nicholas Mosley, the latter from the novel by L. P. Hartley. I would also mention Bryan Forbes, author of *The Angry Silence* (Note 54). Actor, writer, director, in 1969 he was appointed managing director of Associated British, after it had been absorbed by EMI. Although he held the post for only two years, he was responsible for the production of several fine films, including E. Nesbit's *The Railway Children*, and *Tales of Beatrix Potter*, both classics of English literature and cinematic successes.

58 See *Sight and Sound*, autumn 1982.

59 Goldcrest paid £½ million towards script development for *Chariots of Fire*. Production cost of £6 million was met equally by American and Egyptian sources. See *The Times*, 2 November 1981.

60 Another interesting newcomer in the 1981 list was Channel Four, which financed three films with BFI, one with the Irish Film Board, and also backed two films on its own.

61 By way of example, in alphabetical order: Robert Bolt, Agatha Christie, Ian Fleming, Winston Graham, Graham Greene, Frederick Forsyth, Alistair MacLean, W. Somerset Maugham and Bernard Shaw. Bolt and Greene were also successful scriptwriters.

CHAPTER TWELVE

1 Soon after the war, the Screenwriters' Association severed its practical connection with the Society of Authors and, with the advent of commercial television in 1954, competed actively with it for the representation of TV writers, although both sides managed to collaborate as members of the Television Writers Council and of the Radio and Television Safeguards Committee. Eventually a truce was arranged. The Radiowriters' Association (of the Society) retained radio, the Screenwriters' Association films and TV, and to this end changed its title—first to the British Screen and Television Writers' Association in 1956, when it was registered as a trade union, then to the Screenwriters' Guild in 1961, and then to the Writers' Guild of Great Britain in 1965, in which year it became affiliated to the Trades Union Congress. At the same time the Society continued—as it does today—to advise individual members in regard to contracts and other business involving films and television, as well as book and subsidiary rights in general, and to administer the Broadcasting Group (successor to the Radiowriters' Association) consisting of members concerned with all aspects of the medium.

2 Towards the end of the war, the Screenwriters' Association shared a small room in Albemarle Street with the Composers' Guild. It then took temporary quarters in the basement of Le Petit Club Français, run by Olwen Vaughan, who was also Secretary of the London Film Society. For a time it operated a restaurant club of its own near the Dorchester Hotel, but this generated problems among the membership and had to be given up. Later the Association moved its office to an address in Harley Street, and finally to 430, Edgware Road, its present address (1983).

3 *The Author*, spring 1957.
4 Although the Writers' Guild incorporated a Guild Shop Clause in all its agreements, it was careful to explain that this did not amount to a 'closed shop' in the exclusive sense. The following is a quotation from the *Writers' News* of November 1966.

> A closed shop sets down restrictions upon the entrance to a profession, e.g. doctors, lawyers, printers, and some grades of electricians ... A Guild Shop, however, doesn't lay down any primary restrictions upon entrance into the profession, but it does maintain the following: That any person may write his first contribution, be it an episode of a series or serial, be it a screenplay for a TV film, but after his first contribution, and before being contracted for a second, he must be an accepted member of the Guild. Essentially the argument ... is that if the Guild has struggled and fought, and expended a great deal of its members' time, energies and finance to obtain improved remuneration and status for the writer, it is only just that other people should not gain these benefits without identifying themselves with the majority.

5 Allan Prior was one of the original writers of *Z Cars* and wrote 150 episodes of that series and its successor, *Softly, Softly*. He has also written many original plays for television.
6 On a personal note, I was offered £350 per script in 1964 for two 40-minute scripts in the BBC TV series, *The Great War*. Neither was used, but I acted as an historical adviser for the period 1916–17.
7 *The Author*, winter 1978.
8 *The Author*, spring 1979.
9 *BBC Annual Report and Handbook*, p. 22.
10 *Ibid.*, p. 26.
11 *Writers' News*, November 1968.
12 Indeed at the time of writing (1983), there is a surprisingly large number of television scriptwriters, earning in excess of £50,000 a year.
13 *The Stage and Television Today*, March 1980.
14 Eric Paice also told me: 'I once had to keep a note of writers who had met their Maker. The mortality rate among television writers is quite staggering. Of the last ten to die, only one reached the age of 60. Seven didn't make 55.'
15 See 'Video Report' by Brian Norris in *Sight and Sound*, spring 1983.
16 In practice it is highly likely that, for reasons of cost, only urban areas will be cabled.
17 In a White Paper issued in April 1983, the Government proposed a) to set up a Cable Authority which would award franchises to operators and act as general overseer; b) to require all cable systems to carry the public services and those of the satellite on which the

BBC has two channels to be in service by 1985–6; c) to forbid anything approaching a 'porn channel' and to insist that the Cable Authority keep a close watch on the requirements of taste and decency. These proposals were substantially confirmed in 1983.

17 Quoted from an article by the Reverend Edwin Robertson in *The Author*, summer 1981.

Selective Index

Not every item or personal name occurring in the text and Notes is included in this Index, which is confined to entries of prime significance only.

General Subjects

Authors/authorship/Authors' organisations
  Authors, The Society of
    General 13–15, 20, 21, 22, 23, 25, 28, 29, 30, 32, 33, 34, 35, 36, 38, 39, 43, 46, 48, 49, 50, 51, 52, 53–6, 58, 59, 60–3, 64–5, 66, 68, 69, 72, 73, 74–5, 77, 78, 79, 80, 82, 83, 85, 87, 88, 92, 93, 95, 98, 99, 100, 102–3, 107, 108, 110, 112, 113, 120–2, 126, 127, 128, 130, 131, 132, 134, 141, 151–2, 157, 184–5, 186, 190, 206, 212, 214, 215, 220, 221–2, 224–8, 231, 232, 238, 245, 298, 299, 301, 302, 303–4, 306, 307, 308, 309, 311, 312, 314, 316
    Authors' Planning Committee 60–1
    Authors' National Committee 62
    The Author 13–14, 23, 25, 29, 30, 33, 43–4, 49, 66, 69, 71, 73, 75, 83, 87, 88, 93, 97, 99, 100–1, 109, 111, 116, 120, 127, 128, 129, 137–8, 173, 213, 218, 219, 222, 223, 276, 297, 298, 302, 304, 307, 308, 310, 311, 312, 314, 315, 316, 317, 319, 325, 326
    Collection Bureau (agency) 23, 54, 70–1, 76–7
    Critical Times for Authors 92–3
    Trade Union 49, 120–5, 170, 307, 324
    The Book Writers: who are they? 95–7
    Welfare schemes 23, 30, 80
    What are Writers Worth? 93–5
  Authorship
    General 14–16, 20, 66–8, 89–92, 138–9, 147–9
    Earnings 46, 89, 96–8, 143–7, 163–4
    Social security 84–5
    Surveys 46, 91–100, 139, 141, 145, 305
  Authors' Lending and Copyright Society (ALCS) 128, 131–2, 308
  Group, The Writers' Action (WAG) 107–9, 127, 131
  Guild, The Writers' Guild 15, 82, 98, 99, 126–7, 131, 132, 189, 196, 238, 281, 293, 308, 312, 316, 324, 325
  PEN 63–4, 159
  Poetry Society/*Poetry Review* 33, 34, 159
  Royal Literary Fund 14, 15, 85, 151, 153–4
  Royal Society of Literature 83, 151, 153–4
  Theatre Writers' Union – see under Drama
Authors' Agents
  General 69–74, 88, 93, 185, 297, 303
  Association of Authors' Agents 78
  Firms/Individuals: A. M. Burghes 70; Christy and Moore 70; William

Firms/Individuals—cont.
   Morris Colles 70–1, 152; Curtis Brown 36, 70, 73–4, 78; Mark
   Hamilton 78; A. M. Heath 78, 303; David Higham 74, 76, 303; Hughes
   Massie 70; Galloway Kyle 33–4, 70, 298; A. D. Peters 60, 61, 77–8, 88,
   303, 305; J. B. Pinker 26–8, 63, 70; Raymond Savage 73, 303; A. P.
   Watt 36, 70, 76
   Society of Literary Agents 73

Books/Booksellers/Book Trade
   General 14, 21, 24–5, 34, 56–60, 68, 86–7, 88, 92–6, 100–1, 137, 157–8,
      162, 163, 298, 301
   Book clubs 57–8, 61, 87, 93
   The Bookseller 44, 58, 111, 133, 302, 311
   Book Tokens 58, 301
   'Charity books' 29–30
   National Book League 15, 51, 83, 157, 159, 312
   Net Book Agreement 21, 57, 88
Broadcasting
   General 20, 23, 46, 50, 58, 66, 72, 232–6, 315
   Association of Broadcasting Staffs 238, 316
   Broadcasting Group 127, 308, 315, 324
   British Broadcasting Corporation (BBC) 59, 76, 97, 134, 188, 190, 205–28,
      229–35, 283, 284, 288, 289, 313, 314, 315, 325
   Radio 14, 20, 205–39, 314, 315
   Radiowriters' Association 126, 127, 227, 228, 229, 232, 234, 308, 314,
      315, 324
   Screenwriters' Association – see under *Cinema*
   Television 14, 20, 126, 127, 134, 135, 136, 189, 218, 228, 236, 283–96,
      308, 315, 321, 325

Cinema
   General 14, 20, 72, 117–18, 189, 240–82, 317, 319, 321, 322, 323, 324
   Screenwriters' Association 51, 126, 189, 256–60, 285, 287–8, 316, 318, 324
Copyright
   General 20, 23, 30, 50, 55, 58, 71, 83, 101–2, 141, 142, 143, 204, 243,
      293, 308
   Acts (1709) 19; (1842) 19; (1911) 13, 14, 19, 20, 50, 71, 128, 163, 170,
      209, 297, 300; (1956) 102, 103, 106, 128
   British Copyright Council 82, 128, 130, 131, 308
   Crown copyright 130
   Government green paper (1981) 130–1
   Infringement/piracy 56, 133–4, 308
   International 128, 129, 132, 184
   Licensing organisations 132
   'Moral' rights 129–30
   Out-of-copyright/public domain 92, 93, 94–5, 97, 98
   Term of copyright 92, 130
   Whitford Report 128–32

Dartington Hall 13, 231, 314, 319
Defence of Literature and Art Society 117
Drama/Dramatists/Theatres
   General 21, 115, 167–204, 302, 309, 310, 311, 312
   Amateur 176–9, 310
   Arts Council 193, 194–8
   British Drama League/British Theatre Association 176, 310, 312
   Council for the Encouragement of Music and the Arts (CEMA) 158, 191,
      193
   Entertainments Duty 169, 171, 202, 263, 265

Dramatists' Guild (USA) 182–3
League of Dramatists 22, 51, 71, 126, 184–90, 310, 314, 316
National Theatre 115, 188, 193, 195, 196
Royal Court Theatre/English Stage Company 182, 188, 195, 197–8, 312
Stage censorship 22, 114, 170, 174–5, 310
H.M. Tennent 192, 311
Theatre-in-the-Round, Scarborough 199–201
Theatre Writers' Union 190, 196, 204, 312

Illustrators 307

Journalism/Journalists/Journals
General 27, 28, 44, 45, 47, 58, 72, 79, 87, 88, 89–90, 93, 97, 98, 99–100,
   111, 120, 133, 140–6, 161, 300, 304, 308, 309, 319
Institute of Journalists 122
'Little' magazines 146–7
National Union of Journalists 120–2, 126, 127, 145, 238, 308, 316
Press Charter 121–2
Rates of Payment 145–6
Schools of Writing 147–9
The Author – see under Society of Authors
The Bookseller – see under Book Trade

Libel/Defamation
General 39, 49–50, 118–20, 301, 306, 307
Faulks Report 119–20
Libraries
General 14, 21–2, 101–3, 105, 106, 297, 298
Public Lending Right – see under that heading

Music 23, 50, 66, 209, 214–17, 314, 319, 324

Obscenity/Censorship
General 26–9, 110–18, 305–6
Obscene Publications Act 1959 103, 110–15, 116
Obscene Publications Act 1964 114, 115, 116
The Rainbow case 26–9
Stage censorship 22, 114, 170, 174–5, 310
Williams Report 117–18, 279

Patronage
General 14, 150–1, 154–6, 164, 309, 311
Arts Council(s)/Arts Associations 46, 83–4, 104, 105, 115, 146–7, 157,
   158–63, 193, 194–8, 309, 311
Awards/Prizes/Honours 49, 83–4, 156–7, 159
British Council 56
Civil List Pensions 70, 151–3, 154, 309
Council for the Encouragement of Music and the Arts (CEMA) 158, 191,
   193
Grants 83–4, 157–63
Royal Bounty 152–3
Performing Right Society 50, 107, 108, 128, 215, 216, 224, 309, 314
Public Lending Right 22, 93, 97, 98, 100–9, 110, 127, 130, 131, 132, 160,
   163, 204, 305
Publishing/Publishers/Publishers Association
General 20, 21, 24, 26–8, 30, 31–2, 34, 36, 40, 46–7, 49, 51, 53, 56–9,
   62, 68–9, 73, 74, 76, 77–8, 80, 82, 83, 86–8, 90, 91, 93, 94–5, 98, 99,
   105, 106, 112, 114, 134, 136, 137, 138, 157–8, 297, 298, 300, 301,
   304–5, 308, 314

Contracts/Rights/Royalties 23, 30–2, 35–7, 59, 61, 77–8, 80, 87, 88–9, 93, 95, 98, 139–40, 142, 304–5

Recording, Audio, Visual 14, 20, 135–8, 295–6, 325
Reprography 132, 134

Secrecy
   Access to Government records 120, 307
   Official Secrets Act 120

Taxation 59–60, 78–84, 163, 169, 171, 192, 202, 263, 265, 294, 304

World War I 23–25, 44, 66
World War II 55–6, 59–65, 66–9, 78, 86, 120, 139, 158

Principal Personalities

Agate, James 313
Aldington, Richard 25
Allen, Walter 91–2, 305
Amis, Kingsley 117
Archer, William 168
Armstrong, Anthony 61, 310
Asche, Oscar 171
Asquith, Anthony 180, 252
Asquith, Cynthia 28
Asquith, H. H. 28, 309
Astley, George 76, 303–4
Attenborough, David 291
Auden, W. H. 47, 256, 319
Ayckbourn, Alan 198–201

Baily, Leslie 313, 315
Baker, Denys Val 89–90, 92
Baker, John 56, 90–1
Balchin, Nigel 305, 317
Balcon, Michael 44, 240, 252, 266, 267, 268, 269, 271, 272, 279, 320
Balfour, A. J. 29, 309
Barber, M. Elizabeth 51–5, 69, 74–6, 187, 259, 301, 302, 306
Barker, Harley Granville 168, 169, 170, 185
Barker, Ronald 105–6
Barrie, James 22, 43, 44, 170, 186, 187, 246, 310, 316
Bates, H. E. 67–8, 302, 304, 305
Beach, Rex 247
Beith, Ian Hay 24, 48, 50–1, 53–4, 178–9, 183, 217, 218, 298
Bell, Julian 47
Belloc, Hilaire 44
Bennett, Arnold 21, 44, 46, 71, 140
Bennion, Francis 306
Benson, E. F. 25
Beresford, J. D. 28
Besant, Walter 13, 20, 33, 69, 70, 110, 215, 299
Betjeman, John 47
Black, Cyril 117
Blackwood, Algernon 25
Blunden, Edmund 25

Bolt, Robert 198, 203, 310, 324
Bond, Bligh 300
Bonham-Carter, Victor 76, 104, 303–4, 305 307, 309, 314, 325
Bottome, Phyllis 25
Boucicault, Dion 168
Bowen, John 290
Boyle, Andrew 83
Braddon, Miss 25, 298
Braine, John 278
Bridges, Robert 44
Bridie, James 179, 197, 224, 257, 259, 310, 319
Briggs, Asa 217, 313
Brighouse, Harold 173
Brittain, Vera 25
Brooke, Rupert 25
Brophy, John 100–1, 102, 103, 109
Brophy, Brigid, 107, 109
Brown, Ivor 311
Bryant, Arthur 64
Bull, Donald 286
Burns, Jim 147
Buxton, Sydney 20

Calder, John 114
Campbell, Roy 47
Cannan, Gilbert 28
Carton, R. C. 22, 170, 173, 245
Carver, David 305
Catty, Jon 202
Causley, Charles 92, 230
Caute, David 98
Cavalcanti, Alberto de Almeida 268, 269
Cecil, Henry 130, 308
Chesterton, G. K. 44, 52, 310
Cheyney, Peter 81
Church, Richard 305
Clarke, T. E. B. 240, 260, 269–73, 321
Clunes, Alec 176
Connolly, Cyril 47, 144, 147
Conrad, Joseph 44, 152, 162
Cooke, Alistair 217
Cooper, Lettice 107
Cornford, John 47
Cross, Nigel 151–3, 164, 308, 309
Crossman, R. H. S, 60
Coward, Noel 46, 175, 179, 186, 197, 262
Cummins, Geraldine Dorothy 300

Dane, Clemence 57, 179, 258
Danischewsky, Monja 240, 266–7, 268, 271, 272, 273, 321
David, Toby 116
Davies, Walford 28
Davies, W. H. 152
Day-Lewis, Cecil 47–9, 91, 104, 159, 301, 302, 319
Dean, Basil 168, 245
Deeks, Florence 42
Deeping, Warwick 25
De la Mare, Walter 28, 152, 302
Delaney, Shelagh 277
Denny, Ernest 173

Dingle, Captain A. E. 222
Donaldson, Lord 109
Douglas, James 27
Drabble, Margaret 157
Drinkwater, John 44, 175, 184, 207
Druten, John van 174
Duffy, Maureen 107, 109
Dukes, Ashley 44, 175, 185, 218, 314
Dunhill, Thomas 175, 216–17, 218
Durell, C. V. 46

Eccles, Lord 106
Eliot, T. S. 92, 175, 196, 217, 302
Elmhirst, Leonard and Dorothy 231
Elwin, Malcolm 46
Ervine, St. John 61, 62–3, 174, 176–7, 179, 184, 224, 310, 314
Evans, Christopher 136

Fagan, J. B. 176, 245
Faulks, Mr Justice 119–120
Findlater, Richard 15, 93–8, 99, 100, 106, 139, 169, 303, 305, 309, 310,
    311, 312, 313
FitzGerald, Scott, 240, 248–50, 254, 317
Foot, M. R. D. 120, 307
Foot, Michael 121, 224, 268
Forbes, Bryan 288, 323–4
Forster, E. M. 28, 61, 217
Forsyth, Frederick 281, 324
Francis-William's, Lord 305
Fraser, Lady Antonia 120, 125, 130, 307
Fraser, Hugh 112
Frazer, Sir James 152
Freitas, Denis de 108, 128–9, 132, 308
Frohman, Charles 168
Fry, Christopher 192, 196
Fuller, Roy 92

Galsworthy, John 22, 29, 44, 79, 168, 170, 207, 210, 299
Garnett, Constance 152
Garvice, Charles 28, 29, 79, 304
Gascoyne, Bamber 291
Gibson, Alan 231
Gielgud, Val 213–14
Gilardino, Caterina 55, 301
Gilbert, Michael 131, 306
Gissing, George 140, 152
Gittings, Robert 99–100
Godwin, Tony 94
Goodman, Lord 81, 104, 159, 259
Gorell, Lord 48–51, 53, 118, 301, 314
Gosse, Edmund 23, 44
Graham, Gordon 137–8, 139
Graves, Robert 25
Gray, Terence 176
Greene, Graham 47, 197, 312, 317, 318, 324
Greenwood, Frederick 21
Grein, J. T. 168
Grierson, John 260–1, 319
Grigson, Geoffrey 47, 48, 314, 315
Grundy, Sydney 167, 170

Haggard, Rider 23, 25
Hall, Radclyffe 111
Hamilton, Cicely 25
Hanley, James 111
Hardy, Thomas 22, 44, 210, 246
Harmsworth, Alfred 21, 140, 147
Harris, Frank 140
Hartley, L. P. 323
Hawkes, Jacquetta 305
Hawkins, Anthony Hope 23, 44
Henley, W. E. 140, 152
Hepworth, Cecil 241, 316
Herbert, A. P. 60, 82, 93, 103–4, 106, 110–116, 118, 131, 159, 175, 259, 260, 279, 285, 301, 304, 305, 306, 310, 354
Hewitt, C. R. 113, 305, 306
Hilton, John 60
Hodson, J. L. 88–9, 224
Holbrook, David 116
Holroyd, Michael 105, 120
Hopkins, John 291
Horniman, Annie 168
Household, Geoffrey 318
Housman, A. E. 44, 207
Housman, Laurence 175, 307, 310
Howard, Elizabeth Jane 117
Huberman, Leo 74
Hudson, W. H. 44, 152
Hughes, Richard 213–14, 313
Huxley, Aldous 255

Ibañez, Vincente Blasco 248
Innes, Ralph Hammond 81–2, 304
Irving, David 119
Isherwood, Christopher 47, 256

Jacobs, W. W, 54, 207
James, David 106
Jameson, Margaret Storm 62–5, 224, 301
Jenkins, Hugh 108–9
Jenkins, Roy 82, 112, 305
Jepson, Edgar 245
Jones, Henry Arthur 44, 167, 169, 172, 246
Joyce, James 44, 111, 153, 162

Kaufmann, Stanley 112
Kavanagh, Ted 228, 315
Kee, Robert 291
Kelsey, Gerald 127
Kennedy, Margaret 44, 256–7, 258, 319
Kernon, A. P. 83
Keynes, John Maynard 155, 158, 191, 311
King, Francis 107
Kingsford, R. J. L. 56–8, 301
Kipling, Rudyard 29–30, 44
Korda, Alexander 240, 252, 265, 317, 318, 319, 321, 323
Kurnitz, Harry 270, 271

Lambert, Jack 198–9, 312
Lane, John 31
Langridge, R. H. 143

Larkin, Philip 92
Launder, Frank 257–9, 285, 319
Lawrence, D. H. 26–9, 44, 111, 114
Leathes, Stanley 28
Lee, Jennie 104, 106, 159
Le Fanu, Mark 74, 76, 100
Lehmann, Helen 232, 234, 304, 315
Lehmann, John 46–7, 144, 153–4, 300, 315
Lehmann, Rosamond 80, 315
Leon, Jack de 176–7
Levy, Benn 184–6, 258, 310
Lonsdale, Frederick 46, 174, 179
Losey, Joseph 323
Lowndes, Mrs Belloc 28, 44
Lynd, Robert 27
Lynd, Sylvia 57

McCarthy, Justin Huntly 173
MacDermott, Norman 175
McGuigan, Jim 161
Mackenzie, Compton 80–1, 268, 304
MacLiesh, Philippa 75–6, 129–30, 303, 307, 308
MacNeice, Louis 47, 92, 233, 302, 319
Machin, David 76, 99–100, 133–4, 308
Mailer, Norman 111
Mann, Christopher 258
Manvell, Roger 316, 317
Marsh, Edward 153
Marshall, Norman 175
Masefield, John 24, 44, 49, 61, 87, 170, 217, 224, 302
Mason, A. E. W. 71
Mathis, June 248, 316
Maude, Aylmer 28
Maugham, W. Somerset 44, 71, 170, 174, 179, 248, 259, 317, 324
Maxwell, W. B. 49, 298
Mercer, David 198, 291
Meredith, George 22
Milne, A. A. 174, 179, 209–11, 212, 313
Mitford, Jessica 148–9, 309
Monck, Nugent 176
Money, Ernle 108
Moore, George 44
Morgan, Charles 79, 179, 224
Morgan, William de 26
Morrell, Philip and Lady Ottoline 28
Mortimer, John 190, 198, 254, 284, 310, 311, 318
Murry, John Middleton 28

Nettal, Reginald 230
Nevinson, Henry 61
Newnes, George 21, 140

O'Casey, Sean 174, 197
Orczy, Baroness 29
Orwell, George 47
Osborne, Charles 161
Osborne, John 182, 188, 197–8, 277, 310, 312
Ould, Herman 64
Owen, Wilfrid 25

Paice, Eric 293, 325

Parsons, Ian 77–8
Payne, Ben Iden 168
Peach, L. du Garde 214, 227, 311, 314, 315
Pearson, Cyril 21, 140
Pearson, George 241, 316
Phelps, Gilbert 231, 314
Phillpotts, Eden 25, 71
Pinero, A. W. 22, 44, 167, 170
Pinter, Harold 125, 198, 233, 323
Playfair, Nigel 175
Post, Laurens van der 125
Postgate, Raymond 48
Potter, Denis 291
Pound, Ezra 153
Powell, Anthony 47
Priestley, J. B. 46, 57, 61, 62, 92, 134, 179–80, 197, 218, 224, 227, 285, 310
Prior, Allan 287, 288, 294, 325
Pritchard, Hesketh 223
Pritchett, V. S. 61, 224, 305, 315

Rackham, Arthur 28, 29
Raleigh, Cecil 243–4, 316
Rattigan, Terence 180–2, 197, 287, 310, 317
Raymond, Ernest 44, 61, 219
Raymond, Harold 58
Read, Piers Paul 130
Reade, Charles 168
Reith, Lord 205–6, 313
Roberts, Denys Kilham 43–4, 51, 52–5, 60–2, 63, 69, 73, 74–5, 77–8, 79,
    87, 258, 259, 299, 300, 301, 305, 314, 319
Roberts, Michael 47
Roskill, Captain Stephen 307
Rubinstein, Harold 71, 187
Russell, Bertrand 44

Sale, Geoffrey 230
Samuel, Lord 22
Sassoon, Siegfried 25
Saunders, Hilary St George 68, 222, 302
Sayers, Dorothy 60, 217
Scammell, Michael 121–2, 306, 307
Segrave, Edmond 44, 68, 111
Shaffer, Peter 198
Shaw, George Bernard 14, 21, 22, 28, 29, 33, 36, 39–42, 43, 45, 50, 58, 61,
    69–70, 71, 73, 79, 110, 124, 134, 140, 168, 169–70, 172, 177–9, 184–5,
    186, 207–8, 209, 217, 225, 246, 250, 258, 259, 263, 297, 298–300, 303,
    309, 310, 314, 324
Shearman, Hugh 66–7
Shepherd, Rev. Dick 217
Sherriff, R. C. 174, 197, 255, 310
Shorter, Clement 27
Sillitoe, Alan 277
Sitwell, Edith 302
Sitwell, Osbert 61, 64, 80, 224, 302, 314
Smith, E. P. 79, 227, 304, 310
Spender, Stephen 47
Squire, J. C. 26, 28, 44
Stead, W. T. 21
Steiner, George 117
Stevas, Norman St John 108, 305

Stevenson, R. L. 71, 221
Stopes, Marie 174–5, 245, 246
Stoppard, Tom 198
Storey, David 198
Strachey, J. St Loe 142
Strachey, John 54, 61, 64, 313
Strachey, Lytton 44
Streatfeild, Noel 305
Strong, L. A. G. 60, 222–3, 259, 315
Sutro, Alfred 170
Symons, Arthur 152
Symons, Julian 145–6
Syrop, Konrad 315

Taylor, William 105
Tennyson, Lord 22, 156
Terson, Peter 198, 311
Thomas, Dylan 47, 233, 302
Thomas, Edward 153
Thomas, Hugh, 125
Thring, G. H. 23, 25, 27, 28, 30–41, 43, 50, 51, 73, 74, 173, 183, 205–6,
    209, 212, 298–300, 313
Trevelyan, John 278
Trewin, J. C. 312

Unwin, Stanley 34–40, 44, 298

Vachell, Horace 25
Vowles, Hugh P. 38–40, 50

Wales, Robert 289, 291
Waller, Robert 229, 230, 231
Walpole, Hugh 28, 44, 45, 53, 57, 255–6, 298
Wareing, Alfred 168
Watts, Stephen 276
Watts-Dunton, Theodore 26
Waugh, Evelyn 47, 284
Wedgwood, Dame Veronica 125, 134
Welland, Colin 284
Wells, H. G. 21, 25, 30, 38–40, 42, 45, 50, 140, 217, 262, 297, 298, 299, 300
White, Alan 103, 104, 131
White, Eric Walter 104, 160, 309
Whitehouse, Mrs Mary 117
Whitford, Mr Justice 128–30
Whiting, John 197, 312
Whitworth, Geoffrey 176
Wilcox, Desmond 134
Wilde, Oscar 167
Williams, Bernard 117–18
Williams, Emlyn 179, 310
Williams, J. B. 258, 259
Williams-Ellis, Annabel 48
Williamson, Henry 25, 230
Willis, Lord 109, 127, 188–90, 260, 288, 310, 311, 315, 321
Wilson, Harold 264–5
Wodehouse, P. G. 46
Woolf, Leonard and Virginia 45–6, 300
Wright, Basil 317–18
Wyatt, Woodrow 80

Yeats, W. B. 44, 152